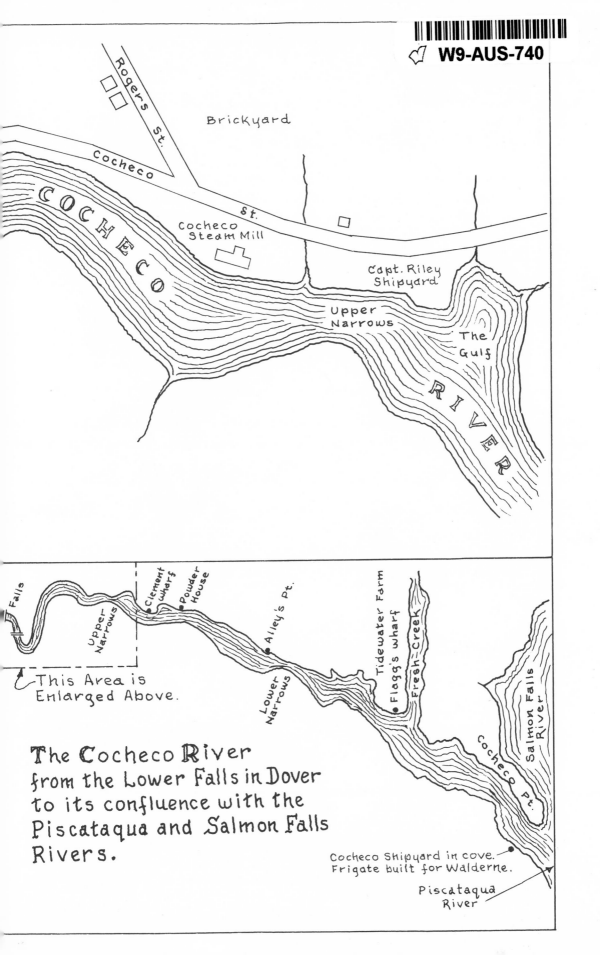

Rogers St.

Brickyard

Cocheco St.

Cocheco Steam Mill

Capt. Riley Shipyard

Upper Narrows

The Gulf

COCHECO RIVER

Falls

Clement Wharf

Powder House

Upper Narrows

This Area is Enlarged Above.

Alley's Pt.

Lower Narrows

Tidewater Farm

Flagg's Wharf

Fresh Creek

Salmon Falls River

Cocheco Pt.

The Cocheco River from the Lower Falls in Dover to its confluence with the Piscataqua and Salmon Falls Rivers.

Cocheco Shipyard in cove. Frigate built for Walderne.

Piscataqua River

Port of Dover
Two Centuries of Shipping on the Cochecho

Port of Dover
Two Centuries of Shipping on the Cochecho

by Robert A. Whitehouse
and Cathleen C. Beaudoin

The Portsmouth Marine Society
Publication Eleven

Published for the Society by

Peter E. Randall
PUBLISHER

A publication of
 The Portsmouth Marine Society
 Box 147, Portsmouth, NH 03801

Frontispiece: View of Cocheco Manufacturing Company Mills from
Dover Landing, c. 1799-1812. Painting by William Stoodley Gookin. G.B.

Library of Congress Cataloging-in-Publication Data

Whitehouse, Robert A. , 1918-
 Port of Dover : two centuries of shipping on the Cochecho / by
Robert A. Whitehouse and Cathleen C. Beaudoin.
  p.   cm. -- (The Portsmouth Marine Society ; publication 11)
 Bibliography: p.
 Includes index.
 ISBN 0-915819-10-4 : $24.95
 1. Harbors--New Hampshire--Dover--History 2. Inland water
transportation--New Hampshire--History. 3. Shipping--New Hampshire-
-Cocheco River--History. 4. Dover (N.H.)--Economic conditions.
I. Beaudoin, Cathleen C., 1952- . II. Title. III. Series:
Publication (Portsmouth Marine Society) ; 11.
HE544.D6W45 1987
386'.8'097425--dc19
87-29214
CIP

Other Portsmouth Marine Society Publications:
 1. John Haley Bellamy, Carver of Eagles
 2. The Prescott Story
 3. The Piscataqua Gundalow,
   Workhorse for a Tidal Basin Empire
 4. The Checkered Career of Tobias Lear
 5. Clippers of the Port of Portsmouth
   and the Men who built Them
 6. Portsmouth-Built
   Submarines of the Portsmouth Naval Shipyard
 7. Atlantic Heights
   A World War I Shipbuilders' Community
 8. There are No Victors Here
   A Local Perspective on the Treaty of
   Portsmouth
 9. The Diary of the Portsmouth, Kittery
   and York Electric Railroad
 10. Port of Portsmouth Ships and the Cotton Trade

In memory of my father, Clyde L. Whitehouse,
who inspired my love of history;
and George Maglaras, Sr., who loved the Cochecho

Contents

Acknowledgments

THANKS ARE OFFERED to the many people who have helped me bring this six-year research project to fruition. Dover's history as an important inland seaport and its shipping heritage on the Cochecho River formed a story begging to be told and I am grateful to those who made this effort possible:

To Cathy Beaudoin, my co-writer, for suggesting that all my notes, taken during long days spent in the Dover Public Library, could be transformed into something publishable;

To Tom Wells for his splendid maps of the Dover waterfront and the river;

To Allan Gillingham for his thoughtful editing;

To Richard E. Winslow III who kindly passed on to me many interesting historical bits;

To Ray Brighton for his book, *Port of Portsmouth Ships and the Cotton Trade*, especially the chapter on Dover's ships;

To Major Wilbur Hoxie who provided much useful material on dredging;

To David Goodman for his valuable information on the Portsmouth Bridge lawsuit;

To my wife, Madaleine, for her support and encouragement.

And for their many contributions and courtesies, I also thank the following institutions:

Dover Public Library, Dover, New Hampshire

Northam Colonists Historical Society, Dover, New Hampshire

Woodman Institute, Dover, New Hampshire

Portsmouth Athenaeum, Portsmouth, New Hampshire

Maine Maritime Museum, Bath, Maine

Old Berwick Historical Society, South Berwick, Maine

Special Thanks to the Portsmouth Marine Society, Joseph Sawtelle, and talented publisher, Peter Randall.

Robert A. Whitehouse

Introduction

IN ALL THE HISTORIES OF DOVER, little has been written about
the city as an inland port and shipping center. Yet from its begin-
nings in 1623 when Edward Hilton settled at its southernmost tip,
Dover's heritage has ever been tied to the waterways that form its
boundaries. It was because of the abundant fishing grounds around
Great Bay and its tributaries and because of the numerous falls on
the Cochecho River that could supply power to run sawmills that
Dover was developed at all. It was the river that inspired local
entrepreneurs to build, in the 1820s, the sprawling mill complexes
that today ironically impede our view of these important waters and
stymy our appreciation of the Cochecho River's historic contributions.
It was the river that led to the incorporation of the Dover Navigation
Company, a highly successful shipping line during the last quarter of
the nineteenth century. It was the river and its comfortable
surroundings that beckoned a dozen wealthy deepwater sea captains
to make Dover their home. It was the river that hastened the growth
of commercial Dover and its downtown merchants. It was the river
that led to the development of the Landing with professional offices,
stores, warehouses, taverns, fire companies, and a school. And it was
the river that eventually moved the heart of the town from its
founding spot at Dover Neck to its present location, originally known
as the Village at Cochecho.

Dover, with its connection by water to Portsmouth and the
ports of the Atlantic, and its connection by land to the smaller back-
country towns north and west to Winnipesaukee, was an important,

thriving inland seaport. "Portland, Boston, New York, and even the West Indies, knew of this tidewater trading place."[1]

The development of Dover as a shipping and trading center, and eventually its decline as a seaport can be seen in three distinct stages.

Stage 1—1623-1785

During this stage, the Cochecho River was the focus of Dover's livelihood. Every inhabitant's existence was tied in some way to the water as the main source of food, trade, and transportation. Yet these were individual efforts; there was no organized body that encouraged the growth of the town and the use of the river as a community resource until 1785 when town selectmen voted to sell or lease lots at the Landing in order to encourage and promote trade. This planned incentive led to the second stage of development of Dover and the Cochecho as an important water port.

Stage 2—1785-1842

Soon after the town of Dover began leasing acreage at the Landing, development followed. River traffic increased as scores of stores and businesses opened along the waterfront during the 1820s. Trade with Portsmouth was augmented, as well as trade with inland towns in Strafford, Carroll, and Belknap Counties. Numerous gundalows and packets plied the waters on daily scheduled runs to Portsmouth and semiweekly trips to Boston and Portland. River captains were able to make a good living delivering freight and passengers to distant towns and cities. There was even talk of digging a canal from Dover to Winnipesaukee in order to connect even more New Hampshire towns to the sea. The Cocheco Manufacturing Company had thousands of tons of coal delivered annually to its wharves on the river, and business boomed. Dover was becoming so successful, in fact, that the Boston and Maine Railroad determined to run its tracks into downtown. When the railroad did connect to Franklin Square during 1842, that signaled the decline in river freighting at the Landing.

From 1842 until after the Civil War, little river news is available to report. Dover's citizens appear to have focused entirely on the new technology of the iron horse, and later to have concentrated on the war and not on the development of the Cochecho River. About the year 1870 however, news of the arrivals and departures of schooners on the Cochecho starts to pick up once again. As railroad freight charges increased steadily and businessmen turned once again to the river and its cheaper methods of transport, another era, a renaissance in Dover shipping, began.

Stage 3—1870-1914

During the last quarter of the nineteenth century, a concentrated effort was made by city officials to develop the Cochecho River by easing navigation into the port. Federal funds for dredging the shallow beds of the river and blasting submerged ledges were secured so that larger vessels with greater drafts could come directly into the Landing to unload. A local businessmen's conglomerate built the Dover Navigation Company from one schooner in 1877 to a fleet of ten huge vessels by 1890. Businesses along the waterfront like Charles Trickey's Coal Company and Converse and Hammond's Lumberyard flourished. The 1880s were the heyday of Dover shipping with as many as seven or eight vessels docking here each week. Imagine, if you will, a three-masted ship like the schooner *J. Frank Seavey:* 144 feet long, thirty-four feet wide, and over ten in depth, carrying 1,200,000 pounds of coal docked at Dover Landing. This sight was quite a common occurrence to our citizens and a source of great pride to all.

The demise of the shipping industry in Dover was brought on by two factors, one local and one national. The great storm and flood of March 1, 1896, known as Dover's Black Day, crippled many local waterfront businesses and redeposited much of the silt, sand, and debris that had been dredged out of Dover's river during the previous twenty-five years. As a result, the great-sized schooners that had visited here so frequently in the past were unable to get into port again. And the Dover Navigation Company, whose main business had been freighting, dissolved in 1914, a victim of the nationwide shift to railroads and modern trucking on interstate turnpikes.

The glorious days of the Cochecho River as the key to Dover's commercial and industrial success are gone forever, but it is still to the river that we must turn to discover the rich heritage of the past. And as we come full circle, it is once again the river that is becoming the focus of Dover's development in the 1980s.

(above) Early square-end gundalow 20 to 30 feet long. (below) Gundalow with spoon bow and stern, 60 to 70 feet long. There were ten such gundalows in use at Dover by 1810. Models by Clyde L. Whitehouse. OBHS

I *The Early Years,*
1623-1785

LONDON FISHMONGERS Edward Hilton and his brother William
sailed from England and came up the Piscataqua River to Dover Point
sometime during the year 1623. The exact date of their arrival, the
name of their vessel, and most of the names of their exploration party
are unknown. There exists even today an unspoken rivalry between
Dover and Portsmouth as to which settlement was the first in New
Hampshire: David Thomson at Little Harbor or the Hiltons at Dover.
Alonzo Quint, John Scales, and George Wadleigh present credible
arguments for Dover in their histories of the city.[1]

In any event, the Hiltons did begin a small settlement at
Dover Point, then called Wecanacohunt by the local Indians. At the
southern-most tip of Dover Neck, bounded by the Piscataqua (or
Fore), Bellamy (or Back), and Cochecho Rivers, this point was an
ideal location for a colony. Quint says:

> The spot of the first settlement is given by tradition, and the
> tradition seems probable. It was at the extreme southern
> point of Dover. The view southward is across the broad, deep,
> and rapid Piscataqua, which flows from Great Bay; westward
> it is over the Bellamy River and fertile meadowlands beyond;
> eastward it is across the Newichawannock (Salmon Falls),
> which now separates Maine and New Hampshire, and to the
> Eliot fields and Agamenticus. Here the settlers "set up their
> stages" and on the land arrayed their flakes. The great river
> at proper seasons was richly supplied with fish.[2]

George Wadleigh concurs, yet adds another reason for settling this site:

> The location at the Point was doubtless first selected for the convenience of trading with the Indians about the falls of the Cochecho, a favorite resort with them. It was also in the vicinity of good fishing ground, for the various branches of the Piscataqua, up to their first falls, must at that day have swarmed with fish, and there was no need of going far to the coast to hook and obtain them. Its advantages must have been soon seen and appreciated.... They could hardly have found a more inviting place than the Point, either for fishing, planting or trading with the Indians, exchanging such articles as they brought with them from England for the Beaver skins and other peltries of the Indians.[3]

Wadleigh also suggests that safety was a high priority with the settlers and that this narrow neck of land with its boats docked nearby provided an excellent means for a quick escape should one ever be needed. The small community grew slowly from a transient trading and fishing post to an organized village by 1630.

Edward Hilton was formally granted possession of the land from Hilton's Point to the falls at Squamscot and three miles into the mainland. Jeremy Belknap prophetically described that land as "a ridge rising gently along a fine road and declining on each side like a ship's deck."[4] The grant today would include all of Dover, Durham, and Stratham, and parts of Newington and Greenland.

By 1634, the first meetinghouse for public worship was built at Dover Point and more land grants had been made. In 1639, the settlers formed their community into "a body politic."[5] This action was followed by the union of Dover with the government of Massachusetts in 1641 and the adoption of the laws of that commonwealth.

Shortly after this, development began at the Lower (First) Falls of the Cochecho River. *Cochecho* was an Indian word meaning "swift, foaming water." The river rose among the ponds of New Durham and Middleton and emptied some thirty-three miles and nine falls later into the Piscataqua at the junction of the Newichawannock (or Salmon Falls) at Cochecho Point.

Recognizing the usefulness and profitability of trading with the Indians who lived around the falls of the Cochecho, and possibly even foreseeing the upcoming great demand for timber abroad, settler Richard Walderne (Waldron) began a second settlement about 1642 at what is now downtown Dover.

Dover's first industry was fishing, but Walderne started a second: a sawmill at the Lower Falls prior to 1647. In fact, laws concerning the fair disposition of those large quantities of fish and those huge timber stands at Cochecho formed the bulk of the earliest ordinances passed by the town.

> April 20, 1644:
> It was ordered that Mr. Edward Starbuck, Richard Walderne and William Furber be Wearesmen for Cotcheco falls and river...paying yearly six thousand Alewives for rent to the town. The first fish they catch are...for the use of the Church... and the first Salmon...to the pastor or teacher, and none are to fish in said falls or weares but the above written. The said wearesmen are to have (the next) six thousand of fish each of them. Church officers are to be served with fish [as are] all that bear office in the Commonwealth and the most ancient inhabitants.... And it is ordered that no man shall molest the said Wearesmen...upon pain of nineteen shillings....[6]

> Oct. 12, 1648:
> There was granted to Richard Waldron fifteen hundred trees, either oak or pine, for the accommodation of a sawmill...set up at or upon the lower fall of the river Cochchecho. The said Richard Waldron is to pay three pence per tree.[7]

The issues to which Dover paid attention in the 1640s were land grants, fishing rights, and sawmill profits—all concerns dependent on the river which provided these livelihoods. It is not surprising, therefore, that by 1650 interest in the river would lead Dover to develop its third industry, shipbuilding. Enterprising townsfolk like Richard Walderne could envision the exportation of cured fish to foreign ports, and planks and masts to England where the demand for good lumber was high.

Records indicate that a frigate was built in a cove at the junction of the Fore and Cochecho Rivers prior to 1650, probably for Walderne, who embarked on a trade business with the West Indies and Europe. Local laws were quickly passed to assure quality workmanship by boatbuilders.

No lengthy descriptions or ship's captains' accounts exist today to give us an accurate picture or count of the first vessels built in Dover, but John Scales speculated that the first ships were "large for those days,"[8] "clumsy little sloops and ketches"[9] of forty to sixty tons and "commanded by hardy, keen-minded and fearless men [who] voyaged farther and farther away from Dover as profitable trade lured them on."[10] Also in use on the Cochecho River at this time were the gundalows, a unique river craft indigenous to the Piscataqua

Region. The first models of these boats were little more than barges. In use before 1659, the gundalows were square-ended and flat-bottomed without a sail or rudder. They were about twenty to thirty feet long and were guided by a crew of two or three men "poling" or using long sweeps. The vessels had no deck except for small platforms at each end where the men could stand while steering with their poles. Cargo (cords of wood, etc.) was carried in the open middle of the boat, yet even when fully loaded, the gundalow drew no more than two feet of water.

Captains were dependent on the winds and the tides for their movements, but the key to the success of the gundalow in this region was its utility. At this time period, there were few wharves on the river, but the gundalow could come right up to the bank. Being sail-less, the vessels could negotiate easily under low bridges, and being flat-bottomed could travel almost any shallow tributary. Despite their hulk, the gundalows were quite easy to maneuver in the swift currents of the Piscataqua and provided an extremely cheap means of transportation for bulky freight like lumber or marsh hay.

Gundalows were not built to go to sea (though some did), and their captains were often held in lower regard than the men who commanded the sloops, packets and schooners, but they were the workhorses of the rivers around Great Bay. It was the gundalow that was able to sail from Cochecho Landing three miles downriver to Cochecho Point and unload the larger vessels arriving laden with cargo from the West Indies. It was this ugly little barge that helped develop Dover's export business. By the year 1700, Dover ships carried cod and salmon to Spain, Portugal and cities along the Mediterranean coast, lumber and barrel staves to Barbadoes and the West Indies, and cut timber, masts, and pelts to England. They imported finished goods from Europe, sugar, molasses, and great quantities of rum from the Caribbean. The Village at Cochecho (from Tuttle Square to the Falls) had grown to contain just as many taxpayers as the settlement at Dover Neck and a new meetinghouse was built in 1713, equidistant between the two villages. More boat-yards produced bigger and better ships, and Dover's attachment to the Cochecho River grew too.

It is interesting to note that there were many more place names for points along the river than there were for streets or locales in town. Mary Thompson's *Landmarks in Ancient Dover* lists locations such as Clement's Point, the Horse Races, Boiling Rock, Long Reach, Nancy Drew's Point, Trickey's Cove, Langstaffe Rocks, Shag Rock, the Narrows, the Pulpit, Freeman's Point, Ham's Point, and the Gulf.[11] Directions were given in relation to how close a certain

Piscataqua House at Dover Point. Thomas Trickey's ferry ran from Dover Point to Bloody Point in Newington in 1840. RAW

point was to a known location at the water's edge.

Because roads were poor and bridges almost nonexistent, ferries ran between Dover Neck and Bloody Point (Newington), Kittery (now Eliot), and Fresh Creek (now Rollinsford). Rights to operate a ferry business were also controlled by the town, and permits were handed down in families from generation to generation or could be sold for a considerable price. Clark's, Trickey's, Knight's, and Henderson's were some of the more famous ferries that brought freight and passengers from one side of Little Bay to the other.

By 1766, business was so good on the river that the town voted to build a hostelry at Dover Point:

> The town voted to erect a dwelling house, stable, ferry ways, etc. at Hilton's Point for the convenience of travellers and a committee was appointed to obtain subscriptions to defray the expense.[12]

In 1767, a census was conducted and showed Dover's population to be 1,614, an increase of about 500 over the previous century even though "old Dover" had contained the now setoff towns of Durham, Lee, Newington, and Somersworth. The entire region's total was 3,465, a goodly population for that time. The Revolutionary War considerably slowed Dover's import and export trades, but shipbuilding continued at a steady pace. In 1785, a sixty-ton schooner was hauled from its boatyard at Garrison Hill to be launched on the Cochecho River. The vessel was built by Captain Richard Tripe "and landed on the ice a few rods below the lower bridge. The snow covering the earth this time was not less than three feet deep."[13] But the Landing at this time had been little developed. The riverbanks were principally used to store lumber waiting for shipment and the only business was a cooper's shop for producing barrels. "There was little trade in the town; the few articles for consumption or wear not produced at home were bought of itinerant dealers or procured at Portsmouth."[14] The town fathers, recognizing the need for Dover to grow and become more self-sufficient, voted in 1785 to sell lots on the Landing "for the purpose of promoting and encouraging trade."[15] More lots were sold or leased in succeeding years, and ever so slowly, the Landing began to emerge as the center of Dover's activity. The 1790s were the turning point for Dover as an inland port. A conscious decision was made to direct the town's industrial growth to reap the benefits of the Cochecho River and to build Dover as a commercial center.

This shift in focus did not occur overnight. A noted traveler in these parts, Yale president Dr. Timothy Dwight, visited Dover in 1796 and wrote these blunt remarks:

> The site of Dover is chiefly a declivity. The buildings are substantial and decent, but formed with very little taste or beauty. A small number of them only are painted: and most of these with a dull disagreeable color. There is nothing sprightly in the appearance of the town, except the activity of its inhabitants. The commerce in Dover consists chiefly in lumber. The material is daily diminishing, and in a short time will probably fail. Whether a substitute can be found by the inhabitants, I am ignorant.[16]

A more than suitable substitute was eventually found—cotton manufacturing, but Dover actually began to turn around long before the mills were built. It was to the Cochecho River that the town owed its promise and its past. And it was to the development of the Landing that Dover gave its attention in the nineteenth century.

II *The Growth Years, 1785-1842*

IN 1785, THE SELECTMEN OF DOVER voted to sell and/or lease some of the town-owned land bordering the Landing on what are now Cochecho, Portland, Young and Water Streets. Up until this time, the lots had been used chiefly for storage of cargo or cordwood that had been delivered by gundalows or that was awaiting shipment from Dover to larger vessels in Portsmouth harbor. Town fathers, anxious to build up Dover's treasury so that improvements to the village could be made, discovered that the lease of these lots to enterprising businessmen for commercial purposes could benefit the town not only through the collection of rental fees, but also because these enterpreneurial merchants soon attracted other businesses to the area. Men with a keen eye for economics saw the potential in this area and rightly predicted that Dover was about to blossom. The population of the town did not increase greatly during the last decade of the eighteenth century, but the volume of activity involving deed transfers and land acquisitions was phenomenal. The new breed of men moving into Dover were not the "old families" but innovative risk-takers gambling on future prosperity.

During the 1790s, with shipbuilding on the increase, there arose a need for goods and services at the Landing that could supply those ships and their crews, take their items in trade for necessary provisions, and provide outlets for the sale of the imported goods which those ships brought to Dover. Joseph Smith, a native of Newburyport who came to Dover about 1794, opened a bakery on Main Street. Smith supplied a basic foodstuff to incoming ships and his big ovens were right on the river so that the freshly baked loaves could be loaded still warm onto the boats in port. By 1799, Smith had expanded his interests and was also dealing in tobacco and finished goods. Another entrepreneur, Nathaniel Ela, opened a tavern on the corner of Washington and Main Streets. Shortly after the turn of the century, several other new stores were dealing in East and West India goods, molasses, and rum. William and Samuel Hale operated a hardware store opposite Ela's tavern, and nearby Nahum French had a dram-shop, Enoch Nutter a clock-making business, and Dover's third newspaper, *The Sun,* was started at the Landing in 1795. A school was established as were a distillery and a tannery. Several lawyers opened new offices in the area and the focus of Dover's commercial activity began to slowly shift from The Corner at Tuttle Square to the bustling Landing.

Notice.

THE subscriber respectfully informs his customers, friends, and the public in general, that he intends to navigate the Cocheco River, the coming season with Packets, Gondolas, &c. suitable and convenient to take all kinds of freight to and from Dover and Portsmouth, at his usual prices. Having employed first rate men to navigate said boats, which, with his own exertions, will be able to freight Goods with the greatest dispatch.

The Packets *FOX* and *TRAVELLER* will run daily, Sundays excepted, and Gondolas will be ready, at all times, to carry freight to any amount. I take this opportunity to return thanks to all persons who have employed me, and hope by attention to the business to have a continuance of the same.   STEPHEN TWOMBLY.

Notice   SE   Dover, Feb. 4, 1810.   34

Quint described Dover at the turn of the century: "Its merchants dealt with all the surrounding country up to and beyond... Winnipesaukee Lake and the White Mountains. On a winter's day... the country teams coming into town in the morning frequently extended from Ela's tavern to near the foot of Garrison Hill."[1] The revenue generated by these businesses helped the town of Dover build a new courthouse in 1789, establish a Social Library in 1792, construct a bridge over the Bellamy River in 1793, and buy an engine for the fire companies in 1800. "The courthouse, bridge, library and fire society are examples of the movement toward social improvement which coincided with the introduction of new merchants into the area. The spirit of growth which the town must have experienced brought with it a pride and ambition for improvement."[2]

As the volume of activity increased on land surrounding the Cochecho River, it doubly increased on the waters themselves. Gundalows had been operating in the Great Bay and Little Bay for several decades already and their traffic into Dover was climbing steadily. Larger vessels like the schooners could not sail all the way into Dover. The channel just was not wide nor deep enough. The gundalows' job, therefore, was to meet the big ships about three miles down the Cochecho, unload their cargo, and bring it up to Dover wharves.

In Dover, by 1810, there were as many as ten gundalows in constant use on the Cochecho River to Portsmouth. Each boat could carry from thirty-two to thirty-six tons of cargo or eighteen cords of dry hardwood. They could come up to the Landing at halftide with a fair breeze to move them along.[3] Captains Moses Young, John Sayles, Joseph Dame, Benjamin Ford, and Stephen Twombly delivered between 20,000 and 30,000 tons of cordwood annually to the brick-yards along the river. The hulky craft had evolved somewhat from the square-ended scows of the early eighteenth century: the Piscataqua gundalow adopted a spoon bow and stern and a lee board on the port side, a cuddy (or cabin) aft, and a "lateen" triangular sail attached to a short ten- or fifteen-foot mast and a yard arm as long as the vessel. The sail could be lowered quickly when going under bridges.[4]

Another type of river craft, also unique to the Piscataqua region, was developed at this time. The "packet" (a catch-all term that applied to almost any vessel not a gundalow or a full-sized schooner) was:

> a curved-hull, keel boat, thirty to forty feet in length, of about twelve to eighteen tons in carrying capacity, lateen–rigged, on a single stump, to pass beneath bridges, and carried her cargo below deck. Obviously, these vessels were not able to navigate in the shoal water of this region. It was necessary to keep to the deepest channels and take full advantage of high water.[5]

These vessels were also referred to as sloops, transients, or coasters, and as early as 1807, a Captain Clements was sailing regularly from Dover to Boston.[6] During the summer there were two daily packets, commanded by Clements and taking light freight and passengers, running between Dover and Portsmouth.

River Captain Charles Young described the activity at Dover Landing during the first half of the nineteenth century:

> I commenced going in a packet between Dover and Portsmouth (in 1815)...continued in that business...until 1827. From the spring

Piscataqua packet. Model by Capt. Edward H. Adams (1860-1951)   GB

of 1828 to December 1831, I was engaged in the coasting business, that is, sailing between Dover and Boston. During the time I was in the packet business between Dover and Portsmouth I should think there were as many as eight or ten gundalows owned in Dover whose business it was to ply on the river. And all of said time in summer months there was one, and a considerable portion of the time...two daily packets between Dover and Portsmouth. There was one sloop owned and commanded by Captain Clements which ran regularly between Dover and Boston. One small pink-stern schooner commanded by Captain Peirce also run for one or two years during said time between said places. He afterwards built a large vessel and run her one or two years. He and Captain James Wentworth built a schooner of about seventy tons and run her as a regular coaster between said places one or two seasons.

About the time the two small vessels were built as above, a schooner of about fifty or sixty tons, called the *Cordelia* commenced running from Dover to Boston, to Newburyport, to Cape Ann, Thomaston, and Portland.... She was called a transient vessel.

About the same time a schooner of fifty tons or upwards, was owned in Dover. She was engaged in the fishing business, called the *Laurel*, and afterwards engaged in the Southern trade.

Another schooner, called the *Marion*, of about forty tons burthen,...was employed as a transient vessel between Dover and other ports. She was owned in Dover about two or three years. About 1826 or 1827 a sloop called the *Satellite* was bought by people in Dover and Great Falls Company. She was of about sixty tons....

Around 1830, a schooner called the *William Tell* was put on the course between Dover and Boston. She was of about seventy tons....Shortly after,...another schooner of about thirty tons called the *Young Tell* was bought by Moses P. Perkins of Dover and was employed one or two seasons as a transient vessel. About the same time,...another schooner of about forty or fifty tons was bought and put on course from Dover to Boston.... She ran a part of two seasons–owned partly in South Berwick and partly in Dover and named *Volusia*. About the same time the *Volusia* was bought or a little before, a sloop called the *Flash* was put on the course between Dover and Boston.... She was owned by the Great Falls Manufacturing Company and by citizens of Dover and rated about fifty tons. A sloop called the *Sally*, of about thirty tons, commenced running about the time the *Cordelia* did and run until the *Satellite* was bought, for which she was in part exchanged.[7]

Another packet commander, Daniel Trefethen of Dover, testified in court that he had been "coasting" since 1827 and annually made between twenty and twenty-five trips to Boston and back.[8] His brother, Archelaus, had done the same. Andrew Peirce Jr. reported that he had begun navigating in packets about 1807 between Dover and different ports in Massachusetts.[9] Several other river captains, including James Wentworth, George Young, Enoch Dunn, James Dore, Ivory and George Chadbourne, Abram F.J. Channel, Benjamin Ford, Thomas and Henry Card, Joseph Dame, Eli Cole, Charles and George Spinney, Stephen Twombly, Moses Varney, Moses Young, and John Sayles accounted for their gundalow and packet sailings from as early as 1790.[10] Several of these men even had more than one boat under their command and all were able to make a satisfactory, even comfortable, living from plying the coastal rivers of the northeast, a testament to the volume of activity on the Cochecho River.

This shipping industry on the river spurred even more commercial activity at the Landing. In 1815, the first brick block of stores was built on the east side of Main Street by Joseph Smith and Rogers and Patten. The Dover Cotton Factory, which had been incorporated in 1812, had begun production at their Upper Falls mill two miles north on the Cochecho, but its owners were anxious to relocate closer to the Lower Falls just above the Landing as much of their raw material was arriving at the port of Dover. Dr. Timothy Dwight, who had pronounced Dover "a declivity" in 1796, revisited the town about 1813 and declared, "I found Dover considerably improved since my last visit, and, what was not a little gratifying to me, furnished with a good Minister of the Gospel."[11] Religious adherence notwithstanding, Dover was also suddenly concerned with improving its homes' and its citizens' appearance. George Wadleigh in his *Notable Events* remarks:

> J. Mosely, "Fashionable Hair Dresser, Cutter, Shaver and Boot Blacker", offers his services to the public, and assures his friends of his "assiduous endeavors to prove himself worthy of their patronage." L.S. Parmly, a travelling dentist, offers to furnish "durable enamel artificial teeth".... About this time also, William Palmer, well-known mason…, offers to build… "Russian stoves, on a new and improved plan, with or without fireplaces." All of which furnishes indications of the progress which Dover was making in "modern" fashions and improvements.[12]

Gordon Grimes in his *History of Dover* concurs:

> After almost three decades of growth, Dover had become a rather sophisticated little village. While the population had grown by only 800 during the preceding thirty years, another

Folsom DE

type of growth had occurred. The economy had matured and was more diversified, no longer dependent upon lumber and produce alone. The town was the trading center for the county and numerous merchants sold East and West India goods to the farmers who came to Dover to buy. In addition, specialty artisans turned out products ranging from watches and clocks to paintings and sofas. The economy was no longer one of subsistence living but almost of consumerism. Satisfying basic needs was not enough.[13]

Michael Reade House, 43 Main Street, Dover. An Irish immigrant who came to Dover during the late eighteenth century, Reade was one of the wealthiest and most influential merchants at the Landing by 1800. His home, now listed on the National Register of Historic Places, was built in 1780 when Dover's commercial growth in that area was in its infancy. DPL

Michael Reade, son of Irish immigrants, who had moved to Dover in the 1770s (and whose home still stands at 43 Main Street), was one of the early entrepreneurs who had made a great deal of money in commercial and real estate dealings when the land he had owned surrounding the river suddenly became a gold mine. Reade kept an *Almanack* from 1812 to 1864 and one of his entries from February 1818 shows his delight in his good fortune: "To the Landing teamsters from up country came to town with their loads of produce and exchanging them for the goods that the store keepers were well supplied with, in great variety. Business was excellent."[14]

The Landing was the hot coal of Dover, NH enterprise.... Nothing was done in local trade elsewhere in town. The river afforded a channel to Portsmouth, and so on out to sea, and the outer world.... So the Landing outpaced other sections of the town. There came to live within its borders the bold and energetic, as

Young's storehouse with its overhanging second floor for gundalows to pass under. The fourth building is the old Flax Mill, later D. Foss & Son's mill. RAW

well as the possessors of ready money, and, if a forceful man lived elsewhere, he spent his busiest hours near the waterfront.

In a neglected locality...where still existed some traces of the ancient forest, there grew up a thriving business with the north country, and paying relations with distant coast towns.[15]

A ledger account dated 1820-21 from Nathaniel and Jerry Young's Wharf and Warehouse at Dover Landing attests to the abundance and diversity of goods that were shipped to and from Dover and housed in Young's storehouse. The following items were brought by gundalows and packets during that year: A wide variety of food including salt fish, rice, flour, corn, rye, sugar, spices, bacon, turkey, butter, mackerel, flounder, tongue, halibut, tea, coffee, lemons, molasses, vinegar, chocolate, raisins, nuts, grapes, fig, and peas; all kinds of liquor and wine; some ready-made clothing and lots of fabrics such as cotton, flannel, wool, leather, flax, horsehides, sheepskins, feathers, buttons, thread, yarn, and lace handkerchiefs; building materials including iron, nails, wood, clapboards, copper spikes, glass, tin, ash, grindstones, varnish, lead, plaster, scythes, mud, logs, pipes, paint, chalk, lime, shovels, barrel staves, hoes, and oak planks; household necessities and niceties like kettles, tallow, candles, writing paper, guns, gunpowder and shot, carpeting, furniture, frypans, earthenware, books, mirrors, cigars, gravestones, and even a sundial. Young's also rented gundalows for about one dollar a day and took passengers for a twelve and one-half cent fare. As a sideline business, the Youngs also trained dogs and dealt in hides for the home shoe industry. (Young's Warehouse eventually was put up for auction in 1864 after the brothers' deaths.)

Also during 1821, owners John Williams and Isaac Wendell of the Dover Cotton Factory were able to purchase the land at the Lower Falls that they had coveted for a mill. The company increased its capital to $500,000 and in July laid the cornerstone of its new brick factory, called Mill #2 to distinguish it from the first wooden mill upstream. (A nail factory was also begun there in 1821 but being unprofitable, was abandoned in 1826.)[16] The new #2 was opened in 1822 and the huge amounts of brick, mortar, and wood needed for its construction were delivered by the gundalows. The large group of about 300 workmen employed in the construction of the building meant that more goods and services were needed in the town as Dover's population increased even before cotton production began. And when the factory actually started work, the influx of mill

Wharf property at auction DE

operatives, mostly young women from outlying communities, added even more to the demand for consumer goods.

In 1823, with the takeover by Boston-based investors led by William Payne, the company increased its capital to $1,000,000, changed its name to the "Dover Manufacturing Company," and opened Mill #3 at the Lower Falls. Mills #4 and #5 were built in 1825, and in 1827, the factory changed hands once again and became the "Cocheco Manufacturing Company"[17] with capital of $1,500,000.

In the decade between 1820 and 1830, Dover's population had almost doubled, rising from 2871 to 5449 as the mills physically altered the face of downtown and significantly changed its character. Life on the river was busier than ever as gundalows brought up raw cotton and cordwood for the factories, and packets took the finished products down to Boston.

But it was not just Dover that was booming. In 1822, due to greatly increased traffic going across the river from Portsmouth to Kittery, Maine on the cumbersome and infrequent ferry, a bridge was built crossing the Piscataqua River to ease the land-travelers' route. However, the Portsmouth Bridge proved to be a serious navigational problem for Dover river boat captains, who now had to battle not only swift currents and tides but also bridge supports which were, most Dover commanders thought, too close together. Accidents at the bridge increased dramatically and captains unfamiliar with the currents often declined to try to make the trip up to the Cochecho River if they had to pass under the bridge at less than high tide or in the dark. Several days passage time could be lost waiting for a safe time to pass under the Portsmouth Bridge. The town of Dover eventually filed suit against the proprietors of the bridge for its removal, but the lawsuit was unsuccessful.[18]

But dangerous or not, traffic on the Cochecho River and activity at the Landing continued to increase. An aqueduct company was chartered in 1823 to supply fresh water to homes surrounding the Landing area.[19] In 1824, a local group was formed to petition the State Legislature for two major river improvements: first, the digging of a canal from Dover to Lake Winnipesaukee so that the trade routes could be facilitated to the north country, and second, the dredging of the Cochecho River so that larger vessels could dock at Dover's inland port. The prohibitive $700,000 estimated cost of such a canal led quickly to the demise of that idea, but the dredging plan, which could be federally funded, was not forgotten for long because the volume of Dover's coasting business made news even in Boston:

> Goods are shipped from Boston to Dover, NH at $1.00 per ton, and packets are about to be established to run in a regular line

Hosea Sawyer block at the corner of Main and Portland Streets on Lafayette Square. It was built in 1825 for $8766.26 and is today listed on the National Register of Historic Places. CLW

weekly, between the two places. ...The trade of Dover has lately revived and (is) expanding. ...It bids fair to become a great seat of the manufacturing industries.[20]

In 1825, when Revolutionary War hero General Lafayette visited Dover on his tour of New England, it was to the Landing that he was taken by Dover dignitaries, so proud were town officials of their booming port. The junction of Main and Portland Streets, dignified with the recent completion of Hosea Sawyer's new brick block with its graceful curved front, was renamed Lafayette Square in the General's honor. Dover's burgeoning pride was deeply reflected in a Fourth of July oration given by former citizen John Mellen in celebration of fifty years of United States independence in 1826. Mellen expounded:

It is but 203 years since the first settlement was made in this town, upon the neck; the settlement of this part of Cochecho

---

Dover and Boston Packets.

NEW LINE.

THE public is informed that a line of
Packets is established to run regularly and weekly between Dover and Boston, composed of the
following vessels :
  Sch. Dover Packet,   Capt. Peirce,
    " Boston Packet,   "   Wentworth,
    " Cordelia,   "   Card.
  These vessels are good and adapted to the trade,
two of them being built for the purpose, the present year, and it is intended that one of them may
always be found in each place. The masters are
acquainted with the navigation, and will take due
care of all property entrusted to them, and proper
attention will be paid to passengers who may
be landed, and alsofreight by agreement in passing Portsmouth. Inquiry may be made at No. 29,
Long-wharf, Boston, or at No. 2, Main-st. Dover.
  July 26.

ONE CENT REWARD.

RAN away from the subscriber on the night of
the 24th inst. an indented apprentice boy by
the name of ALVAH HUNTRESS ; the above reward
will be paid to any person who will return said boy
to the subscriber, and no charges paid ; and all
persons are forbid harbouring or trusting said boy
on my account.
            WILLIAM W. STACKPOLE.
New Line NHR Dover, July 26, 1825.

much later. 114 years ago this town was infested with a savage
foe. ...Now instead of the war whoop and savage yell along your
river and the light-oar'd canoe, you have the canvassed vessel,
the heavily-oar'd gondola bearing the product of every clime to
the merchant, the raw material to the manufacture and the
rattling of 10,000 spindles adds to the roar of your cataract.
How changed the scene!... Your commerce and boat navigation
has greatly increased and the amount now employed is not less
than $33,000. The number of your merchants or traders is now
forty-one, and their stock not less than $106,000. The number of
mechanicks regularly settled and in good employment is not less
than 400. The amount employed in your extensive
manufactories is more than $800,000 and affords a source of
employment to more than 2000 persons...[21]

REGULAR LINE OF
PACKETS
Between Dover & Portsmouth.

THE subscriber having purchased of *Stephen Twombly* his BOATS, which said Twombly has run between Dover and Portsmouth, would now say to the public, that he has commenced running a REGULAR LINE OF BOATS between DOVER and PORTSMOUTH, for the purpose of transporting Merchandise, Lumber, &c. consisting of the Sloop WASHINGTON and the Packet MENTOR; and also a supply of GONDOLAS when occasion requires. The subscriber having been engaged for several years in the coasting business between Dover and Boston, flatters himself that he can do the Freighting business between Dover and Portsmouth, in a manner that will be satisfactory to those who may employ him, and solicits a share of patronage.

All orders left with Andrew Peirce, Jr. or Andrew Peirce, Jr. & Son, will receive prompt attention, and satisfaction given or no pay

JAMES WENTWORTH.

N. B. Smallest favors gratefully received.

March 19, 1842.   1S

Packet, James Wentworth RAW

Local businessmen saw the importance of running the coastal packets on regularly scheduled routes to other New England ports. Vessels that ran frequently and on time would gather much of the freighting business from those ships which ran a haphazard schedule. As early as 1825, a newly organized "Line" of packets, run by Andrew Peirce, Jr., James Wentworth, and Thomas Card, Jr., was started to serve the needs of the cotton factory. The *Dover*, *Boston*, and *Cordelia* promised regular trips to Boston and back.[22] In 1828, the *Dover*, the *Boston*, and the *Satellite* (built in 1826) offered Wednesday passages to Boston for freight or passengers through its Masters, Peirce Jr., Wentworth, and George Young.[23] During March 1829, a Boston newspaper noted:

> The last weekly *Dover Packet* from New Hampshire brought nearly as many cotton and woolen goods to this market as were brought by the packet ship *Dover*, and more than were brought by the packet *New England* from Liverpool. Cotton goods which were once purchased in England for thirty-eight cents and thought remarkably cheap, were not better cottons than can now be purchased here at twenty cents.[24]

The Cocheco Manufacturing Company had indeed put Dover on the map. The factory had supplied jobs, spurred growth, both industrial and residential, and had made optimum use of the river as a trade waterway. The town was now the second largest (behind Portsmouth) in New Hampshire. Dover citizens, still wishing to expand the port, petitioned the U.S. Congress for funds to dredge the Cochecho, but the bill was vetoed in 1830 by President Andrew Jackson. Yet business was still good. Michael Reade wrote in his *Almanack* in 1831:

> Good sledding through January and February. Teams came in with loads from up country; merchants were busy with big trade. Sometimes the teams (oxen) would reach from Garrison Hill to the Landing. They had to wait for the team ahead to unload and load up again and start for home.[25]

George Wadleigh added further comment:

> There were belonging in Dover, at the commencement of this year, six sloops and schooners, constituting a regular line of packets, plying between Dover and Boston and other places. Also three daily packets running between Dover and Portsmouth. A steamboat was also run on the river a part of the time.[26]

Shipbuilding at Dover boatyards produced as many as six vessels a year during the 1830s. These boats, ranging in size from thirty tons to 600 tons, were, for the most part, commissioned and owned by wealthy Dover men and were employed in the coasting business. At the Hale Brothers shipyard at Squall Point (now the site of Henry Law Park), 250-ton sister ships, the *Lydia* and the *Martha*, were built for William Hale. On the spot where New #1 Mill was built in 1877 (now Clarostat Mfg. Co.), John Saville built two schooners, the *Charles Henry* and the *Ellen and Clara*, for Andrew Peirce Jr. which were used in trade with Texas. In 1835, Rogers and Peirce launched a 300-ton ship from their yard on the Landing.

The *William Penn*, the *Peirce*, the *Cochecho*, the *Laurel*, the *Marion*, the *Volusia*, and the *Greyhound* were just some of the other ships built in Dover at this time and there were many other vessels owned in Dover, yet built elsewhere. Competition between rival packet boat masters was fierce during the early 1830s as other vessels such as *William Tell*, *Pactolus*, *Banner*, *Washington*, *Young Tell*, *Sally*, *Fox*, *Zimri S. Wallingford*, *Factory Girl*, *December*, and *Lafayette* advertised their capabilities much the way today's myriad overnight delivery services boast their advantages: quicker! safer! on time! guaranteed! low fares!

Yet in 1835, these competing companies suddenly joined together to form one large syndicate called the Despatch Line of Packets. Gordon Grimes, in his *History of Dover*, suggests why:

> The papers had reported in December of 1834, that a railroad was being planned from the Boston area to Lowell. It was suggested that perhaps this steel road might be extended to Dover. Responding to the suggestion, entrepreneurs who had already played such an important part in the development of the town, made what was to become as important a contribution to the town as the cotton factories had been. William Hale, Andrew Peirce, James Bartlett, Joseph Smith, Stephen Hanson, John P. Hale and Asa Freeman incorporated the Boston and Maine railroad in June of 1835.[27]

"Notices began to appear in the papers that a railroad was in process of construction from Wilmington to Andover, meetings were held to aid its continuance to Dover and on the 31st of August, 1835, books for subscriptions to its stock were opened in Dover."[28]

The rival packet boat companies, perhaps in a retaliatory move to the initiation of the railroad plans, consolidated into a syndicate called the Despatch Line of Packets in 1835. "With the collective capital, nearly all the sound and fast-sailing seaboats were bought.... Among the early directors were Moses Paul, Andrew Peirce, Nathaniel Young, Andrew Peirce, Jr."[29] The Despatch Line owned and operated about seven vessels:

Dover and Boston PACKETS.

The regular line of Packets; running between Dover and Boston, viz.

Schooner DOVER PACKET,
Andrew Peirce, Jr. Master.
Sloop SATELLITE,
George Young, Master.
Schooner BOSTON PACKET,
James Wentworth, Master.

Will continue to run during the ensuing season in the following order, (wind and weather permitting) viz.

One of said Packets will leave Dover for Boston on Wednesday, and Boston for Dover on Saturday of each week.

☞ For Freight or Passage, apply

JAMES B. VARNEY, *Agent.*
Dover, April 1, 1828.   7tf

NEW-YORK & PORTSMOUTH PACKETS—Despatch Line.

THE following Vessels will compose the line of Packets for the ensuing season Viz.—

Sloop FLASH, E. Crowell Master,
Sloop AMEY & POLLY, J. Hallett, Master.
Sloop ——, E. Nicherson, Master.

The above are substantial fast sailing vessels and are commanded by men of experience in the trade ; every effort will be made to accommodate shippers by this line, and to ensure regularity safety and despatch. One of said vessels will sail from East side Coenties slip, New-York, and Jaffray's wharf Portsmouth, on Wednesday of each week, wind and weather permitting. Apply on board, or to

VAN NORTWICK & MILLER,
24 Coenties-slip, New-York, and
CHARLES BOWLES,
8   Jaffray's Buildings, Portsmouth.

Dover & Boston Packets SE

Four, from seventy to eighty tons each, are...employed between Dover and Boston. The others, from fifty to sixty tons each, are...employed as transient vessels. ...The amount of freights received...has been on the average about $20,000 a year. That company does none of the freighting to or from Portsmouth. ...The Despatch Line has been in the habit of importing goods from Boston to Dover for the section of the country following—Beginning at Durham, thence to Northwood, to Pittsfield, Gilmanton, Gilford, Meredith, New Hampton, Plymouth, Campton, Sandwich, Tamworth, Ossipee, Effingham, Newfield, Me., Acton, Shapleigh, North Berwick, and South Berwick, Me.[30]

Despatch Line commanders included Daniel Trefethen of the *William Tell*, Archelaus Trefethen of the *William Penn*, John Card of the *Peirce*, Clark Paul of the *December*, James Sterling of the *Lafayette*, and Daniel Card of the *Cochecho*, Masters Charles Young, Paul Burley and Henry Card were also employed by the line,[31] as were the vessels *Cordelia*, *Satellite*, and *Flash*.[32] There were several schooners owned only partly by the shareholders of the Despatch

Line. These included: the *Charles Henry*, John Smith 2d, master, owned by Andrew Peirce 3d and Co., the *Dover Packet,* Tristam Griffin, master, also owned by Andrew Peirce 3d and Co., the *Robert Rantoul, Jr.*, Timothy Newman Porter, master, owned by Joseph Morrill, Nathaniel Demeritt, William F. Estes, Josiah Hall, and William S. McCollister; and the *Washington*, J.B. Guppey, master, owned by Andrew Peirce, Jr., Andrew Peirce 3d and Co., James Wentworth, and J.B. Guppey.[33] These small schooners or coastal packets did not meddle in any of the activities of gundalows or smaller river packets that ran between Dover and Portsmouth. The small river packets, carrying small freight and passengers to Portsmouth, were about thirty feet long and drew only five and one-half feet of water when loaded. They were "rigged with a large lateen sail, bent to a long spruce yard which was slung to a short oak stump by a chain. A rope and block-tackle, attached to the lower end of the long yard and the bow of the boat, served to hold the triangular sail at proper angle when the boat was in motion, and to lower and hoist the same when passing under and beyond a bridge."[34] One of the earliest of these river packets was called the *Fox* and was operated by Captain Stephen Twombly in 1834; a few years later John and George Saville built a beautifully modeled, very fast packet, the *Greyhound*, at Lyman's yard in Dover. It was owned by the Andrew Peirces. The largest river packet, the *Zimri S. Wallingford*, built in Portsmouth by Toby and Littlefield, was commanded by the popular Dover skipper, James Rand, and was shortly joined on the river by William and George Drew's vessel, the *Factory Girl*, and George Dunn's *Eagle*.[35]

Michael Reade's *Almanack* documents the great amount of activity at Dover Landing during the spring of year 1835:

> Monday, April 12, 1835 Schooner Satellite, Capt. Daniel Trefethen, from Boston with freight for the merchants in Dover, Great Falls (Somersworth), North Berwick, and Meredith. Tuesday, April 16, 1835 Arrival of schooner Flash, Master James Wentworth, from Boston with freight for merchants in Dover, Wakefield, Farmington, Berwick. Friday, April 17, 1835 Schooner Cordelia, Master Daniel Card, from Portland with molasses and W. I. Goods for Rogers & Peirce of Dover. Monday, April 20, 1835 Arrival of schooner William Tell, Master Benn, from Boston, with freight for Dover merchants, L. Draper; Moses Paul; S. Snell; E. Young; T. J. Palmer; J. G. Smith; William Hale, Jr.; Prescott & Banks; John Brown; J. B. H. Odiorne; E. J. Lane; Clark & Bennett; J. Smith; and John Williams.

Arrived the same day: Schooner Lafayette, Capt. James Card, from Boston with freight for Dover merchants; Samuel Snell; J. H. Wheeler; Benjamin Boardman; Davidson Webster; David Peirce; R. H. Palmer. Monday, April 27, 1835 Arrived schooner Satellite, Master Trefethen, from Boston with freight for Dover merchants; Moses Paul; J. B. H. Odiorne; Joseph Smith; Ira Christie; Silas Moody and E. H. Nutter. Also for Great Falls, Berwick, Rochester, Farmington and Meredith, New Durham, and Shapleigh, Maine. Friday, May 1, 1835 Arrival of schooner Lafayette, Master Card, from Newburyport with freight for Dover merchants. Monday, May 4, 1835 Arrival schooner Flash, Capt. James Wentworth from Boston with merchandise for parties in Dover, Great Falls, Rochester, Barnstead, Meredith, Sandwich, and Berwick, Maine. Sunday, May 10, 1835 Arrival schooner Volusia, Capt. John Card, from Boston with freight for merchants in Dover, Meredith, Rochester, Center Harbor, South Berwick.

The schooner William Tell arrived the same day from Boston, Capt. Benn in command, with freight for parties in Dover, Rochester, Farmington, New Durham, Meredith, South Berwick and Great Falls. Friday, May 29, 1835 Arrived schooner Flash, Master Wentworth, from Boston with freight for William B. Smith & Co.; A. C. Smith; A Peirce 3rd; H. A. Tufts; L. Draper; George Andrews; M. B. Bird and Moses Paul of Dover. Also for C. P. Weeks of Rochester; Eben Dow of Tamworth; William Ives: Wingate North Co. of Somersworth. Sunday, May 31, 1835 Arrival of schooner William Tell from Boston, with freight for Dover parties and various upcountry towns. Thursday, June 4, 1835 Arrival schooner Strafford, Capt. Eldridge, from Washington, N. C. with cargo of 3900 bushels of corn, 20 barrels of tar; rosin; spirits of turpentine; and a deck load of hard pine plank, all for Rogers & Peirce of Dover.

The above may suffice to show how the Dover merchants were supplied with goods from abroad, and how the up-country towns had to send ox-teams here to get their supply of all kinds of goods they could not make themselves. Dover was then the greatest shipping center of the State.[36]

In 1836 there was, in addition to all the gundalow, packet, and schooner traffic, a steamboat called the *Tom Thumb* in operation between Dover and Portsmouth. Steamboats drew at most two and one-half to four feet of water, could make the passage in an hour, and could come up to Dover Landing even at half tide.[37] The *Tom Thumb* ran about three seasons at Dover, but eventually stopped because of

RATES OF

WHARFAGE & STORAGE,

ESTABLISHED BY THE

DOVER PACKET CO.,

	Warfage.	Storage.
Barrels Apple and Potatoes,	1 cent	2 cent
Do Flour and Bbls. Merchandize,	1	2
do Liquor, Pork Lard and Beef.	2	3
do Beer,	2	3
Bark per Cord,	12	
Boards per thous.	15	
Cases of Merchandize,	3	4
Chairs,	1-2	1-2
do Rocking,	1	1
Corn per Bushel,	1-4	1
Cotton per Bail,	3	6
Crates of Ware,	5	10
Coffee and Bags of Merchandize	1	2
Coal per ton,	12	
Fish per Bbl.	2	2
do per Qt'l	1	1
Grain Per bushel of all kinds,	1-4	1
Glass per Box,	1-4	1
Grindstones per ton,	10	12
Hay screwed per ton,	25	50
Hhd. Empty,	2	
Hhd Hoops per thous.	12	
Teirce, do	8	
Bbls do	6	
Lime per Cask,	2	4
Liquor per hhd and Pipe,	5	8
Molasses per hhd.	5	10
Tierce do	3	6
Barrels do	2	2
Oil per hhd and pipes,	5	8
Tierce do	3	5
Barrels do	2	2
Plank, Oak & Ash per thous.	25	
Potatoes per bushel	1-2	1
Rags per ton,	17	29
Rice per Cask.	3	4
Salt per hhd. lose	3	12
Saleratus per Cask,	3	3
Shingles per thous.	4	6
Shook and heading,	1	2
Sugar per box,	3	5
Hhds do	5	10
Sofas each,	3	6
Stoves and Aperatus,	3	7
Tierces, dry,	3	4
Tea per Chest.	2	2
1-2 do	1	1
Timber per ton, Oak Moulded,	17	
do by the Gundalo load,	1,00	
do Pine "	1,00	
do Oak Timber not hewed,	1,50	
Wood per Cord,	,10	
do by the Gundalo load,	1,00	
All small boxes and Ferkins of Mer-chandize	1	1

☞ This don't meant Goods laided by the Dover Packet Co.

Wharfage and Storage DPL

the difficulties in navigating under the Portsmouth bridge. Potential passengers were too frightened by the possibility of an accident to want to make the trip to Portsmouth by steamboat.

The largest coastal packet in use at Dover Landing drew between seven and eight feet of water when loaded and could come all the way up the Cochecho River at high tide. Vessels drawing ten to eleven feet could come within a mile of the Landing, while those drawing more than seventeen feet could only come up to a point two and one-half miles away from Dover wharves. There, their freight was unloaded by the gundalows, a process called lightering. This inconvenience not only added to the time it took for deliveries to be made, but also to the expense. Businessmen, town officials, and Cocheco Manufacturing Company directors continued to plead for federal funds to dredge the Cochecho River and finally, in 1835, their petitions were granted and $10,000 was appropriated during the next two years. "The navigation was much improved by clearing out the channel, taking out rocks and ledges, and widening the channel at the Gulf and the Narrows."[38]

During 1838, the last ship built in Dover was launched at the deepened Gulf on the Cochecho River. Captain Robert Rogers set sail on the 600-ton *Orinoco* during September. (The vessel unfortunately was lost at sea one year later, Sept. 4, 1839.) That same year, the third big brick block of stores, known as the Nutter and Peirce Block, was constructed at the corner of Washington and Main Streets,[39] and Michael Reade noted in his *Almanack*, "The number of arrivals of vessels in Boston from Dover during the year was ninety-seven–a larger number than from any other place east of New York, except Portland."[40]

In 1840, the Landing's prosperity was at its highest peak ever. It was estimated that between 150 and 200 vessels, from fifty to eighty tons each, navigated the Cochecho River each year to the port of Dover,[41] and this estimate does not take into account the gundalow traffic or transient arrivals. Moses Paul, agent of the Cocheco Manufacturing Company, testified that "the amount of goods and merchandise belonging to said Company that is transported on the river to and from Dover…in packets and gondolas, is in value about $750,000 per year. It would probably average that for the last ten years."[42] The Cocheco Mills had begun to switch, in 1840, from wood to coal for heating the factories and running the looms and had installed huge boilers in the west end of No. 5 mill. The coal was brought up river in gundalows. At first, teams of horses took the coal directly from the Landing to the boiler room at the archway on Washington Street, but soon the Company erected its own coal sheds on the Landing.

Dover, N. H. april 24   1867

Mr   I S abbott

To W. H. & G. K. Drew,
MASTERS OF THE

Dover and Portsmouth Packets and Gondolas.

FREIGHTING OF ALL KINDS OF MERCHANDISE.

	14	Bu Corn	42
april 27	16	" "	48
May 1	16	" "	48
2	12	" "	48
9	14	" "	42
July 9	16	" "	48
22	14	" "	42
27	14	" "	42
aug 3	14	" "	42
22	14	" "	42
30	14	" "	42
Sept 5	14	" "	42
6	14	" "	42
14	14	" "	42
24	14	" "	42
24	14	" "	42
oct 7	14	" "	42
14	14	" "	42
17	14	" "	42
19	14	" "	42
	1	Sail	2 00
22	14	Bu Corn	42
24	14	" "	42
Nov 1	14	" "	42
23	36	" "	1 08
	1	Sail	2 00 14 98

Capt. W.H. & G.K. Drew TH

The gundalows also brought up much of raw cotton for the mills: About one-half of the cotton used at our establishment is imported from the South and landed at Portsmouth. Thence it is taken to Dover in gondolas. All our coal, about 3000 tons per year...is imported into Portsmouth for us, and thence it is freighted up the river in gondolas. We run more than 27,000 spindles.... The other half of the cotton and other materials for our mills come in the packets from Boston.... We send no goods down the river in gondolas; they all go to Boston in the packets.[43]

In July 1842, Andrew Peirce, Jr. estimated that "the value of the goods transported up and down the river to and from Dover to Portsmouth and by Portsmouth, amounts to about $2,400,000 annually. This intends to apply to the navigation of the Cochecho only."[44]

However, on June 30, 1842, the Boston and Maine Railroad reached into Dover and opened a station on Third Street. The people of Dover were hardly aware of the railroad's implications for the Landing and shipping industry, but the trend toward this more modern and efficient method of freight transportation was hinted at only one month after the railroad had been in town. Mill Agent Moses Paul declared, "Since the opening of the railroad from Boston to Dover, a portion of our goods have been transported over the Rail Road...and I have no doubt a portion of our freight will continue to be transported over the Road."[45]

Alonzo Quint in his *History of Dover* summarizes:

...The opening of the Boston and Maine Railroad, and the construction a few years after the Cochecho Railroad to Alton, to both of which Dover people contributed liberally, had a marked effect upon the business of the town. While its local trade and interests were on the increase, its importance as a distributing point for interior trade declined. The Dover Packet Company, which had for many years given life and activity to the wharves and storehouses on the river, soon discharged its last cargo, the Landing ceased to be the center of business, which from this time gathered around the railroad station and the streets leading most directly to it.[46]

All shipping at Dover Landing did not stop. River packets still ran for at least a decade after the Civil War, small schooners delivered lumber and lime, excursion boats took pleasure trips to the Isles of Shoals, and steamers traveled to Boston, but this traffic was minor and infrequent. The *Dover Enquirer* of September 21, 1865 editorialized on the dilemma of the water versus the rails:

The traveller from Dover to Portsmouth has the privilege of going nearly double the actual distance by Railroad at more than double what the fare should be between the two cities, or he can take one of the packets which can only run when the tide serves and when once started may make the passage in one hour or it may be five or six as the wind may be favorable or adverse.[47]

The Dover newspapers of the 1850s and 1860s reported little news of shipping or activity at the port. Consumed by reports from the war-front, Dover citizens had little interest in local enterprise, but after the Civil War, with railroad freighting costs high in an unstable national economy, city officials once more began to investigate the use of the Cochecho River and the possibility of making improvements to its narrow channels and shallow beds. New dredging work began again and the newspaper remarked on the reincarnation of the Landing as a port:

> Years ago some six or eight schooners plied between Dover and different points along the coast. Then came the railroads and all had their merchandise brought by cars, as they could get it so much quicker, and could add the additional cost to the price of goods and make the consumer pay for it. The result was that freighting did not pay and the vessels, with one or two exceptions, were sold and taken from the river. Later still, our traders found that they were being undersold by their neighbor traders where there was railroad competition and consequently cheaper freights, and so many of them are now having their heavier goods come by water. So that it is not unusual to see three or four vessels at our wharves at one time either taking in or discharging Freight.[48]

More entrepreneurial men, that invigorated Dover breed, envisioned yet another heyday for Dover waterways and incorporated in 1877 the Dover Navigation Company,[49] a business that breathed new life into this inland port.

III   *The Town of Dover*
v. The Portsmouth Bridge

IN DECEMBER 1840, THE TOWN OF DOVER filed suit in Strafford County Superior Court against the proprietors of the Portsmouth Bridge for obstructing navigation of the rivers leading to Dover Landing. The Dover complainants declared that the bridge spanning from near Rindge's Wharf, Portsmouth to Kittery, Maine "is destructive of life and property and is a great public nuisance."[1] The bridge had been erected in 1822, and had always caused navigational problems for boats, packets, and gundalows trying to negotiate the swift currents and eddies of the Piscataqua, but what set this suit in motion, almost two decades after the original construction, was the intention, in 1840, of the bridge owners to deposit several thousand tons of stones and rocks into the river to help support the bridge's sagging piers. Dover claimed that this action would further impede access to its Landing by commercial vessels and would greatly hinder the town's shipping economy.

The lengthy testimony given by both the plaintiffs and the defendants paints a generous picture of the seacoast's dependence on shipping and particularly highlights Dover's activities as an inland port from 1810 to 1840.

Dover's suit, filed by Selectmen John Riley, Stephen Toppan, and Sharenton Baker, and presented by Town Solicitor Charles W. Woodman, alleged that while the bridge had always been a nuisance, "the Proprietors of Portsmouth Bridge...have lately entered into a contract with Lewis Hayes of Kittery...for filling up a large portion of the channel of said river...(with) large quantities of stones and

The Portsmouth bridge, built in 1822 to connect Portsmouth with Kittery. OBHS

rock...and...(have) already sunk and deposited...upwards of fifteen hundred tons of stones and rocks...(which) can never be removed."[2]

The selectmen further stipulated that:

> ...the navigation of said river has already become difficult, hazardous, and destructive to life and property, that by sinking and depositing such vast quantities of rock and stone...the river will be...still farther difficult...and be obstructed and rendered inconvenient and unsafe for said Town of Dover and its inhabitants.... Navigation between the harbour of Dover and the harbour of Portsmouth will be wholly destroyed, the river becoming swifter and more impetuous in its current and narrower and shallower in its channel, all which will be to the public damage.[3]

A train crossing over the draw of the Portsmouth Bridge. OBHS

The suit asked the court to rule on whether the bridge did indeed obstruct navigation; whether the gundalows and schooners could pass under the bridge at all times of tide as easily and freely as they could before the erection of the bridge; whether the larger class of vessels and steamboats that frequented Portsmouth harbor could pass under the bridge and whether these large ships couldn't pass all the way to Bloody Point if the bridge was removed; and whether the dumping of stones served any useful purpose.[4] The complainants finally asked the court to issue a restraining order prohibiting any further dumping of rocks, any further obstructions of any sort in the river channel, and any further keeping up and supporting said bridge.[5]

The defendants, Edward Cutts, A. W. Haven, Samuel Lord, Alexander Ladd, William Stavers, Nathaniel B. March, Lewis Hayes,

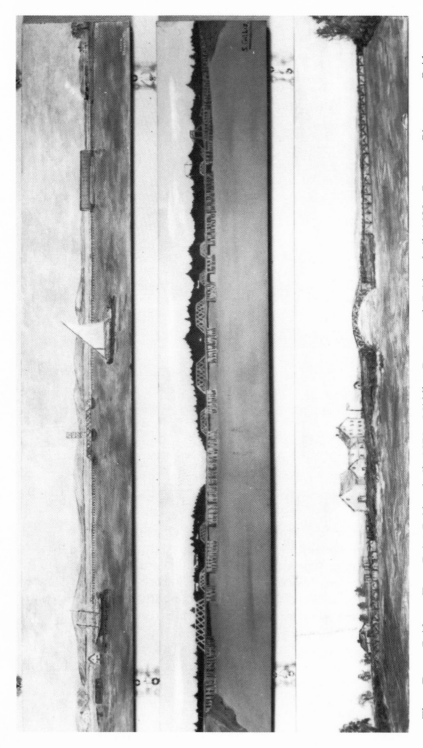

Three Dover Bridges. Top: Point Bridge, built 1871. Middle: Portsmouth Bridge, built 1822. Bottom: Piscataqua Bridge, built 1794, from Durham to Newington, and connecting Dover and Portsmouth, Fox Point on right. CLW

and their legal counsel Ichabod Bartlett, swiftly prepared their rebuttal to the suit, which they claimed contained many "errors, insufficiencies, and other imperfections."[6] They emphatically denied that the Cochecho River above Bloody Point was "navigable for boats or vessels of any description so far as the place called Dover Landing at low water,"[7] but did allow "that at high water the Cochecho is navigable up to Dover Landing for boats, gondolas, and vessels of a small size."[8]

The defendants stressed that the Portsmouth Bridge served a greater good: "the great and main road for the conveyance of the principal mails of the United States"[9] and that a highway connecting New Hampshire and Maine was much more convenient than the ferry boats that formerly ran between the two points. Their defense also cited the legal acts of incorporation that allowed the erection of the bridge in 1822, for $40,000. They further elaborated that "the number of travellers, teams and coaches which now pass said bridge is very great, and constantly increasing and that of stage coaches alone, the average number which now pass over the bridge is from eight to ten each day."[10]

The defendants next provided the proportions of the bridge and detailed the improvements (totaling an additional $30,000), which had been made to improve navigation for vessels passing under its piers.

> The length of said Bridge from the main land in Portsmouth to Ham's Island, is 500 feet in length, and that this portion of the Bridge is constructed with a convenient Draw or Hoist, for vessels to pass and repass, of such width as is convenient for the largest merchant vessels which have ever yet been in the harbour of Portsmouth. And the length of said Bridge from said Ham's Island to the Kittery shore is 1750 feet: and from the bottom of the channel of the River is in some portions of the same nearly seventy feet in height, that the same rests upon parts framed into what are called sections or piers, driven into the bottom of the River.[11]

The Bridge was originally constructed with a draw-hoist "of sufficient width for vessels to pass and repass freely and with two good and sufficient piers made, one...above and the other below the Bridge, and so connected...as to make it convenient for vessels to make fast to, and moor, until wind and tide...admit such vessel...to pass through."[12] The proprietors claimed that the draw was always opened without delay for the accommodation of all vessels.

They also claimed that open boats and gundalows could pass under the Bridge, "at least in one place, exclusive of the Draw...(as) the passage way was of sufficient height and width to pass with safety...at all times of tide."[13] At night, four oil lamps provided suffi- cient light for passable navigation.

Early draw of the Dover Point Bridge, built 1871. DLW

The original draw-hoists were thirty-three feet wide and the arch, or open space, was fifty feet wide. In 1826, improvements were made that widened the arch to seventy feet and added two other open spaces, each seventy feet, for the free passage of gundalows. These renovations cost $4,000. In 1835, for an additional $1500, the draw-hoist between Ham's Island and Kittery was enlarged to forty feet wide and a buoy with a heavy anchor and chain cable was placed above the bridge. In 1838, the draw-hoist between Ham's Island and Portsmouth was widened to thirty-eight feet for an $800 expenditure.

These improvements, claimed the directors of the bridge, were made in consideration of the difficulties some of the vessels had encountered in passing under the original structure. The width of the Piscataqua River itself between Portsmouth and Ham's Island at low tide was 350 feet, at high water 500 feet, and at the main breadth of the Bridge (from Ham's Island to Kittery) the width was 1300 feet at low tide, 1750 feet when high tide. At a point one mile north of the bridge toward Dover, the width of the Piscataqua "is no more than 650 feet."[14] So, the defendants concluded, although some vessels cannot pass through and under the bridge at all tides as freely and easily as they could before its erection, "vessels and steam boats can freely pass and repass through the Draws or Hoists of said Bridge, of a size much large than can at any stage of the tide navigate Cochecho River up to or near or within several miles of Dover Landing where the complainants alleged that they own and occupy wharves."[15]

The defendants further explained that the great force of the currents, tides, and ice had washed away some of the river bed surrounding the piles on which the Bridge rested and that the structure had moved "near seven feet from the direct line in which it was originally constructed"[16] and that the bridge had become "loose and insecure at the bottom and (was)...liable to be destroyed."[17] The proprietors had been advised by structural engineers to deposit the stone under the bridge, and by 1840, some 690 tons had already been thrown in around the pilings. The point was "so far distant from the Arch and the Draw...that these Defendants...believe such stone pier would form no obstruction that the bridge does not now create and produce no effect whatever upon the present ease and facility of navigating said River."[18]

Both sides concluded their initial presentations to the court on December 5, 1840, but depositions by actual witnesses for each side did not take place until December 1842.

Many of the names prominent in the annals of Dover's shipping history were called upon to testify by the plaintiffs' lawyer, Mr. Woodman. Their sworn statements served not only to corroborate the complaints made against the proprietors of the Portsmouth Bridge, but also to give a sound and accurate description of early nineteenth century life in the Piscataqua region.

Isaac A. Porter:
I have hired three lots (of the town of Dover on the Landing)...commenced March, 1836...(and) have used them principally for a lumber wharf—occasionally there has been sea manure laid on them. The principal part of the lumber went down the river to Portsmouth and Boston.[19]

Joseph Smith, businessman:
A resident near Dover Landing for forty years—I was engaged in the lumber business at Dover Landing (and) in the habit of putting...lumber on the town lands. I went down the river, principally to Portsmouth, some to Boston and other places.[20]

George Piper, Town Clerk & Customs Inspector:
From eight to twelve different vessels averaging from fifty to eighty tons each navigated Cochecho River as far as Dover Landing in 1840 and previously, and the number of their arrivals at Dover (was) 150-200 per year. In addition to these...were frequent arrivals...of transient vessels loaded with fish, lumber, etc. The voyages of the regular vessels are from Dover to Boston and back. The transient vessels go to New York, Thomaston, Mobile, etc.[21]

Samuel Kimball, farmer and selectman 1804-1818:
Lots were leased for three years at a time and the money went into the treasury of the town. They were principally used to place lumber on.... The principal part...went down the river in gondolas.... Gondola men call it more dangerous now than before the bridge was built.[22]

George Young:
As many as sixty or sixty-five years ago I have known vessels of 100 tons burthen come up the river and anchor at the junction of the Cochecho and Berwick rivers, about three miles below Dover Landing, and take in their cargoes for the West Indies.[23]

Moses Paul, Agent of the Cocheco Manufacturing Company:
The amount of goods and merchandise belonging to (the Cocheco Mfg. Co.) that is transported on the river to and from Dover and passing under the Portsmouth Bridge in packets

and gondolas, is in value about $750,000 per year.... About one half of the cotton...is imported from the South and landed at Portsmouth. Thence it is taken to Dover in gondolas. All our coal, about 3000 tons per year...is imported into Portsmouth for us and thence...freighted up the river in gondolas. The other half of the cotton and other materials for our mills come in the packets from Boston.... We send no goods down the river in gondolas; they all go to Boston in the packets.... Since the opening of the Railroad from Boston to Dover, a portion of our goods have been transported over the Railroad.[24]

Charles Young, packet commander:
Since the organization of the Despatch Line of Packets, they have owned and kept in their employ about seven vessels. The Portsmouth Bridge has always been considered a great obstruction to the navigation of the river. It has been considered dangerous for any but experienced persons to pass the bridge.

Since the Bridge was built, gondolas have to wait until a slack tide or nearly low water before they can go down through the arch with safety.... It [is] difficult and dangerous to pass it when a strong current is set up the river.... The natural current...is not at right angles with the Bridge.... I have seen several gondolas that were upset against the Bridge, and have seen their lading, being wood, float down the river.... It was not considered safe to pass the draw by night, and was scarcely ever if ever attempted to my knowledge.

The gondolas usually start from Dover...at or about high water, and being rowed down the Cochecho to the Piscataqua river, and then being permitted to float with the tide they would reach the bridge at about slack tide.... It would take about four and one-half hours to row a loaded gondola from Dover Landing to Portsmouth Bridge. In leaving Portsmouth, there is a necessity to leave as the tide begins to flow. Since the erection of the bridge, the gondolas have diminished at least one half from Dover to Portsmouth.[25]

Archelaus Trefethen, packet commander:
The construction of the Portsmouth Bridge is such that boats and vessels cannot and do not pass freely and easily through it except when the wind and tide are favorable.... It is necessary to cast anchor nine times out of ten.... Even then we very often meet with damage...by striking against the bridge.... I should consider that the damage to the Despatch Line of Packets in

consequence of the bridge..., would be at least $1000 yearly....
We sometimes in consequence of being detained at the bridge
have lost the change of a favorable wind and have...been detained two or three days on the voyage to Boston.

     The navigation of the river is much impeded in the
winter...in consequence of the obstruction the bridge makes to
the free passage of ice out of the river. The ice collects against
the bridge and dams up the passages when the tide is on the
ebb, so that there is no passing...until the tide shifts.... The
tide does not rise so high at Dover Landing from six to nine
inches as it would if the bridge were not made. On full flood
tide the water is two feet higher on the lower side of the bridge
than it is on the upper side.... Commanders of vessels not
acquainted [with the river] necessarily obtain a pilot.... I
scarcely ever knew a captain who was a stranger to come up
the river but once.... In consequence of the bridge we are compelled to have extra rigging and extra help.[26]

Paul Burley, navigator:
At the time of the building of the bridge I noticed that the tide
fell off, or did not rise so high as before.... I am satisfied that
the water at common high tides does not rise so high now by
ten inches as it did before the bridge was built.... When I first
moved to Dover (1816) it was the practice for men and
women...to do...their marketing in Portsmouth. They went
down in boats and returned both by night and by day. My wife
was...managing a boat to and from Portsmouth by night and by
day. Since the building of the bridge, the practice...has
decreased and my wife ceased going down or up by night....
Since I have lived at Dover the market at Dover has much
increased and the people now in my neighborhood do most of
their marketing at Dover.[27]

Daniel Trefethen, packet commander:
In the year 1827 I commenced coasting from Dover to Boston....
I generally make from twenty to twenty-five trips to Boston
and back each year. [The Bridge] is more difficult to pass than
any other with which I am acquainted.... This arises from the
rapidity of the tide and direction of the current and the eddies
formed in the current.... Were it not for the bridge I think twice
as many strange vessels would come up to the Dover Landing
as now come up.... I have heard captains say that they would go
up to Dover if it were not for the bridge. The duration of still
water at the bridge does not exceed one half hour at a time.[28]

Steamer Pioneer *DE*

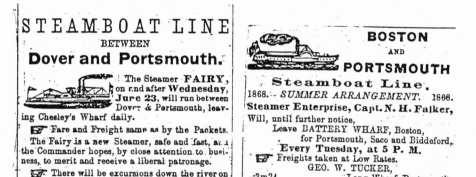

Steamboat Line DE

Andrew Peirce, Jr., businessman:
I have acted as agent for...the Despatch Line of Packets.The anchorage on either side of the river above the bridge is bad, and there are no safe eddies to lie in.... The freighting business has gradually increased at Dover for six years past.[29]

James Wentworth, gundalow and packet captain:
Once, about fourteen years ago, I started with a packet for Boston and was detained at the bridge in consequence of the ice, eight days.... It [always] took one extra hand in consequence of the bridge; and we considered the voyage to Boston half performed when we had gotten through the bridge.

The difficulty in passing is occasioned by the course and rapidity of the current. There is no difficulty...if we get there at slack tides. If there is to be a bridge in the neighborhood anywhere below the narrows, I do not know but it is as good a place as any other.... It is easier passing the draw since it has been altered and vessels are not so frequently damaged.[30]

George Young, gundalow captain:
Never, since the bridge was built would I have trusted myself
with a loaded gondola to pass the bridge when the current ran
fast.... The business of gundolaing has diminished since the
bridge was built, I should think. I do not know whether the
bridge injures the gondola or coasting most. The accidents to
gundolas are most numerous.[31]

Bartholomew Wentworth, farmer:
I cannot at times obtain sea manure (seaweed) at what I
consider a reasonable price. People will not fetch it.... Those
that bring up gondolas of sea manure now are men well skilled
in the navigation of the river. None besides those attempt it.[32]

Enoch Dunn, gundalow captain:
From [1818 to the present], I have had charge of one or more
gondolas. One year I run three gondolas. About one quarter
part of the time I run two gondolas. They were all of the large
class of gondolas, carrying from thirty-two to thirty–six tons....
Were it not for the bridge we could come up by night.... About
fifteen years ago, I saw three gondolas loaded with wood upset
against the bridge at one tide and within about half an hour.
The wood was all thrown out. At this time one man was
drowned.... A gondola of large size will carry from sixteen to
eighteen cords of dry hard wood.... [The bridge] occasions loss of
time and thereby makes expenses greater for boarding hands, etc.
    The gondola business on the river has increased for the
past twenty years. The articles brought up by gondolas from
Portsmouth to Dover are coal, cotton, flour, plaster of paris,
lime, etc. For five or six years past, five or six gondolas have
been regularly employed on Cochecho river between Dover and
Portsmouth.[33]

James Dore, gundalow and packet captain:
I have helped persons off from the bridge in distress and have
seen gondolas that were capsized against the bridge and the wood
floating around.... I have broken perhaps a half dozen oars....
The bridge lessens the number of craft that would ply on the river,
and also the number of trips made by those who regularly run.[34]

Stephen Hanson, butcher:
There was occasion to ship to Portsmouth a lot of beef and pork
and...cut nails.... They were put on board a gondola

commanded by Joseph Young...at the Dover Landing. The gondola went against the bridge, was capsized, and the cargo lost. The loss of beef, pork, and nails amounted to about $600.[35]

Abigail Nutter:
On [January 23, 1838], a Mrs. Hanscom was desirous of being carried to Portsmouth. My two sons, John, age then about fifteen, and William, age then about eleven, took our boat and Mrs. Hanscom.... It was a pleasant day. The boat broke against the bridge and all three were thrown into the river.... Mrs. Hanscom and John were picked up and saved. John was injured in his stomach. He held on to the bridge. William was lost and his body was never found.... My said two sons were in the habit of going down to Portsmouth in a boat together without any other person in the boat. I used to send them down on errands frequently to Portsmouth.[36]

Stephen Twombly, packet and gundalow captain:
The arch is not in a proper location. The spaces in the middle of the bridge are not wide enough nor high enough. A gondola load of hay could not go under them at one third ebb tide. At full tides a gondola load of wood could not go under at high tides. I have seen the water...rise to within three feet of the stringers of the bridge.... I have met with frequent accidents there...a damage to me of at least $500. I commenced the gondola and packeting business on the Cochecho river from Dover to Portsmouth in 1829. The amount of freight received by me annually from that time to this, has been from $1000 to $4000. It would average at least $2000 per year. For ten years past I have had in constant employment, on an average, four gondolas and two packet boats.... I have had three gondolas capsize.... I have had many hit there.[37]

Henry Card, packet and schooner master:
I should judge that not more than one third as many gondolas passed Dover Point now as did as long ago as I can remember. I have quite often seen fifteen or twenty at one time coming up the river Piscataqua....
   If the bridge were not there we could come up from Portsmouth to Dover Landing with fair wind in two hours. We consider ourselves fortunate if we get through the bridge in one hour after we begin to take in the sails. That hour's delay often prevents our coming up to Dover with that tide....

Taking all the branches of Piscataqua river into consideration, there is not more than one half the quantity of wood and lumber seeking market below that there was as long ago as I can remember. There is but little wood and lumber that now goes down the Cochecho. Most of what lumber now goes down goes in the packets coastwise to Boston.

I do not know whether the bridge obstructs the vessels or gondolas most. But the most serious losses have happened to the gondolas. Comparatively little property has been lost by coasters.[38]

Moses C. Young, packet commander:
I have suffered there by several accidents myself. In 1825 or 1826 I capsized a gondola load of boards against the bridge.... At the same tide Captain Rogers had a three-masted schooner go down. She was towed by a gondola. The schooner was anchored near the bridge...tripped her anchors and smashed [the gondola] against the bridge. Twelve hands were in the gondola.

I once went against the bridge with a sloop gondola...about 1834.... The sails and rigging were somewhat injured....

I once went against the bridge with the packet *Strafford*... in 1835 or 1836. A hole was broken in her and the sail was torn.... I have frequently seen gondolas capsized.... I have also seen them broken lying against the bridge. I have also heard men screaming, and helped...them off from under the bridge in the night....

I commanded the sloop gondola from 1831 to 1833 called the *Express*. She averaged about four trips each week. From 1833 to 1837 I commanded a packet. She run six trips each week for eight months in a year.[39]

John Sayles, steamboat pilot:
Since I have lived in Dover, five different steamboats have commenced running regularly from Dover to Portsmouth. They did not run but a short time each. I went in two of them, but the owners stopped them on account of the dangers incident to the passing of the bridge. The steamboats were injured in passing, and I know of some women who refused to go on account of the bridge.... I heard the captain of the *Tom Thumb*, Mr. Porter, say...damages sustained in passing the bridge took off too much of the profits. These steamboats drew from two and one half to four feet of water and could make a passage from Portsmouth to Dover in an hour were it not for the bridge. They could come up to Dover Landing at half tide.

Those steamboats were named *Tom Thumb*, *Dolphin*, *Suffolk*, *Minerva*, and *Jefferson*. The *Jefferson* was the largest and about seventy tons burthen. The *Dolphin* was the smallest and of about forty tons.[40]

The sworn testimonies of these people presented the case for Dover with great vehemence and conviction but under cross examination, many of these witnesses were forced to admit that navigational conditions had improved somewhat since the alterations to the bridge in 1826, 1835, and 1838; and that many of the accidents they had witnessed had happened because a vessel's captain was unwilling to wait until slack tide when the passage would be easier. The bridge definitely caused long delays and made navigation on the river more difficult, but a safe voyage was quite possible if the right tide conditions were in effect.

In October, 1842, Samuel Hill, clerk/treasurer of the Portsmouth Bridge, testified for the defense as to the "greater good" for seacoast area citizenry that the bridge was providing.

> ...Said bridge is of great advantage to me, and...of great advantage by the people of Elliot [sic]; that there is a great deal of travelling...from...Maine into...New Hampshire...and that said travel has greatly increased since the erection of said bridge. I well remember the dangers and difficulties attending the passage across said river by the ferry.... It was troublesome and expensive and occasioned a great loss of time, and was difficult to cross at all times of tide, particularly when the wind blew hard. Now we have not difficulty...we are never hindered...; it makes a good highway...to pass in safety, at half the price that was charged over the old ferry.
>
> The travelling across said bridge is very great, and it is the great U.S. mail route from Maine to Georgia. The Navy Yard is also connected with Portsmouth by this bridge.... If this bridge should be taken away, the loss to the citizens of Maine living in York County, would in my opinion be very great, their farms would depreciate in value very much, their privilege in going to the Portsmouth market would be nearly cut off.[41]

The eventual decision made in the case of Dover versus Portsmouth Bridge was handed down by the Strafford County Superior Court in July 1845. The evidence cited by both parties in the case was outlined:

The plaintiffs produced evidence of the ownership and occupation of the wharves stated in the bill, the character and number of the vessels navigating the river Cochecho to Dover Landing, the building of vessels at said Landing, with evidence of the position, plan, dimensions and construction of the bridge, the depth and currents of the river, the navigation of the Piscataqua and Cochecho rivers; of appropriations and expenditures by the United States Government to improve the navigation of the latter river; and of the obstruction of, effect upon, and danger in navigation caused by the bridge. The defendants produced their charter, with evidence of the approval, by the judges of the Superior Court of New Hampshire, of the plan upon which the bridge was constructed, of alterations in said bridge, to meet the wants and desires of the people of Dover and other towns in the vicinity, and evidence in rebuttal as to the effect of the bridge upon navigation, especially subsequently to such alterations.[42]

The final judgment was to dismiss the suit filed by the town of Dover and to allow the proprietors of the Portsmouth Bridge to go ahead with their plans to deposit tons of stones around the bridge's pilings. The court gave three reasons for its verdict: First, "a town cannot maintain a bill to abate a nuisance, upon the ground that individual inhabitants are affected in their private interests.... The town of Dover does not, as an owner of wharves, appear to have sustained any injury by the bridge, other than such as is common to private owners of like property.... [If] the plaintiffs have sustained any special damage thereby, not common to others, they may have a private suit."[43] Simply, a town government cannot sue for injuries sustained by private business owners. "The town of Dover cannot come here as a public prosecutor. They cannot come here unless they show any injury to their wharves; and the case shows no such injury. All cases of injury referred to in the plaintiff's argument are those sustained by the public."[44]

Second, the court stated, "All the navigation which ever came to the plaintiffs' wharves comes there still."[45] Merely causing delay and inconvenience is not considered a public nuisance.

Finally, the ruling concluded, "If...the design or principal effect of this bridge was to destroy commerce, obstruct the collection of revenue, or prevent the navy from resorting to navigable waters...its existence would be truly a nuisance which ought in some form of proceeding to be abated.... But nothing of that kind is even suggested in this case."[46]

The Dover complainants were obviously disheartened at the verdict. Their case was well presented and well documented but they were defeated on what seemed to them mere legal technicalities and convoluted interpretations of the law. But the judgment at this time, almost five years after the initial suit was filed, was nearly moot anyway.

The Boston and Maine Railroad, which had come into Dover in 1842, was highly successful and ever-expanding its reaches into inland New Hampshire. This new method of transportation, with its speed and efficiency, was doing more damage to the Dover shipping industry than the Portsmouth Bridge could ever do. It would almost appear that the Dover plaintiffs may have filed their initial suit against the proprietors of the Portsmouth bridge in some sort of futile attempt to rescue their shipping interests. In 1840, the plans of the B & M Railroad to expand into downtown Dover were certainly known and the businessmen of Dover who were dependent on the river for their livelihoods may have convinced the town selectmen to tackle a lesser giant than the railroad magnates who seemed unstoppable. With the Portsmouth bridge, at least they stood a chance of winning some restitution. Unfortunately, they won nothing, and the final verdict of the Superior Court was tacitly accepted as another blow to the floundering industry.

IV *The Dredging of the Cochecho River*

THE EARLIEST RECORD OF AN ATTEMPT to secure United States government funds for the improvement of the Cochecho River was in 1830. A River and Harbor Bill containing an appropriation of $4200 "for improving the Cochecho branch of the Piscataqua river from Dover Falls to its confluence with the Piscataqua"[1] was vetoed by President Jackson on April 13 of that year. No further action was taken until 1834 when a committee of ten was chosen at a Dover town meeting to lobby Congress for money to remove obstructions in the river. The appointed committee was successful as $5000 was appropriated in 1835, and $5000 more in 1837.[2] As parts of the Cochecho were cleared and navigation improved, so did the amount of river traffic increase. Through 1842, as many as ten gundalows, each carrying from thirty-two to thirty-six tons of cordwood, were in constant use on the river from Dover to Portsmouth. The packet business, too, was booming at Dover Landing: "a circumstance without parallel at this season of the year."[3]

In May 1868, a local effort was made to clear out obstructions near the city's commercial wharves. The directors of the Dover Gas Light Company asked the City Council to appoint a special committee to examine the Moses Page wharves on the Cochecho in the hope that the Gas Company and the city might share the expenses in clearing out the obstructions near these wharves. The matter eventually came to the attention of the Dover Board of Trade, whose opinion it was that the federal government should bear the cost of any river improvements. A committee, whose members included Mayor William S.

Stevens (owner of Wiggin and Stevens Glue Factory), John Bracewell (officer of the Dover Navigation Company), Moses D. Page (former owner of Trickey's Coal Company), and A.C. Chesley (former owner of Converse and Hammond Lumberyard), was instructed to inform local congressman J.H. Ela "that the people of his district are more vitally interested in the subject of Navigation of the Cochecho River than any other one thing in which he can aid us."[4] Representative Ela was able to get things in motion within a year, and on August 4, 1870, General George Thom,[5] U.S. Topographic Engineer, arrived in Dover for a preliminary inspection of the river. Thom was "furnished with important information by his Honor, the Mayor, and taken down the river by Alderman Page and Captain Trefethen on a tour of inspection. We shall expect favorable results to follow."[6]

In January 1871, the Dover Board of Trade was still waiting for those survey results. At their annual meeting, the Board stressed "the matter...in which every citizen should feel interested...the deepening of the channel of our river. There is now a prospect that their efforts in this direction will prove successful."[7] And indeed they were, although only partly so. In March 1871, Congress appropriated $10,000 for the Cochecho River, "about one-fourth as large as it should be, but once begun the work will undoubtedly be pushed forward until vessels of large size can reach our wharves. Too much praise cannot be bestowed upon our Board of Trade for their successful efforts in bringing about this desirable result."[8] Committee members Bracewell, Stevens, and Page were immediately nominated to attend to the money's dispersal.

In April 1871, General Thom submitted requests for proposals to various dredging contractors and by June 29 had hired, with the consent of Mayor Stevens, the firm of Morris and Cummings of New York to excavate a channel at the Lower Narrows for $7,000. The channel would be seventy-five feet wide and four feet deep at low tide, eleven feet at high tide. "The parties have arrived with a gang of hands, and tools are already at work."[9]

The hard work continued throughout the summer of 1871:

> The work of clearing out the river at the Narrows is being pushed rapidly forward, which can but result in great good to the "commercial interests" of our city. An explosive substance called "duelline"[10] is used for blasting, and an explosion has the force of 264,000 pounds to a square inch, or eight times that of powder. At a blast last Saturday a rock weighing nearly 100 pounds was thrown a distance of seventy or eighty feet in the air, while another weighing 4000 pounds

was started from the bed of the river. Mr. Bracewell a few
days since had a portion of the channel at the foot of Perkins
Street cleared out, deepening it some eighteen inches for quite
a distance, to increase the facilities for getting coal to the
Printery coal sheds.[11] The work of cleaning out the Cochecho
River at the Narrows is being steadily prosecuted. The
subcontractors Moore and Floyd, with the assistance of Reuben
Wiley, the submarine diver, are driving the work along
finely.... The ledges are not so hard as they expected, and
consequently they are not obliged to use the steam drill. They
are taking out about four cubic yards daily, and soon the
Narrows will be safe for any vessel wishing to come to Dover.
After removing the obstructions at the Narrows there will still
remain some ugly boulders at Trickey's brook, and another
ledge at the Gulf, which must be removed before we reap any
advantage from the present job, but our efficient Board of
Trade, who procured from Congress the present appropriation
will "push things" until a sufficient sum is secured to complete
the job.[12] The work of clearing out the river at the Narrows is
nearly completed, and the balance of the appropriation is to be
spent in making improvements at the mouth of Trickey's
brook. Mr. Floyd thinks that with another appropriation of
$20,000 our river can be made navigable to vessels drawing
twelve feet of water.[13]

The results of this first major dredging operation on a portion
of the Cochecho River were immediately observable:

Our wharves at this time present a lively appearance. There
are the schooner *Ceres*, Captain Trefethen, loaded with coal for
M.D. Page; schooner *Hattie Lewis*, Captain A. Coleman, with
lime for D. Trefethan; schooner *G. W. Raitt*, Captain Colemen
with salt; schooner *Midnight* with quartz for Wiggin and
Stevens, in addition to the several packets and sail boats,
whose canvas whitens the waters of the Cochecho.[14]

However, this initial successful project did not satisfy the
Board of Trade but only spurred them on to further improve their
busy port. They eagerly sought greater federal appropriations on the
advice of the Engineer Thom.

The Government Engineers are making surveys of the
Cochecho river up as far as the Print Works. The amount
appropriated has been most judiciously and nearly expended.
Gen. Thom will probably recommend an additional

*Coffer dam on the Cochecho River at the Gulf opposite Wiggin & Stevens Sandpaper
and Glue factory, 1873. JPA*

appropriation of $35,000 or $40,000, which he thinks will do
about what is advisable on the river. Our Board of Trade...will
second his efforts in securing a liberal amount to complete the
important work.[15]

That same fall, the schooner *Midnight* of Bath, Maine, with
only a five-foot draft, got caught on some hidden rocks still remaining
in the river. The ship was attempting to get into Wiggins and
Stevens' wharf with a load of quartz for their sandpaper mill. There
was considerable damage to the vessel, but a fire steamer was able to
pump her out and bring her up to the wharf. This small accident only
served to further illustrate the fact that captains unfamiliar with the
narrow, shallow waters of the Cochecho would hesitate to bring their
vessels into Dover unless more improvements were made. The Board
of Trade became more determined than ever to clear out the channel
into the Landing.

Blasting and clearing at the Narrows ended on November 25,
1871. The *Dover Enquirer* intimated that while the city fathers were

Excavating the bed of the Cochecho River at the Gulf in 1873. JPA

happy with the work that had been done, they were not as happy with
the personal conduct of one of the job's subcontractors. Gardner Floyd
of Portland, Maine had been in charge of the men employed in
removing blasted rock from the river bed. On the morning of the 25th,
Floyd went on board one of the scows and "in an abrupt manner,
without any provocation struck one of the hands two or three times in
the face, injuring him severely. This assault could not be accounted
for by any of the men present."[16] The angry Floyd then took a boat to
Eliot in order to avoid Dover constables "who will be likely to find him
when he comes back to this city to settle a few small bills he forgot to
pay previous to his leaving."[17]

In 1872, the Board of Trade was greatly surprised and
disappointed that the River and Harbor Bill passed by Congress
contained no funds for the Cochecho River. Chairman John Bracewell
lobbied vociferously for an amendment to the bill and was ultimately
successful in securing $8,000 for Dover. "We are in hopes of getting
more next year. The committee had...supposed that everything
necessary had been done to have the appropriation inserted in the

original bill, but were disappointed."[18] Still, General Thom was able to advertise in August for proposals to remove 1000 cubic yards of sunken ledge at the Gulf and Upper Narrows. Mr. E.M. Lapham. U.S. Engineer, then surveyed the area to be blasted, and in May 1873, the contract for excavating the Upper Narrows channel was awarded to Edward Moore of Portland for $26.50 per cubic yard. "The work to be done consists of removal of ledge so as to have a channel forty feet in width and four feet in depth at mean low tide. The whole distance for which the channel is to be excavated is about 325 feet, and the average depth two feet."[19]

Ironically, some of the work being done to improve navigation on the Cochecho also interfered with its passability. On June 19, 1873, Captain Trefethen's schooner *Ceres* was forced onto some rocks at the Gulf as she tried to squeeze by the temporary dam that had been built by the contractors cleaning the channel. Fortunately the *Ceres* received only slight injuries to her caulking and soon was able to sail again.

This temporary dam, known as a coffer dam, was constructed at the Gulf during the summer of 1873. This structure enabled the contractors to drain a portion of the river bed so that men and equipment could get in to drill and blow out obstructions. When the river bed had been excavated to specifications, the coffer dam was taken down and the river allowed to flow once again over the deepened channel. The Gulf coffer dam was completed in July 1873 but "not being filled in with clay it was not strong enough to stand the pressure of the tide and...twenty feet of it was carried away."[20] The dam was reconstructed and completed in September, the water pumped out, and a large crew put to work blasting ledge. "A large number of loose stones were found, supposed to be the results of blasting when an attempt was made to clear the channel at this point some thirty-five years ago."[21] The deepening and widening of the river at the Upper Narrows was completed in October 1873 "for the present or until another appropriation is made"[22] and the coffer dam was removed.

In May 1874, $10,000 more was awarded to Dover in the U.S. River and Harbor Bill, and in August, the dredging contract was once again given to Colonel Edward Moore. The temporary coffer dam was reconstructed at the Gulf in September and the water pumped out of the work area. By October, the job was complete and the water was able to run once more in the new channel. A distance 165 feet long by forty feet wide had been cleared "which, added to what has previously been done, makes 530 feet in length by forty feet in width, and giving depth of ten to fourteen feet of water according to the tide."[23]

The improvements in the navigation of the Cochecho River and the great amount of ship traffic which now flowed into the port of

Dover made it easy for the Board of Trade to plead their case for additional federal funds. They had little difficulty in securing the large sum of $25,000 from Congress in 1875 for continuing the dredging work. General Thom reported that the next area to be cleared would be at the ledge opposite Collins' wharf, where 484 cubic yards of rock would need to be blasted, and that 9000 cubic yards of dredging would continue from that point to the packet landing place at Clements' Point shoal and Trickey's shoal. He wished the work to be completed by November 1875.

Despite some delays in building another temporary coffer dam—"a series of misfortunes or blunders,"[24] the work was eventually completed in September: "The deepening of the Gulf was finished Tuesday. All who want to see the bottom of the Cochecho River must go this afternoon as it will probably never be uncovered again, at least in our generation."[25] General Thom accepted the work of ledge removal and ordered the dredgers to begin on September 23; the job was finished on schedule.

The improvements on the Cochecho directly benefited all of the businesses at the Landing. Because larger vessels could now come into port without difficulty, bigger cargoes could be brought in more cheaply and the Dover consumer was able to purchase goods at lower prices: "C.H. Trickey and Co. have on hand the best and greatest variety of family coals ever offered in this section. The facilities for getting it are superior, as they ship directly to our wharves, and they sell a good article at the lowest prices for the same qualities."[26]

> C.H. Trickey and Co. are enlarging and rebuilding their coal sheds, making them about double the present capacity. When completed they will occupy a space 75 x 72 feet...with much better facilities for receiving coal from the vessels. Their increased business renders this enlargement absolutely necessary.[27]
>
> In consequence of the improvements already made in our river, C.H. Trickey and Co. are enabled to freight their coal in much larger vessels, which makes it come cheaper to them, and which they say their customers shall have benefit of. The schooner *Odell*, Captain Winslow, a large, handsome vessel of some 250 tons, arrived recently, much larger than we have been accustomed to see at our wharves.[28]

Additional blasting at the Lower Narrows continued throughout the summer of 1876 while the Board of Trade worried about a further appropriation of $14,000 that had been requested of Congress. In August, their fears were allayed as "notwithstanding the cutting down of appropriations by Congress, and the cutting of them off in many cases, the $14,000 for improvements in our river passed through all right."[29]

In May 1877, John Bracewell traveled to Portland to see General George Thom about finishing the dredging on the Cochecho and constructing "a basin for them to lay in while waiting for a chance to discharge their cargoes."[30] Work started immediately. "Solan S. Andrews, who has charge of the submarine work in improving the channel...such as blasting, removing boulders, etc., has arrived with steam drills, batteries, etc., and commenced operations at a point near the Powder House."[31]

Work on the basin was completed in August and the shipping business was booming in Dover. "Our harbor presents a lively and business-like appearance on Saturday last when there were five vessels at the wharves loaded with coal for Trickey and Co., lumber for J. Converse, lime and cement for Captain Trefethen, coal for the Dover Gas and Light Co."[32]

From August to September 1877, the dredgers and submariners moved downstream to Dover Point "to remove an enormous large rock which has always been dreaded by the mariner. "This rock is situated in the channel in twenty-six feet of water at high tide and stands up fourteen feet higher than the surrounding bottom; at low water there is but four feet of water over this dangerous rock which weighs over 200 tons."[33] Divers drilled holes into the rock and then filled the holes with explosives. A large crowd of spectators gathered at the Dover Point Hotel to witness the explosion. "The job was a grand success"[34] and again the businesses and industries dependent on the Cochecho River benefited greatly. Bigger and heavier schooners were visiting Dover, each month setting new records for size of vessel and amount of cargo carried into port:

> One of the largest schooners that ever came up to our wharves, if not the largest, is the schooner *J.D. Ingraham*, Captain C.W. Smith, from Philadelphia, which this week discharged a cargo of 250 tons of coal at the wharf of C.H. Trickey & Co. It is in consequence of what has been done to our river that such large vessels can come to this city. This in turn enables us to get our coal cheaper, as the expense of bringing 150 tons of coal in a small schooner is about equal to that of bringing 250 in a larger one, and what is saved in freight the consumer gets the advantage of. We are now getting coal at the same rates as the citizens of Portsmouth; but before the improvements we used to have to pay from fifty cents to one dollar per ton more, the

additional expense of getting it up the river, as much of it
formerly had to be transferred to gondolas and brought up in
that way.[35]

The largest vessel that we recollect of ever having come
up to our wharves was the schooner *J. J. Little,* N.F. Gandy
Captain, which arrived last week with 254 tons of coal for C.H.
Trickey. She is 110 feet long, twenty-three feet wide, and eight
feet deep. This large cargo was discharged in forty-eight hours,
which is considered lively work.[36]

It was also in 1877 that a group of Dover entrepreneurs,
perhaps inspired by the great improvements on the river and the size
of the vessels they saw docking at the Landing, formed the Dover
Navigation Company[37] and built a fleet of ten schooners that traveled
the globe from this humble port. By 1878, it was not unusual for
seven vessels to visit Dover in one week's time and the federal
appropriations continued with $6000 more for Cochecho coffers. "Six
schooners were in our river on Tuesday with cargoes of coal. A
striking contrast with business at our wharves before the
improvements in our river when only one or two schooners were seen
then at a time, and sometimes none."[38] More size records were set,
with the schooner *Surprise* arriving in port with 375 tons of coal on
August 8, 1878. All were indeed surprised when the vessel, 150 feet
in length and twenty-two feet wide, arrived at high tide without
having to be lightened. The dredging continued during that summer
near the old Cushing steam mill with a new machine called "Little
Giant" in charge of Thomas Symonds.

In the six months between March and August, the *Dover
Enquirer* boasted that 3,558 1/2 tons of coal had been brought up river
and 100 vessels had come to port so far during 1880. Local
businessmen were expanding their facilities: a new wharf for the
Dover Gas Light Company, a storehouse for Joseph Hayes, a cotton
storehouse for the Cocheco Manufacturing Company, a lumber storage
wharf for Converse and Hobbs and more coal sheds for Valentine
Mathes. "There were nine schooners moored at one time in the lower
Cochecho recently. A grand sight, prophetic of the brilliant future
awaiting Dover as a port of entry."[39]

Work on the river continued in 1882. Captain Thomas
Symonds was supervising the removal of ledge ridges which had
accumulated on the riverbed near the Cocheco Manufacturing
Company's wharf. "Little Giant," three scows, a steam tug, and a
large force of workmen were on the job. A $27,000 appropriation from
Congress was approved in April 1883 for finishing the dredging. The
proposals for final improvements included:

A "cut-off" for the river through Alley's point, at the Lower
Narrows, so as to give a straight channel having a depth of five
feet at mean low water, and a width on the bottom of fifty feet
with sides sloping forty-five degrees. Above and below cut-off a
channel will be dredged requiring the removal of about 16,000
cubic yards of material. Second, the present channels at
Trickey's Shoal and Clement's Point are to be widened and
deepened so as to be sixty feet wide at botton, with mean low
water depth of five feet, requiring the removal of 2,530 cubic
yards of material (hard-pan and boulders) at Trickey's Shoal
and about 730 cubic yards at Clement's Point (also boulders
and hardpan). All the work to be done to the satisfaction of the
U.S. Engineer in charge.[40]

In July 1883, the *Dover Enquirer* sent a reporter for an eyewit-
ness account of the dredging work:

We had the pleasure Wednesday afternoon of going down to
Alley's Point and making some slight inspection of the work
that is being done by the Government at that point. We rode
down to Barney McCone's farm where we left our team. We
went down to the river and signalled the workmen on the other
side, and Captain Symonds answered our call by sending over
a boat which took us across and we were courteously received
by the Captain, who is doing the job by contract. He showed us
what had been done and what he expects soon to have done.
He took us aboard the Dredge boat and explained the action of
the complicated machinery, by means of which the jaws of the
dredger were worked. It will lift a stone weighing three tons.
The length of the cut, through the point, is 400 feet; the depth
of cut, from top of the hill to the bottom, will be fifty-two feet.
The work is being rapidly advanced and Captain Symonds
thinks he can have all the channel all completed there in about
ten days so that any of Dover's schooners can come up through
it, safe from all danger.[41]

In August, Captain Symonds moved the dredge from Alley's
Point to a position near the powder house and continued work until
November.
"He has completed the dredging at all points below Trickey's
Brook and will now work from there up the river as fast as possible.
What the Captain don't know about dredging is not worth knowing."[42]
The river was straightened and deepened from Alley's Point to
Clement's Point to a depth of five feet at a low tide, a great improve-
ment for heavily loaded schooners.

The remaining job, deepening the river bed from Clement's Point to the coal docks, would be completed with $28,000 in additional funding granted by the Senate Commerce Committee in June 1884. Captain Symonds returned to Dover in September with submarine divers and four steam drills. About 2000 cubic yards of ledge remained to be removed–an estimated nine-month job. Symonds put a swing bridge over the Cochecho River, four feet from the water, on which he placed his drills. The bridge was able to swing out of the way when the large schooners came up the river so commercial shipping in Dover was able to carry on as usual. Work stopped for the winter on December 5, 1884 and the dredging equipment was hauled up for storage at Portsmouth.

On May 29, 1885, Captain Symonds recommended dredging for three months, until this phase of the work was completed. Carl Berrier, government engineer in charge of the project, estimated that an additional $20,000 would be needed to enlarge the Basin to such a size that larger schooners would be able to turn around in. "That is what is needed so that Dover can have first class accommodations for its splendid line of schooners. Our Congressmen and Senators should see that Dover has the needed appropriation when the proper time comes."[43] Senator H.W. Blair of New Hampshire submitted an amendment to the River and Harbor Bill asking for a $30,000 appropriation for the Cochecho River, but disappointingly only $2000 was received. From June to September 1887, Captain Symonds continued widening and deepening the river from Trickey's wharf to the Cushing saw mill, and in March 1888, $9000 more in federal funds was awarded. Dredging began once more in October:

> The present job of dredging on the lower Cochecho by Captain Symonds is being pushed rapidly along, and when completed will finish the work under the old survey. This has been an appropriation made by Congress for a new survey for the enlargement and deepening of channel from the wharfs to the mouth of the river, so to provide for the increasing amount of shipping that is coming to this city.[44]

Symonds continued work from April to November 1889, and in December of that year, an ambitious proposal was developed for further improvements.

> Colonel Smith, U.S. Engineer, has made a report to Congress...and has recommended a scheme for improving the channel which will admit the passage of vessels of much larger tonnage than those which arrive at our wharves at present.

The estimated amount necessary...is placed at $175,000...to have the channel at least fifty feet wide in the rock, sixty feet wide at hard pan, and seventy-five feet wide at soft soil; depth in the rock seven and one-half feet at mean low water, and in other places not less than seven feet.[45]

Buoyant emotions were riding high in Dover and the *Dover Enquirer* teased its rival port: "Our Portsmouth friends appear to be frightened; Don't be alarmed, good people, those schooners were simply on their way up river to Dover, where businessmen are wide awake."[46]

New dredging began in the summer of 1891 with a fleet of six scows under the direction of the New England Dredging Company. The work was inspected in July 1892 by a federal engineer in the company of the highly interested parties of Charles Trickey, John Holland, and J. Frank Seavey. On the inspector's approval, $15,000 more was approved for Dover on April 6, 1894. Twin drills ran until 9 o'clock every night during that summer.

If you have chanced to be walking or riding down Portland Street on any weekday between 7 A.M. and 12 midnight during the past eight or ten weeks, as the Trickey wharves were passed, you have without doubt noticed an object on the river which looked greatly like the third story of a tenement house that had been torn from its foundation by a Western cyclone and landed in a neighboring stream. If you were of an inquiring nature you probably asked your companion for an explanation, and if he or she knew, your wishes might be gratified but if not, the answer probably reminded you of a woman's description of a football game. Our reporter was of this inquisitive nature, and one afternoon having plenty of time but no companion, he proceeded to the river's edge to find that the float on the Cochecho with noisy machinery was rock drilling apparatus of Rogers and Fitzpatrick of Plattsburg, N.Y. Seeing no means of conveyance and not being well informed in this branch of science, a guide and instructor was sought in Mr. James Rogers, son of the contractor, who was found at Superintendent Fitzpatrick's headquarters. Our man was told that the work now in progress is the drilling and blasting of the ledge in close proximity to the river's channel with a view of widening that channel with the appropriation of $15,000 made recently for the purpose of the U.S. Government. The contractor and his crew of nine arrived here April 11, and on May 1st began the work, the intervening time being taken up in the erection of the drill float. They began operations at the "deep hole" on a line with the point on the land numbered "68" by the surveyor and working up the north side of this hidden ledge as far as the Mathes coal wharves, a distance of 550 feet, blasted enough rock to make the channel ten feet wider. The drills began hammering on the other side, the second cut as it is called, last Monday, and will keep at it four weeks longer. This crew does the drilling and blasting simply, leaving the dredger, which by the way is expected here within four weeks, to pick up the pieces. Through the further kindness of Mr. Rogers, a visit to the float was made in a boat at least water-tight if not a pleasure boat with all modern appointments. Although the raft now rests in the middle of the space between the banks, a little nearer the north side if anything, it is on the edge of the channel which at this point runs very close to the northern shore. The float rests on spuds which stand firmly on the rocky bed beneath, and it can be raised or lowered as the height of the tide requires to keep it touching water at all times. It is thirty-one feet long, twenty feet wide with open sides, covered by a roof which is supported by sixteen posts giving the men a chance to work, rain or shine. The boiler at one end supplies the two Rand drills and the air-pumps with a hundred pounds of steam. Each drill has a drillman and his helper who work by ten hour shifts. They work extra half shifts when the tide permits. When the float and its burden are in position and everything is ready, the large air-pump with a two and one-half inch hose clear the spot to be drilled of all obstructions, and an iron cylinder is lowered over the bare space. A drill varying from four to fifteen feet in length and starting a hole two and one half inches in diameter is put to work, with deafening noise as one result. As soon as the drill enters the rock two feet, a new one of smaller diameter is put in its place until the bottom of the hole measures only one and three quarter inches across. These holes vary from three and one half to seven and one half in depth, always drilled two feet below grade, and one of the machines can accomplish the work in little over an hour. A diver with his additional 300 pounds of clothing puts the explosives in position. Four pounds of dynamite constitutes a charge which the diver receives on the end of a long pole. Two tons and a half of dynamite will be consumed in the work. After six to twelve holes have been treated in this way the charges are connected with the exploder and the float is removed to safer ground, a hundred feet away. They wait for high tide, since the destructive power of the explosion is proportional to the mass of water pressing down on it and then fire the charge which breaks up the ledge and sends the water fifty feet in the air. Then they begin over again. We do not need to say that this work is being done in excellent shape since the good work done by the Company elsewhere is sufficient to prove that the same is being done here. As we said above, the Government is paying for this at the rate of $6.44 a cubic yard, in place, and until the $15,000 is used up our river will continue to be improved.[47]

The painstaking work of Captain Symonds and his crew continued during the summer and fall of 1895, but as the project drew near its close, disaster struck.

A late winter storm ravaged the Dover area with an intensity never before seen in the Seacoast. A driving rain began on Saturday, February 29, 1896 and continued unabated all day Sunday. The Cochecho River rose alarmingly and by March 1, between six and ten feet of water were pouring over the downtown dam at the Lower Falls. Huge ice flows broke loose upriver and crashed into Dover's bridges. Three of these spans were destroyed: the Central Avenue bridge, the Lower Washington Street bridge, and Watson's bridge. The Bracewell Block, housing nine businesses, had been built on piers across the Central Avenue bridge and one-third of this block was swallowed by the raging flood. Electric wires were downed and the city watched the destruction helplessly in the dark. "The volume of water was so great that it ran almost smoothly over the falls in one vast sheet; the ledge beneath it could only manifest itself when huge cakes of ice came over the dam and plunged into the gulf below, ice, timber, and debris of every sort came constantly over the dam."[48]

Nine carloads of lumber were washed off the wharves of Converse and Hammond and 1500 barrels of lime at the lumberyard combined chemically with the waist-deep water to cause a fire that blazed uncontrollably. The Cocheco Mills did not run for three days. After twelve hellish hours, the storm abated and damage was assessed at $300,000. The flood was christened "Dover's Black Day" and likened to the famous Johnstown flood.

The bridges were shortly rebuilt and businesses soon reopened. Buildings were repaired and the Lower Falls dam was reconstructed. But irreparable damage was done to the bed of the Cochecho River. All the sand, silt, and debris that flowed over the dam lodged in the dredged out areas at the Landing and the Cochecho River was essentially back at its starting point with a narrow, shallow port of entry unable to accommodate large commercial vessels. All the work that had been completed from 1835 to 1895 was now undone, and the $164,000 that had been appropriated for river improvements during those sixty years was now wasted.

Although small dredging operations were continued through 1906, the death knell for Dover as a seaport had been sounded. The Dover Board of Trade seemed to accept their city's fate and did not push for any further federal monies for river dredging.

V   *The Dover Navigation Company, 1877-1914*

THE DOVER NAVIGATION COMPANY was organized in 1877 by an ambitious group of Dover men looking for a profitable investment. They foresaw the growth in commercial shipping by schooner and knew, because they were local businessmen, the industrial and mercantile needs of Dover. These men decided to build a vessel capable of hauling large cargoes, particularly coal, right into downtown wharves. Thomas B. Garland, clerk of the Cocheco Manufacturing Company, the largest user of soft coal in Dover, was elected president of the group and B. Frank Nealley, a dry goods merchant, was made secretary-treasurer.

Initially, the members of the Dover Navigation Company found it difficult to sell stock in their first proposed vessel. Cautious investors did not yet hold much faith in the fledgling company. They did manage to raise the necessary capital, however, and when their first schooner, the *John Bracewell* was launched in 1878, it was an instant commercial success, not only because there was lots of business for the ship, but also because it was owned locally and could work for the interests of Dover people, not compete with them. Cargoes were delivered to landing wharves with maximum efficiency and minimum cost. From that point on, the Dover Navigation Company had little difficulty in recruiting investors for subsequent stock offerings in additional vessels.

The Company was able to build a new schooner each year for the next four: the *Charles H. Trickey* in 1879, the *B. Frank Nealley* in 1880, the *Thomas B. Garland* in 1881, and the *Zimri S. Wallingford* in 1882.

Although the costs of building the vessels increased from $13,000 to $19,000, so did the sizes of the schooners (from 113 feet to 130 feet), their net tonnage (from 224 tons to 280 tons), and their profits. Each of those four years, the Dover Navigation Company was able to declare semi-annual dividends of at least ten percent for their stockholders.

The *Dover Enquirer* regularly reported on where the schooners were, what they were hauling, and what weather conditions they had encountered. The city was proud of its fleet and eager to boast of its success: "Upwards of $110,000 of Dover capital is invested in schooners; it has been a very paying investment thus far."[1]

In 1883, the Dover Navigation Company bought a small brick schooner, the *J. Chester Wood*, in 1884 added the *John J. Hanson*, (capable of carrying nearly 1000 tons of coal, but too big to visit Dover), and in 1886 built the *Jonathan Sawyer*, with a 600 ton capacity.

At their 1886 annual meeting, President Thomas B. Garland reported:

> The capital stock of this company was increased a year ago to $114,770.43 by the building of the schooner *John J. Hanson*. Taking the first five vessels of the fleet, representing a capital stock of $81,498.06 and an average service of 5 1/2 years, they have returned to stockholders $60,335.32 in dividends, besides a further sum of $24,787.34 which has been returned to the vessels in the way of renewals and repairs, making a total of $85,122.66, net earnings.[2]

In 1888, the company sold the *Charles H. Trickey* and built the *J. Frank Seavey,* a schooner with an innovative new design that allowed her to sail right into Dover wharves loaded with 600 tons of coal without having to stop at "the lightering place" to discharge some cargo onto barges. (The lightering place was located down the Cochecho River about two miles from Dover wharves. Here cargo was discharged to barges or gundalows when low tides would not allow the vessel to sail into port fully loaded.) The *Seavey* was the vessel the Navigation Company owners had long been dreaming of. She was enormous, yet agile enough to navigate the shallow waters of the Cochecho River. The successes and profits of the Company continued to grow: "Our Dover schooners earned $18,393.42 during the year 1889. The Dover Navigation Company declared a six percent dividend the first six months and seven and three-quarters percent the last."[3]

In 1889, the *B. Frank Nealley* was sold, and in 1890 the Dover Navigation Company added a tenth schooner to the fleet. The *John Holland,* a four-master costing over $54,000 and capable of carrying 1800 tons of coal, was by far the largest schooner owned by the Company. It could never dock in Dover, but did a hugely profitable business at East Coast deep water ports.

In 1892, at the annual meeting of their stockholders, officers of the Dover Navigation Company reported on the status of the eight still-active schooners. The following dividends were declared: *John Bracewell* ten percent; *Thomas B. Garland* ten percent; *Zimri S. Wallingford* twelve percent; *John J. Hanson* twelve percent; *Jonathan Sawyer* eleven percent; *J. Frank Seavey* ten percent; *John Holland* fifteen percent; and *J. Chester Wood* two percent.

> The Dover Navigation Company is a corporation of which Dover people have always been proud for it has grown from at first an experiment to a large corporation with a big capital and a fleet of some of the ablest vessels on the Atlantic coast. The company commenced business in 1878 with a capital stock of $13,121.92. The capital stock stands today $192,226.73. On this capital dividends have been paid back to the owners amounting to $185,035.77 – a most excellent showing.[4]

In 1892, the unprofitable brick schooner *J. Chester Wood* was sold, leaving seven active vessels in the fleet. In 1893, their largest schooner, the *John Holland,* sank in a collision with another ship off the coast of Virginia, but the Dover Navigation Company was eventually able to recover some of the damages. In the company's annual report for the year 1894, Treasurer B. Frank Nealley sounded the first warning note: "Rates of freight have ruled very low throughout the year and expense on vessels for repairs have been exceptionally large being over forty percent of the net earnings."[5] Sales of the *Trickey*, the *Nealley* and the *Wood* and the loss of the *Holland* reduced the capital stock to $123,534.26. Then in March 1895, the *Zimri S. Wallingford* was lost in a fire in Virginia.

The company was still making a profit, however. The annual report for 1897 declared an eight percent dividend on the *Thomas B. Garland* and the *Jonathan Sawyer*, nine and one-half percent on the *John Bracewell*, seven percent on the *J. Frank Seavey,* and six percent on the *John J. Hanson* with total net earnings of $11,950. In 1898, they earned $8,821.

It appeared that the boom in commercial shipping was indeed slowing, yet the Dover Navigation Company was still held in high esteem by the people of Dover.

> The capital stock of the company is at present $104,522.21 and between July 1878 and July 1898, $238,110.66 has been returned to the stockholders in dividends. ...The company has done much to promote and stimulate the commerce of the city which has derived decided advantages from the success of the undertaking.[6]

And in 1890, the following account had appeared:

That the prosperity and development of the community are directly dependent upon the transportation facilities available is a self-evident proposition.... Those manufacturers and merchants who enjoy the best facilities for the reception and shipping of goods are best prepared to meet the sharp competition.... The present importance of Dover as a manufacturing and trade center is of course largely due to advantages of location, but these...would have availed nothing and in less enterprising hands would not have been nearly so well utilized as is now the case. The undertaking carried on by the Dover Navigation Company is of almost inestimable benefit to this city...for the company offers exceptionally desirable transportation facilities and...has shown most commendable enterprise. Some of the most prominent businessmen in this section...are identified with it and naturally...render much more intelligent service under these circumstances than would be possible were its affairs controlled by residents of other sections. The vessels are in first-class condition, are in charge of experienced and reliable men, and enable the company to offer a service unsurpassed for economy and practical efficiency.[7]

That the trend toward motorized and steam-run ships had taken hold and railroads were expanding greatly did not mean the Dover Navigation Company should be considered a failure. Its era was ending and a new one was beginning. The venture had been good for Dover and profitable for her investors.

The *Jonathan Sawyer* was lost in a 1907 storm off the coast of Maine, the *John Bracewell* and the *Thomas B. Garland* were sold in 1911, the *J. Frank Seavey* was sold in 1912. Company Treasurer Mr. B. Frank Nealley had written in January 1910:

During our more than thirty years in the coasting business we have never found the business so poor as in the past two years, both in the difficulty of finding business for the vessels and the low rates of freight paid for carrying.... I do not look for much improvement for coasting conditions have entirely changed from what they were when these vessels were built. Our vessels are old and it costs more from year to year to keep them up. For years the enterprise has been a waning one...I am entirely satisfied...that we ought to sell the vessels for what they will bring in the market and wind the business up.[8]

In 1914, this "winding up" finally occurred. The money in the

Schooner John Bracewell *at Provincetown, Massachusetts. She was the first vessel built for the Dover Navigation Company in 1878. CLW*

treasury was divided among the owners, and the Dover Navigation Company, a proud symbol of a past era, was no more. A detailed accounting of each vessel's history follows:

Schooner John Bracewell
(1878-1911)

Specifications: Tonnage-Gross 224.63, Net 213.40, Cargo 350 tons; Length 113.6 feet; Breadth 29.2 feet; Depth 9.1 feet; Built 1878 in Bath, Maine; Cost $13,121.92.

After the Dover Navigation Company was established in 1877, the incorporators' first venture was to commission Goss & Sawyer of Bath, Maine to construct a three-masted schooner to be used for commercial trade.

> The contract price of the vessel, which is to be of oak and hackmatack, is a little over $13,000. About 16,000 tons of coal is used annually in our city, and we are glad that a few of our citizens are enterprising enough to wish to retain some of the profits of the carrying trade in coal in this city instead of paying to ship owners elsewhere. We think it will pay better dividends than any other stock, as the business must be permanent and bringing coal direct to Dover must take a great saving over re-shipping at Portsmouth, as has been done with much of the coal for this city.[9]

The schooner, named for Dover businessman Colonel John Bracewell, would be primarily used to haul coal into Dover for the Cocheco Manufacturing Company and for the firm of C.H. Trickey. The vessel was launched at Bath in June 1878, and captained by C.W. Chatfield. Charles Trickey, who attended the launching ceremonies reported that "she went off in fine style and sits upon the water like a duck."[10]

The newspaper reported:

> The government tonnage is 225 tons, but she will carry 400 tons. She is built of white oak and hackmatack and is one of the best vessels afloat. She is to take in a load of ice Thursday of this week for Baltimore, and there load with coal for the Cocheco Manufacturing Co. All will see the wonderful enterprise in building this vessel, one of the largest and best that ever came to Dover.[11]

When the *Bracewell* arrived in Dover for the first time in July 1878, the citizenry were enthralled. "She is the handsomest and best built vessel that has come to Dover.... She had about 350 tons (of coal) for a cargo, but was soon unloaded and started for Kennebec for a cargo of ice."[12]

The schooner was immediately profitable, much to the delight of the Dover Navigation Company investors. By the fall of 1879, the vessel had "thus far paid twenty percent which should be satisfactory to any shareholder,"[13] and by the end of 1880, after running two and one-half years, "has given its shareholders fifty percent of its cost, besides paying $2,000 for improvements."[14]

The *Bracewell* sailed continuously up and down the East Coast, her cargo mainly coal, but on occasion carrying seashells from Florida and bat guano fertilizer to Virginia. In early spring, the vessel would deliver ice from Maine to Atlantic City and Baltimore for $1.50 a ton. In 1881, the vessel made a long voyage, 5500 miles, from Baltimore to Galveston, Texas to Pensacola, Florida and ended with a load of lumber for New Haven, Connecticut.

The schooner's captain and crew often battled storms and dangerous gales, and a particularly perilous trip was recounted by a clergyman, the Reverend James DeBuchananne, who sailed on the *Bracewell* enroute to Baltimore:

> Outward bound from Gloucester, in attempting to cross Nantucket shoals, the vessel was driven by the wind back again into Gloucester harbor, there remaining for twenty-four hours. On a second attempt to make their destination, when off the New Jersey coast, in about the latitude of Philadelphia, a great storm arose and the vessel was driven 200 miles out to sea. It was a lively business with them all for a time, all hands furling sail, while the Parson, lashed to the wheel, kept the schooner nose into the wind. He proved himself equal to the demands of the emergency, and in heroic qualities not lacking, he arrived safely at Baltimore....[15]

The schooner sometimes could not return to its home port of Dover. When ice blockaded the Cochecho River, the vessel was destined to spend the winter months in a warmer climate. Stay in icy water even a day too long and getting "frozen in" became a distinct possibility. This happened, in fact, to the *Bracewell* in January 1884 in Lynn, Massachusetts. The ship didn't get back to Dover until the next April. In March 1893, the schooner was blockaded again by "a half mile of ice, six inches thick"[16] at Bridgeport, Connecticut.

On other occasions, the ship, loaded with cargo, was too heavy and drew too much water to come all the way up the Cochecho to the

Schooner John Bracewell coming up the Cochecho River with coal; the tug Cocheco is along side. OBHS

Landing at Dover. Sometimes local tugs like the *Ann* and the *Mystic* could guide her in, but at other times, depending on tides and water depths, the *Bracewell* had to be lightered a couple miles from the wharves before sailing the rest of the way home.

But when conditions were right, the *John Bracewell* was a speedy, efficient schooner. In 1888, news came that:

> The schooner *John Bracewell* has just made one of the fastest trips on record to New York. She went down the river Tuesday afternoon and sailed from Portsmouth at 4 o'clock. C.H. Trickey received a telegram early this morning announcing her arrival at City Island in New York harbor. She made the trip in about thirty-six hours.[17]

And in 1889, "The schooner *Bracewell*...beat two other schooners which started from Philadelphia at the same time; the *Bracewell* is a fast sailer."[18]

In her later years, the schooner carried loads of sand, stone, paving materials, bricks, and railroad ties: materials for a booming economy.

After a profitable thirty-three year run which netted her owners a 266% profit, the Dover Navigation Company sold the *Bracewell* to Captain A. P. Ginn of Rockland, Maine on January 27, 1911 for $2500.

Schooner Charles H. Trickey
(1879-1888)

Specifications: Tonnage-Gross 281.03, Net 266.98; Cargo 350 tons; Length 120.1 feet; Breadth 32.2 feet; Depth 8.1 feet; Built in 1879 in Bath, Maine; Cost $14,372.30.

Glowing in the early successes of their first profitable schooner, the investors of the Dover Navigation Company decided to build a second vessel, this one a little larger in size and capable of carrying more coal.

> A plan is on foot, and most of the stock has been subscribed, to build a schooner especially adapted to such carrying business as is done up and down our river; such as freighting coal, ice, and lumber. It is to be named for Charles H. Trickey, one of our most enterprising and successful businessmen, who deserves, from his efforts to increase the business and facilities of Dover, this distinguished honor.[19]

Trickey, one of the charter member of the Dover Navigation Company, was the owner of the largest coal and wood supply business in Dover, and naturally had a great interest in developing the shipping industry on the Cochecho River.

In May 1879, the schooner *Charles H. Trickey* was launched from the Goss and Sawyer shipyard at Bath and was ready on May 10th to haul a load of ice from the Kennebec River to Atlantic City. The newspaper reported the ship to be "a splendid vessel built of the best material and in the most thorough manner."[20] The editor also hinted that "there is business enough here for five or six vessels of this size."[21] The *Trickey's* captain, also part owner, was Gustavus Kelley of West Harwich, Massachusetts who made sure the vessel contained the most up-to-date equipment including "the Hyde patent iron windlass and a full set of Oregon Spars. She has all the conveniences of a first class vessel."[22]

On June 5, 1879, the *Trickey* docked at Flagg's Wharf on her first Dover visit. She arrived with 350 tons of coal for the Cocheco Manufacturing Company.

> This is her first trip and several of our citizens paid her a visit while she is waiting there to be lightered so that she can come up the river. She is a handsome craft...a splendid sailer. She draws ten feet of water, instead of nine, as the contract speci-fied, and her owners are talking of having another built to take her place, as our channel is not deep enough to have her come up in safety with a full cargo.[23]

On June 12, the vessel's stockholders were welcomed aboard for an excursion ride to Fort Constitution. The men dined on oyster stew and ice cream and returned to Dover that evening, some on the tug *Ann* and others on the Dover and Portsmouth Railroad. The *Trickey* and her crew immediately set to work upon the East Coast waters, and by October 1879, had already paid back her owners twenty percent of her building cost.

The *Dover Enquirer* regularly reported the comings and goings of the *Charles H. Trickey* as she hauled coal, phosphate, granite, paving stone, feldspar, and ice from the Penobscot to the Potomac.

Like her predecessor the *Bracewell*, the *Trickey* was a fast vessel, but also, it seems, a lucky one. Twice, while coming up to Dover loaded with 350 tons of coal, Captain Kelley was able to reach the Cocheco Manufacuturing Company's wharf at the Landing without lightering, "though drawing over ten feet of water. This is without parallel as there is surely only nine feet of water at high tide."[24] This remarkable occurrence happened again on June 4, 1886 when the Trickey docked at midnight in downtown Dover. Imagine the surprise of the locals when they saw that sight the next morning.

The *Trickey* was also spared from two near disasters. In June 1883, the vessel was grounded on one of the shoals around Nantucket and was thought unsalvageable. But wreckers were able to pull the ship off the rocks, and repairs cost only $240. The *Trickey* was soon on her way to Boston with a load of coal from Philadelphia.

On another occasion, in mid-August 1886, the *Trickey* was overdue to arrive at Dover wharves and some citizens were worried. But on August 19, a disastrous fire on the Cochecho River destroyed many of the Landing docks. "Had the *Trickey* arrived it would have been burned without doubt."[25]

In 1888, the members of the Dover Navigation Company sold the schooner *Charles H. Trickey* to a company in Portland, Maine for $8200. In nine years, the vessel had earned $19,442.72 for its stockholders, a profit of 136%.

In September 1893, the *Trickey* collided off Cape Cod with another schooner, the *Governor* from Castine, Maine. The *Governor* was lost, but her crew was taken aboard the badly damaged *Trickey* and the vessel was towed to Vineyard Haven where an inspection proved her salvageable. The *Enquirer* smugly noted that, "The schooner *Trickey* was formerly of the Dover Navigation Line, but was sold in 1888."[26]

Schooner B. Frank Nealley
(1880-1889)

Specifications: Tonnage-Gross 274.27, Net 260.56; Cargo 375 tons; Length 123.6 feet; Breadth 30.2 feet; Depth 8.8 feet; Built 1880 in Bath, Maine; Cost $16,480.

As confidence in their shipping venture grew, so did the size of the Dover Navigation Company's fleet. When the company commissioned the building of a third schooner in 1879, it was ordered to be an even larger vessel than the *Bracewell* or the *Trickey*. The owners wanted a ship capable of carrying even bigger cargoes of coal, over 350 tons, but which could still navigate the narrow channels and shallow depths of the Cochecho River.

All the shares in the new schooner, built to do business on our river, have been subscribed, and the vessel will probably soon be put under contract. It is to be 120 feet keel, thirty feet beam, and not to draw over nine feet of water when loaded. It is to be finished by the first of April. The largest proportion of the stock is owned here.[27]

The new schooner would be named for the Dover Navigation Company's secretary-treasurer B. Frank Nealley and built by Goss, Sawyer and Packard of Bath, Maine. Her captain would be John M. Handy of Cotuit, Massachusetts, "a gentleman of experience in coasting trade."[28]

The *B. Frank Nealley* was launched March 25, 1880 from the Bath shipyard with the hope that this vessel would solve the navigational problems faced by the first two schooners on the Cochecho.

> The problem which this company is trying to solve is this: with a guarantee of nine foot draught of water to all vessels coming into Dover river, to build a schooner that will bring 350 tons to our dock on the river without being lightened. They have failed to accomplish this with schooner *John Bracewell* by 100 tons coal, and with the *C. H. Trickey* by fifty tons coal. It is expected that the new schooner will be a success in this respect. If she is not, the company will undoubtedly try again.[29]

But the *Nealley*, although a sound ship with good speed, did not meet the expectations of the Dover Navigation Company. The schooner still had to be lightered when carrying a full cargo. For the next nine years, the *Nealley* worked constantly hauling coal, ice, pitch, brick, stone, and sand to such ports as Annapolis, Boston, Baltimore, New York, and Philadelphia. She performed her job admirably, yet occasionally the Dover newspapers would allude to the unsolved lightering problem:

> *April 1883*—The schooner *B. F. Nealley* arrived as far up the river yesterday afternoon as Clement's wharf, near the glue factory, where it had to stop to be partially unloaded.[30]
> *December 1887*—The schooner *B. Frank Nealley* arrived at the lightering place today with coal from New York for C. H. Trickey & Co.[31]
> *May 1888*—The schooner *B. Frank Nealley* has come up to the lightering place with coal for the Cocheco Mfg. Co. from Philadelphia.[32]

But her skipper, Captain Handy, was proud of his vessel's accomplishments, even with her limitations. In 1881, he had presented Mr. Nealley with an oil painting of the schooner under full sail passing Boston Light: "the picture is 24 x 36 and was painted by Stubbs of New Bedford. Captain Handy is proud of his craft as is Mr.

Nealley and all stockholders for she is a noble vessel."[33] The Dover
Navigation Company eventually sold the *B. Frank Nealley* in 1889.
John Lowe, Jr. of Key West, Florida bought the schooner "thoroughly
inspected...and...as sound as when she was built"[34] for $12,000 cash.
"She was one of the fastest sailing vessels of the Dover fleet and had
paid her owners 113%..."[35]

Schooner Thomas B. Garland
(1881-1911)

*Specifications: Tonnage-Gross 319.13, Net 303.17; Cargo
500 tons; Length 126 feet; Breadth 32 feet; Depth 11 feet;
Built 1881 in Bath, Maine; Cost $18,515.55.*

For the fourth time in so many years, the Dover Navigation
Company added another schooner to their commercial fleet. The first
three vessels had been built to navigate the shallow waters of the
Cochecho River without drawing over nine feet of water. If the ships,
loaded with coal, could sail all the way to the Landing docks without
lightering at deeper spots downriver, considerable time and money could
be saved. Unfortunately, while built to the Dover Navigation Company's
exact specifications, the first three schooners could not, in most cases,
travel freely into port when heavily loaded. By 1881, the members of the
Company seem to have realized the impossibility of building such large
ships with small drafts and abandoned the idea of direct sailing into
downtown Dover. When the fourth schooner was commissioned of
shipbuilders Goss, Sawyer, and Packard, it was ordered to be even larger
than the other three vessels and to draw eleven feet of water. It would be
capable of carrying nearly 500 tons in its hold.

> We learn that the Dover Navigation Company has placed
> under contract...for a three-masted schooner: 120 feet keel,
> thirty-two feet beam, depth of hole eleven feet with a flush
> deck. The vessel...will rate about 500 tons capacity with all
> the modern improvements.[36]

The *Thomas B. Garland* was launched at Bath in August 1881
and was commanded by Captain Gustavus Kelley, former master of
the *C. H. Trickey.*

> The owners of the schooner *T. B. Garland* who visited the
> vessel while she lay at her moorings in Saco express

themselves as having been highly pleased with the appearance of the craft and all join in the opinion that it is the finest of the fleet owned in Dover.[37]

The *Garland* brought to Saco the largest cargo ever landed there by any schooner and made quite an impression on those viewing her in port.

In December 1881, the big schooner visited Dover for the first time and Captain Kelley there predicted a brilliant and successful future for the *Garland*. For the next nine years, the schooner made numerous trips to Philadelphia and Richmond to pick up coal and often traveled from the Maine coast to southern coast cities delivering ice. Her owners were able to declare yearly a ten per cent dividend for all her stockholders, and in 1888 changed captains, giving W. B. Crosby command of the schooner.

In 1900, the *Thomas B. Garland* was in a bad collision with a ferry boat, the *Snug Harbor*, while sailing up the East River in New York City. A lawsuit ensued with the courts eventually placing the blame for the accident on the ferry. The Dover Navigation Company was able to recover all damages.

The *Garland* was sold in 1911 to Captain Jesse Smith of Vineyard Haven, Massachusetts for $2250. Profits on the vessel for her thirty year run were almost $40,000, another good investment for the Dover Navigation Company's shareholders.

Schooner *Zimri S. Wallingford*

(1882-1895)

Specifications: Tonnage-Gross 295.76, Net 280.98; Cargo 450 tons; Length 127.7 feet; Breadth 30.3 feet; Depth 9.1 feet; Built 1882 in Bath, Maine; Cost $19,012.

The fifth schooner built by Goss and Sawyer shipyard for the Dover Navigation Company was launched from Bath in July 1882.

Commanded by Captain John Willett of Philadelphia, who also supervised her construction, the *Zimri S. Wallingford* was a model of new building ideas. "She is expected to combine the two very desirable qualities in a coasting vessel: large carrying capacity, and light draft of water."[38]

The vessel was named for the agent of the Cocheco Manufacturing Company, Zimri Wallingford, "a fitting compliment to one who is actively engaged in pushing the interests of the Cochecho River. Mr. Wallingford is an owner in this vessel and a member of the building committee."[39]

A navigational and commercial success, the *Wallingford* was able to pay ten per cent dividend to her stockholders by January 1883. In May of that year, however, the schooner collided with another ship, the *Norman* from Mobile, Alabama.

> The circumstances of the collision showed grave carelessness on the part of the captain of the *Norman*, the *Wallingford* having the right of way and keeping her proper course. It carried away channels, stove rails and bulwarks, and stove a hole in the port quarter. The *Wallingford* was repaired, as good as before, in New York and the owners of the schooner *Norman* have paid the bill.[40]

But this accident did not slow down the hectic schedule of the *Wallingford*. Besides delivering many cargoes of coal to Dover, the vessel also carried lumber, stone, ice, and phosphorus to Florida and in 1888 even hauled a cargo of 3000 barrels of apples to New York City!

There was in Dover a great deal of pride in this schooner's accomplishments and abilities. She possessed beauty: "a beautiful boat kept in first class order by her worthy Captain John Willett;"[41] speed: "arrived at Richmond from Charleston only seventy-four hours from dock to dock...extraordinary time and...well pleased with the achievement;"[42] and above all, navigability: "contained 432 tons for the Cocheco Mfg. Co., ninety tons of it was taken off (at the lightering place) and...arrived at wharf at 1 A.M.; quick work."[43] In 1892, the Dover Navigation Company declared a twelve per cent dividend (second-highest return in the fleet) on the *Wallingford* and her stockholders forecasted a long and profitable future.

Unfortunately, the *Wallingford* was totally destroyed by fire on March 17, 1895 at Montompkins Inlet, Virginia. The blaze was discovered at 7 A.M. just as she was getting ready to depart the harbor, and in no time, with a cargo of dry lumber and strong winds blowing, the schooner burned to the water's edge. The captain and crew escaped safely but lost all their personal effects.

The *Wallingford* had earned $23,577 for her owners, a profit of 124% and was insured for another $12,000. A sad loss for the Dover Navigation Company.

Schooner J. Chester Wood
(1883-1892)

*Specifications: Tonnage-Gross 69.99, Net 66.50; Cargo 55
tons; Length 68.6 feet; Breadth 23 feet; Depth 5.5 feet; Built
1881 in Cherryfield, Maine.*

The Dover Navigation Company deviated from their large
three-masted schooner formula when they bought a small brick
schooner, the *J. Chester Wood* which had been built in 1881 in
Cherryfield, Maine. The vessel was probably purchased by the
company sometime after April 1883 as the *Dover Daily Republican* for
April did not list the *J. Chester Wood* in its report of "all the schooners
which will be engaged in carrying bricks from the yards along the
Cochecho this season."[44]

By April 1884 however, the *Wood*, Captain Jack Sanders in
command, was busy delivering to Boston cargoes of brick made at
Dover Point.

> Schooner *J. Chester Wood*...with a cargo of 800 casks of lime,
> was lying at Portsmouth bridge, bound to Dover. After
> discharging she will load with 60,000 bricks at Lucas' yard at
> Dover Point for Boston.[45]

This workhorse schooner was in constant use through 1888,
but her troubles also began in that year.

> Though Captain Sanders...has had some losses this summer such
> as anchor and cable, broken booms, etc. his vessel has paid very
> well and a dividend of ten per cent has been declared on her.[46]

The following September, the *J. Chester Wood* was in collision
with another schooner as both ships were attempting to clear the
mouth of the harbor. "The schooner *Wood* lost her davits and had her
mainsail badly torn."[47]

By 1892, the Dover Navigation Company was only able to
declare a two per cent dividend on the *Wood*, the lowest rate of return
among their eight-schooner fleet, and disposed of the ship when the
trend toward hauling bricks by barges became popular. "Brick
manufacturers have come to the conclusion that shipping by barge is
the proper method and the day of the schooner is past."[48]

Schooner John J. Hanson
(1884-1914)

Specifications: Tonnage Gross 685.77, Net 651.49, Cargo 1000 tons; Length 150.4 feet; Breadth 34.8 feet; Depth 18.7 feet; Built 1884 in Bath, Maine; Cost $29,400.

The next addition to the sailing fleet of the Dover Navigation Company, a huge schooner with a double deck, the *John J. Hanson*, was built by the New England Shipbuilding Company in Bath. The vessel was launched from the Maine port on December 12, 1884 and captained by L. J. Stevens, formerly of the schooner *John Bracewell*.

> This vessel is 140 feet keel, thirty-four and one-half feet beam, thirteen and one-half feet lower hold, four and one-half feet between decks, being a double deck vessel. Mr. Hanson is the largest owner in the vessel and he has presented her with a new "Suit of Colors." It is expected she will carry 900 tons of coal.[49]

The *John J. Hanson* was so big that even though Dover was designated as the schooner's home port, it was never able to navigate the Cochecho River to the Landing. The closest the vessel ever got was Portsmouth. On her first trip, the *Hanson* carried 1,002 tons of coal from Baltimore to New Bedford and made her maiden voyage "in fine style."[50] It was reported that "the cargo on the schooner would make five trains of cars, thirty cars to a train, each carrying six tons."[51]

The *John Hanson* transported mainly coal, but also carried ice from the Kennebec River and phosphate rock from North Carolina. Ironically, as the trains versus schooners argument was raging about which method of transportation was the most cost efficient, the *Hanson* was bringing in thousands of tons of coal for the Boston and Maine Railroad. And when Captain Stevens attended the meeting of the Dover Navigation Company, he had to leave his ship in Portsmouth and arrive on the 10:36 train.[52]

Eventually, after a thirty year life at sea, the schooner *Hanson* was abandoned on February 15, 1914. The vessel was deemed unseaworthy when a storm caused her to begin sinking. She was carrying a load of molasses from Puerto Rico and was bound for Boston. The crew was saved by the steamer *Coamo* and put ashore at San Juan. The *Hanson's* final profit was $80,072.79, at 272% gain for the owners of the ship.

Jonathan Sawyer's prestigious residence near Sawyer Mills. The eighth schooner built by the Dover Navigation Company was named for Sawyer. CD

Schooner Jonathan Sawyer
(1886-1907)

Specifications: Tonnage-Gross 399.15, Net 350.56; Cargo 600 tons; Length 140 feet; Breadth 33.3 feet; Depth 10.3 feet; Built 1886 in Bath, Maine; Cost $19,404.

The eighth vessel to be owned by the members of the Dover Navigation Company was the *Jonathan Sawyer*, built at Bath in 1886 by the New England Shipbuilding Company. "The committee appointed to notify Jonathan Sawyer of the vote...to call the new schooner after him called at his residence, and upon hearing that the wish was unanimous, Mr. Sawyer accepted the honor."[53]

The schooner was launched on April 12, after an on-site inspection by Colonel Charles H. Sawyer, C. H. Trickey, John J. Hanson, and B. Frank Nealley. The news reported the *Sawyer* "going into the water like a thing of life, without accident in any way."[54] Its commander was famous Dover sea captain Benjamin Oliver Reynolds.

Schooner Jonathan Sawyer, *built in Bath, Maine 1886 for the Dover Navigation Company. Photo taken from the Dover Point bridge as the vessel traveled to Dover Landing with coal. ES*

The *Sawyer's* first visit to Dover occurred in August 1886. The vessel arrived at the lightering place on the 20th "with 600 tons of coal, the largest cargo ever brought to Dover."[55] Two lighter loads had to be taken off the schooner before it could sail the rest of the way into Dover Landing. Jonathan Sawyer and his family, anxious to see their namesake, sailed out to visit the *Sawyer* at the lightering spot "and spent a very pleasant afternoon on board, they were very much pleased with the new vessel."[56] On August 27th, the ship was able to dock at the Landing and was "greatly admired by a large number of visitors. It is estimated that over 1000 persons went down...to see the new schooner...which is the largest except the schooner *John J. Hanson*."[57]

Perhaps because of her famous captain and his renowned exploits, the citizens of Dover followed the voyages of Captain Reynolds[58] and the *Jonathan Sawyer* with great interest. The local newspapers regularly reported on their trips to Philadelphia, Galveston, Mobile, Nicaragua, Cuba, and the West Indies with cargoes of coal, stone, sugar, paving stone, and sewer pipe.

For much of her sailing life, the schooner contracted to work out of Saco, Maine for the York Corporation mills and in 1886 had iron plates installed on her bow to help protect her planking from the ice in cold Maine waters.

In March 1896, the *Jonathan Sawyer* was nearly lost when she ran aground in a heavy gale near Sandy Hook, New Jersey. Captain Reynolds would not abandon the ship and stayed aboard to help the two tugs sent to pull the *Sawyer* off the shoal. Part of her cargo, sugar from San Domingo, was discharged and the vessel was floated again after two days hard work.

> All concerned, Dover people in particular, have reason to congratulate themselves. The *Sawyer* is ten years old...it is one of the best ships in the fleet and is handled by a throughly good seaman who is an efficient and most popular captain.[59]

Minor repairs were made and by April 17, 1896, the *Jonathan Sawyer* was at work again, sailing from New York to Philadelphia. She was back in Saco by May 15th.

The schooner was tragically lost at sea on November 6, 1907 near Cape Porpoise, Maine. She was on her way to Saco with a load of coal from Philadelphia when a storm forced her to wreck on Goat Island. No lives were lost, but the Dover Navigation Company, although they'd made a 157% profit of $30,464.28, had to bear the brunt of the loss of yet another of their fleet.

Oil painting of the schooner Jonathan Sawyer, *one of the Dover Navigation Company's fleet. ES*

Schooner J. Frank Seavey
(1888-1912)

Specifications: Tonnage-Gross 412.96, Net 392.32; Cargo 600 ons; Length 144 feet; Breadth 33.9 feet; Depth 10.2 feet; Built 1888 in Bath, Maine; Cost $24,040.96.

In April 1888, Captain Gustavus Kelley, originally master of the *Charles Trickey*, and later the *Thomas B. Garland*, reported from Bath, Maine that the Dover Navigation Company's new schooner, its ninth, would soon be ready. "She has the nicest frames, he says, that he ever saw. There is a large crew of men at work on her and they are rushing things along rapidly."[60]

The *J. Frank Seavey*, built by the New England Shipbuilding Company, was launched in July 1888 from the Bath shipyard with all her owners present for the ceremony. With her capacity for 600 tons in her hold and her innovative design, the *Seavey* was able to dock at Dover Landing on December 7, 1888 with "the largest cargo ever brought here by any vessel."[61] She was towed up the river by the tug *Cocheco* and large numbers of Dover residents went down to catch a glimpse: "it being the first time her prow has parted the waters of the Cochecho."[62]

The *Dover Enquirer* boasted:

> The vessel is a beauty and what is better, works like a charm
> at sea. She has 600 tons of soft coal for the Cocheco Mfg. Co.,
> and this is the largest cargo that ever came into the river
> without lightering: and this shows that this is the vessel for
> the port of Dover.[63]

After a decade of trying, the Dover Navigation Company had
finally gotten it right-the perfect combination of enormity and navigability. Captain Kelley sailed her admirably, traveling often from
Philadelphia to Dover with huge coal cargoes. It is no wonder that with
such a successful vessel at stake, Dover Navigation Company officers J.
Frank Seavey and B. F. Nealley went to great lengths to save her in
1896.

The *Seavey* was bound for New Orleans when a tidal wave hit
the Gulf and drove the schooner three miles inland on the Louisiana
flats. The vessel settled into the deep mud, upright but impossibly
stuck. Word was sent back to Dover that the *Seavey* was
unsalvageable and should be abandoned. Mr. Seavey and Mr. Nealley
decided to investigate in person.

> This was a combination that meant success to the undertak-
> ing. Mr. Nealley was deliberate and cautious. Mr. Seavey
> quick, determined and courageous. They went to New
> Orleans, looked over the situation and decided to bring the
> schooner to the Gulf. They went to the banks and business
> houses to inquire for a wrecking company who were responsi-
> ble and could give suitable bond. They were told by all that
> the vessel could not be floated and that all money put into the
> undertaking would be lost. Their reply was, "We are going to
> do it." They evidently were considered a little daft and in the
> hotel and on the street they would hear, "There they go," "They
> are the men," and even at church they heard the remark,
> "Look, there they go." They finally found the right parties who
> took a power boat up one of the small streams. When the tide
> was out the soft mud was scooped up to make a channel.
> When the tide was high the power boat pulled the schooner
> *Seavey* along as far as possible. The work continued for two
> weeks. The cost was about $3000. When the diligent sidewalk
> committee and the businessmen who had given such kindly
> advice saw the schooner *J. Frank Seavey* uninjured, and worth
> $15,000 float out into the Gulf of Mexico, they had discovered
> the true temper of the New England Yankee.[64]

The schooner *Seavey* was sold March 19, 1912 to Captain John
Bennett of Rockland Maine.

Schooner John Holland
(1890-1893)

Specifications: Tonnage-Gross 1165.88, Net 1107.59; Cargo 1800 tons; Length 195.2 feet; Breadth 40.3 feet; Depth 17.8 feet; Built 1890 in Bath, Mane; Cost $54,400.

The last schooner to operate for the Dover Navigation Company was the *John Holland*, built by the New England Shipbuilding Company in 1890 for $54,400. The huge vessel, a four-masted schooner, was launched from Bath, Maine on August 9, 1890 and was commanded by Captain Lucius J. Stevens, formerly of the *John Bracewell* and the *John J. Hanson*.

Because of her enormous size, the *John Holland* was never able to visit her home port of Dover. Citizens there had to be content with viewing several photographs of the ship taken by John Holland and presented to C. H. Trickey, and with seeing a carved model of the *Holland*, five feet long, in the window of the Dover Clothing Company. "The model is the cynosure of all eyes and greatly admired."[65]

The *Holland's* maiden voyage was to Baltimore, so she did not visit New Hampshire waters until November 1890 when she finally docked at Portsmouth.

> The schooner…had all her flags flying in honor of the visit of Mr. John Holland and family and invited friends who came down from Dover to inspect the vessel.[66] The schooner…was visited by a large party of owners and friends from Dover. Captain Stevens went home to Connecticut where an addition of one has been made to his family since his last visit there. The schooner is a model of elegance from stem to stern, the cabin being finely finished in oak. She carries only ten men, the bulk of the work being done with steam. She had a cargo of 1804 tons of coal on this trip.[67]

By January 1892, the Dover Navigation Company was able to declare a fifteen per cent dividend on the John Holland, the highest return ever, and the *Dover Enquirer* glowed:

> The schooner has been running but sixteen months and in that time has earned for her owners, the net sum of $10,800. It should be borne in mind that the rates for all freighting on the coast have been lower during the past summer than ever before. All in all, if a man had money to invest he could not do better than buy stock of the Dover Navigation Company.[68]

Schooner John Holland at Bath, Maine; built in 1890, the tenth ship built for the Dover Navigation Company. MMM

But on June 16, 1893, while bound for Providence from Norfolk with a load of coal, the *John Holland* was struck by an English steamer, the *Michigan*. The ships were about ten miles east of Cape Henry, Virginia when the collision occurred. The *John Holland* heavily laden, sunk in only twenty-five minutes. The *Michigan* received only minor damages and was able to bring the *Holland's* crew, all safe, back to Baltimore.

The Dover Navigation Company, claiming "her officers totally without fault, that the collision was due to the carelessness of the *Michigan's* officers"[69] brought suit against the British ship in U. S. Circuit Court in Baltimore. The suit declared the *Michigan* "did not keep clear of the schooner as required by law, that speed was more than moderate, that she did not change course to avoid the collision, that she did not have fog signals out, and did not attempt to reverse engines."[70]

This first lawsuit failed but an appeal was made, and on January 18, 1895, the owners of the *John Holland* were awarded a check for $39,000, the appraised value of the sunken vessel. The claim had been for $67,750 ($55,000 for the schooner, $12,750 for the cargo), but it appears the Dover Navigation Company was satisified with the settlement after such a long court battle.

Barque William W. Crapo, length 215 feet, breadth 41.8 feet, depth 24 feet. Built in 1880 at Bath, Maine. Captain Washington W. Hardy of Dover was her only captain. MMM

VI · *Dover's Deepwater Sea Captains*

IN ADDITION TO THE GREAT amount of local river traffic on the Cochecho, longer and more treacherous voyages were also the way of life for several Dover citizens. Over a dozen deepwater sea captains made their homes in Dover. These brave, adventurous men were often gone for months at a time, carrying cargo and passengers to all points on the globe. They faced terrible storms, faulty vessels and equipment, and sometimes mutinous crews on board these brigs and barques. They were ever watchful for pirates and always had to be on guard against kidnappers in foreign ports. They battled fires and pestilence and were sometimes forced to survive after shipwrecks on uninhabited isles.

John Scales says:

> Some of the old Dover Ship masters made their voyages overseas without Sextant or "Practical Navigator."…The skipper kept their reckoning with chalk on a shingle…and by way of observation they held up a hand to the sun. When they got him over four fingers they knew they were straight for Whole in the Wall; three fingers gave them their course to the double headed Shop Keys; two fingers carried them down to the Barbadoes.[1]

The local newspapers attempted to keep tabs on these captains and often noted the latest news of their arrivals and departures. The descriptions which follow are based on those news accounts and also on a paper, "Dover Sea Captains," written by Ellen Scales for the Northam Colonists Historical Society in 1915.

Captain John Riley, Sr. (1752-1818)

John Riley was born in London, January 27, 1752, and came to Dover as a teenager with a Captain Hodgdon. He rose quickly to the rank of captain and sailed often to foreign ports. Riley, like other local sea captains of this period, was often at the mercy of plundering privateers. The *Dover Sun* of March 6, 1800 says:

> Arrival at Portsmouth Schooner *Fannie*, Captain John Riley of Dover, twenty-nine days from Martinique. Feb. 12 was brought-to by a French privateer called the *Hassard* from Porto Rico, who ordered the *Fannie's* boat to be hoisted out, in which Captain Riley and two men went on board the privateer. The boat soon returned with five Frenchmen who searched the vessel and took away property to the value of about four hundred dollars and left her.

Captain Riley was not only a shipmaster but also a ship-builder; his shipyard stood where the power station is now on Cochecho Street at the section known as the Gulf. Riley married Mary Hanson on October 13, 1777 in a ceremony conducted by the Reverend Jeremy Belknap, and died in Dover "with his boots on" November 6, 1818 when he fell from the staging of a ship he was in progress of building.

Captain John Riley, Jr. (1781-1842)

John Riley Jr., son of Captain John Riley, was born in Dover on January 24, 1781. He followed in his father's trade and also became a sea captain in addition to managing a fleet of merchant ships doing business abroad. John Jr. married Ann Boardman on October 29, 1812 and for many years served as a treasurer and selectman for the town of Dover and as a representative to the New Hampshire Legislature. Ironically, he was influential in bringing the Boston and Maine Railroad to Dover, a move which hampered the shipping industry at the river not inconsiderably. He died when he was sixty-one, May 21, 1842, just one month before the Boston and Maine completed the track between Arch Street and Franklin Square. The *Dover Enquirer* called Riley:

> Upright and fearless in the discharge of every duty; liberal and generous in the use of that wealth which years of enterprise and industry had accumulated; a friend and benefactor of the poor; a counsellor of the inexperienced; foremost and most

efficient in every good word and worked for the advancement of the prosperity of the town and the welfare of his fellowmen.[2]

The funeral took place May 24, 1842 and was said to be the largest public funeral ever seen in Dover.

Captain John Riley III (1814-1884)

This third generation John Riley was also a sea captain in his early life, but later abandoned the sea and made a fortune on Wall Street. He married Mary A. Pendexter of New York and Newport in September 1840. Riley III served as president of the New York and Pacific Steam Ship Company until his death in New York City August 19, 1884.

Captain William Flagg (1770-1844)

William Flagg was born in Portsmouth April 17, 1770. At the young age of thirteen, he shipped out as a cabin boy on the brig *Sisters* and made his first voyage to Tobago and St. Thomas in the West Indies. On the return trip, William landed in Baltimore and shipped out in 1784 aboard the brig *Friend* bound again for the Caribbean. This vessel developed a leak however, and the crew was forced to land in Charleston, South Carolina.

In Charleston, William worked for a year on the harbor boats, then was persuaded by his brother to return to Portsmouth. Yet by the time he was sixteen, tired of the landbound life, he signed on for a voyage to England, France, and South America. His next trip to France was on a ship carrying American soldiers to fight in the French Revolution.

On his subsequent return to the United States, Flagg became the mate on Captain Benjamin Fernald's brig *Mehitable and Mary* and worked in commercial trade along the New England coast. After a three year apprenticeship, he became captain of the schooner *Truro* and moved back to his beloved Charleston. This southern city, where his brother now lived and worked in the shipping business, became the captain's home for several years (whenever he was not at sea).

In 1793, when he was twenty-three, Captain Flagg took command of the brig *Fame* and sailed to Bordeaux, France. On the return trip, he was captured by an English ship and abandoned in Bermuda where his brig and its cargo were condemned. In 1795, Flagg was able to repurchase the *Fame* at auction and return to Charleston.

Tidewater Farm, home of Captain William Flagg. RAW

The captain's next venture, with war raging between England and France, was in command of the schooner *Eliza* to the Straits of Gibraltar. In this channel, Flagg was again captured by the English and his ship sold. Eventually able to return to the United States, Captain Flagg took charge of another ship, the *Penelope*. This vessel, while on a voyage to Jamaica, was also captured and condemned, this time by a French privateer. When the *Penelope* was sold, Flagg bought it and returned once more to Charleston.

Undaunted by his ill luck, Captain Flagg put out to sea again, this time with a cargo of sugar. A British frigate intercepted his ship and forced the captain to land in Halifax, Nova Scotia. This time, the British wrecked the *Penelope* but Flagg had the ship repaired just enough to allow him to sail back to South Carolina. But this time, the wary captain armed his vessel with fourteen guns.

Soon after these unfortunate setbacks, Flagg enlisted in the United States Navy and became 3rd Lieutenant on the frigate *John Adams*. He served two years and was granted a pension allotment in his old age by a special act of Congress.

In 1801, at age thirty-one he took command of the sloop *Delight* and made several successful voyages to London. But, as was becoming a habit, the captain was captured again, this time off the coast of Cuba with a load of coffee, and forced to dock in Havana. He was able, three months later, to ransom the *Delight* and return to Charleston. Tired of being captured while flying the American flag, the beleaguered captain purchased a schooner, the *Four Friends*, put her under Spanish colors, and sailed to Havana and Tobago. Yet on his return to Cuba, the ship was seized by a Spanish vessel and forced to put back to sea. He returned to Charleston $1000 poorer for this venture, but fortunately, this sixth capture of a Flagg vessel was the last.

The captain refitted the *Four Friends* and sailed to Tobago with a cargo of logwood. From 1805 to 1810, he was engaged in the Southern Coast trade, usually carrying rice or cotton. In 1810, Flagg returned to Portsmouth and joined his brother's shipping and mercantile business. Shortly thereafter, he moved to Dover and built the brick home on the Cochecho, now called Tidewater Farm.

In 1814, together with other seacoast area merchants, Flagg ran a privateering venture along the coast. These entrepreneuring men fitted out a schooner, the *Fox*, for the war-like work of capturing English merchant vessels. Privateering was legal, and even commendable, during the War of 1812. President James Madison, in a document called the Letters of Marque, gave noble citizens the right to arm their own ships and freely capture English ships. Any property seized became the private booty of the brave captors. The rationale was that England had a large, well-equipped navy, so any action that could bolster the power of the smaller, weaker U. S. Navy could only help the American cause. During the course of the next year, Flagg's *Fox* captured several British ships which netted the captain about $236, a considerable sum for those days. He was, no doubt, the richest man in Dover.

His own seafaring days nearing an end, Flagg next became involved in town affairs and in 1813 served as Dover's representative to the New Hampshire State Legislature. He was a devout member of the Central Street Baptist Church and the donor of a bell, said to have been captured from an English vessel in 1814, for the steeple of the Franklin Academy.[3] Captain William Flagg died February 12, 1844, and was buried at Pine Hill Cemetery. His son, Henry, followed in his father's footsteps and commanded several ships, including the *Adelaide Bell* of New York and in 1849, the ship *Pactolus*, carrying railroad iron for the Cocheco Railroad.

Captain Samuel Varney (1797-1875)

Samuel Varney was born in Dover September 16, 1797, the son of Stephen and Susan Varney. When he was just ten years old, Samuel started out on foot, his clothes wrapped in a bandanna and one dime to his name, to see his sister Betsy, a milliner in Salem, Massachusetts.

One of the antique swords presented to Captain Timothy Newman by the Algerian government after the captain paid for the ransom of his kidnapped crew. This sword is on display at the Woodman Institute. WI

This gold-lined silver speaking trumpet made in Sheffield, England ca. 1850 was presented to Captain Timothy Newman Porter of the barque Manchester *by the Cuban families who had been rescued by the Captain in May 1850. WI*

In Salem, Varney learned the barrel-making trade and upon finishing his apprenticeship, sailed on his first and second voyages as ship's cooper.

On June 8, 1827, Samuel married Mary Archer of Salem, a long union that produced five children and seven grandchildren.

By March 31, 1841, when the brig *Thomas Perkins* set sail for Honolulu, Varney was a full-fledged captain and master of the vessel. Over the course of his thirty-year career, Captain Varney made many voyages to distant ports in China, the West Indies, South America, and the Sandwich Islands. He became part owner of a commercial trade barque, the *Angola*, and carried all kinds of merchandise. He was taken prisoner twice and also cast away at sea, but Varney survived to retire back in Dover at a farm in the Blackwater Road area. Varney died there May 6, 1875.

Captain Timothy Newman Porter (1817-1872)

Timothy Newman Porter, son of Mary and Isaac Adams Porter, was born in November 1817. Porter was a well-known captain in many ports of the world and during his thirty year career at sea visited such renowned figures as Nicholas I of Russia, Louis Napoleon, Queen Victoria, and Leopold I and II of Belgium. Porter's involvement with shipping began when he was only fourteen and set out with his friend, Henry Flagg (son of Captain William Flagg) on board a small-rigged vessel commanded by Captain John Rogers. This ship had been built in Dover in the meadow west of the old jail and launched on the Cochecho River.

In 1850, while in command of the barque *Manchester*, Porter landed at Cardenas, Cuba during a political upheaval: Narcisso Lopez (1798?-1851), an infamous buccaneer, was invading the port and a land battle was in progress. The concerned Porter took on board for safe-keeping most of the women and children of the town. When the port was eventually secured, Captain Porter was presented with a silver speaking trumpet by the people of Cardenas. About eighteen inches long, gold-lined, and worth $125 at the time, this sailor's trumpet was engraved with a band around the bell: "Presented to Captain Timothy N. Porter of the American Barque *Manchester* by the families whom he kindly received on board his vessel during the invasion of Cardenas by Narcisso Lopez on the 19th of May, 1850."[4]

During the Civil War, Captain Porter commanded several of the clipper ships owned by Jonathan and I. Salter Tredick of Portsmouth and engaged in the East India Trade. On at least one occasion, Porter's clipper *Simla*, (named for the summer capital of British India and launched at Portsmouth in 1863), narrowly escaped capture by the famous Confederate privateer *Alabama* which hunted for Yankee ships becalmed in the South Atlantic. Porter died June 14, 1872.

Captain Timothy Newman (1760-?)

Captain Timothy Newman Porter was the grandson and namesake of an even more famous shipmaster and naval officer, Captain Timothy Newman, born in 1760. Captain Newman was commanding vessels shortly after the American Revolution when the young United States Republic had no powerful Navy to enforce its rights on the sea. Newman was forced, as were other American captains of that period, to pay a "tribute" to Algiers in order to gain immunity from the seizure of his ship while in the Mediterranean Sea.

This tribute was simply blackmail and offered no real guarantee from capture. Captain Newman, his vessel and crew, and eighteen American merchantmen were captured by Algerian pirates and spent four years at hard labor in a prison in Algiers. Then Newman was paroled on the condition that he return to America to raise funds to ransom not only himself but also his surviving crew members. Eventually, the captain returned to Algiers with 161 kegs of silver currency and the Americans were finally released. Newman was also given two antique swords by the head of the Algerian government for keeping his promise to return.[5]

Captain Newman was then commissioned by President John Adams as a Captain in the first American Navy. He died of yellow fever in Havana while in command of the sloop of war *Essex*. His only son, Midshipman James Newman, died a few days later of the same disease.

Captain John Q. A. Smith (1825-1885)

The sea career of Captain John Q. A. Smith spanned almost forty years. He was born in Dover October 3, 1825 and lived on Brick (now Sixth) Street. Captain Smith was engaged, before the Civil War, primarily in the southern cotton trade and was one of the first shipmasters to visit Galveston after Texas was annexed to the United States. Smith worked a number of years for Thomas Peirce, whose family built the Peirce Memorial Church in Dover, and in fact, the Peirce brothers, Andrew and Thomas, Dover-born Boston-based entrepreneurs, invested largely in Texas properties based solely on

Smith's growing accounts of the wonderful possibilities in that new territory. Later, the Peirces organized the Sunset Railroad from Texas to the Pacific.[6]

During the Civil War, Captain Smith sailed from Galveston to Melbourne, Australia with large cargoes of coal. His son, George, sailed with him during that period. Following the war, Smith's voyages usually started from New York. The *Island City*, the *Herbert*, and the *Rodney* were under his command and carried cotton and grain to England. Smith also commanded a ship in New York for another Dover native, Captain John Riley III of the New York and Pacific Steam Ship Company.

Smith, an Anglophile, greatly enjoyed his trips to England and always returned with great treasures for his wife, the former Mary Riley. Her imported silk velvet cloak was put on exhibit in a New York City store window, and her grass linen handkerchiefs were gifts from the Queen.

Eventually, Captain Smith became a British subject and sailed under the English flag for the firm of Adams, Vedder and Company. He often complained that the United States had failed to protect her citizens and their property abroad. He continued, though, to work out of Galveston, sailing regularly to Liverpool with cotton and passengers. He also visited Dover on occasion, purchasing a flat-bottomed boat from Joseph Young and sailing it between Dover and Boston. Smith eventually sailed that boat all the way to Texas where a tidal wave carried it four miles inland and it was abandoned.

On one of his passenger excursions, two English girls, Mary and Mona Hauslet from Leeds, who had lost all relatives in England, were sailing to Galveston where they had a brother. When the yellow fever epidemic prohibited their landing in Texas, Captain Smith allowed the girls to stay aboard the *Herbert* in harbor until the quarantine was lifted. The young women found out eventually that their brother had died in the epidemic, but Captain Smith was able to locate the remaining family members and settled the two girls with them. To the captain's surprise, one of these girls later wrote a book, *Galveston*, and dedicated it: "To Captain Smith and the officers of the Barque *Herbert* in grateful remembrance of their kindness, this little book is dedicated by the author." The novel was printed in London in 1868 and tells the tale of two English girls, Ida and Amy, and a kindly barque-master, Captain St. Johns. Smith died August 11, 1885 in Newton Center, Massachusetts.

Captain George J. O. Smith (1826-1865)

Captain George Smith, born in 1826, went to sea at an early age and his first command was the *Lucia Field*. He later mastered the barque *Mermaid* in the China coasting trade, running from China to Thailand (then Siam) with rice. His wife was Constance Riley, sister of Captain John Riley III and daughter of Captain John Riley, Jr. Mrs. Smith apparently had the sea in her blood too, as she made several voyages to China with her husband. Smith's *Mermaid* made one of the fastest passages on record between San Francisco and Hong Kong, but unfortunately the ship was wrecked on shoals in the China Sea in 1854.

Captain Smith then fitted out the ship *Beaver* in Boston and continued working in China. He returned home to Dover in the summer of 1860 and the *Beaver* was taken by another captain and lost at sea.

Near the end of the Civil War, Smith thought that since there were few steamers in Chinese waters, he would buy one and sail it to China and sell it. He soon bought an old blockade runner, the *Scotia*, which had been captured during the war. The vessel was cheaply built; its only purpose was to run enemy lines, and it was not suited for a long voyage around the Cape of Good Hope. But Smith, his wife, and her cousin embarked from Boston on Febuary 14, 1865. Heavy storms and gale winds in the Gulf deluged the *Scotia* and the Smiths and their crew were lost. Reverend Ezra Haskell and his wife, a sister of Mrs. Smith's, had been at the wharf in Boston to see them off, and the Reverend was said to have remarked, "That ship won't live overnight." A monument in memory of George and Constance Smith was erected at Pine Hill Cemetery.

Captain Benjamin Oliver Reynolds (1836-1923)

Born in Dover on February 3, 1836, Benjamin Reynolds, son of Oliver and Mary Watson Reynolds, began his sailor's life at age seventeen. During the summer of 1854, Benjamin visited Salem and signed aboard the vessel *Shirley* sailing from New York to Melbourne. From Australia, the *Shirley* traveled to Chile for a load of guano. The coastal islands there had immense beds of that fertilizer deposited by the great flocks of sea birds that came to roost. One thousand tons of the guano were loaded aboard and brought to Baltimore and sold at great profit for $25.00 a ton.

Reynold's second voyage was on board the *Mindaro* as third mate. The ship sailed from New York to San Francisco with a very rough passage around Cape Horn. From the California coast, the trip continued to Manila and from there to Boston via the Cape of Good Hope. This was Reynolds' first trip around the world, but during his half century of life at sea, he was to circle the globe several times.

The third ship on which Reynolds served was the *Aurora*, a voyage from New York to San Francisco. There the ship was outfitted with bunks and took on 500 Chinese passengers for Hong Kong. These men had been working in the California gold mines and had accumulated considerable amounts of money. Reynolds spent much of the voyage refereeing gambling disputes and restoring order among the bettors. At the port of Hong Kong, the crew boarded another shipload of Chinese laborers and transported them to Melbourne and Sydney, Australia. The return voyage, with a load of hemp, finally docked in Boston.

Reynolds' next voyage, aboard the *Malay* as second mate, went from Boston back to San Francisco. There he left the *Malay* to join the *Ocean Pearl* on a voyage to Mexico and the Gulf of California. A load of lumber was loaded there and delivered to London. In England, a cargo of railroad iron was taken on board and brought to New York. In New York, Captain Reynolds left the ship and returned home to Dover in 1869.

In 1871, Reynolds married Martha Dodge White and in 1873, he became captain of the *Formosa,* an American clipper ship owned in Salem, Massachusetts.

July 3, 1873—*Dover Enquirer*:

> We are glad to see our friend Captain Benjamin Reynolds still in town. He is waiting for the completion of a new larger ship than he has here to commanded.

He first saw his eldest daughter Kate when she was thirteen months old on his return from a long voyage in 1874. The family lived on Silver Street in Dover.

In nearly twenty years at sea, the captain had compiled a remarkable safety record with no accidents and no losses. Yet on April 15, 1879, when the *Formosa* sailed from Boston for Madras, India, the lucky streak ended. While on course from India to the Philippines with a cargo of hemp, the vessel went ashore on an uncharted reef in the Java Sea. During the month of January 1880 the captain and crew were stranded, luckily with salvaged supplies from the *Formosa*, on the reef. They were eventually rescued by a steamer, the *William McKinley*. The vessel was insured for $232,000, its full value, and the captain returned once more to Dover by way of the Suez Canal, Amsterdam, and Halifax.

The *Dover Enquirer* for April 15, 1880 says, "Captain B. O. Reynolds returned home on Monday. It will be remembered that his fine ship, the *Formosa*, was wrecked in the China Sea last winter. He received many warm congratulations here that he escaped."

In 1881, Captain Reynolds set sail in January from New York, bound for Shanghai. The folks at home in Dover, keeping track of their wandering captains, read in the *Dover Enquirer* of April 28, 1881:

Friends of Captain Ben Reynolds will be pleased to hear that his ship *Humboldt*...spotted Feb. 7 off Cape St. Roque, coast of Brazil. This looks as if Captain intended to make a quick passage, and he must have just "boomed along" to have been where he was in thirty-five days from sailing. Square away the yards, Captain, and let her boom.

On June 9, the *Enquirer* continued:

The clipper ship *Humboldt*, Captain Reynolds of this city, passed Algier April 11th just 100 days from N. Y. for Shanghai, China. This is a remarkably quick passage, beating the ship *Hoogely* sixty-five days, the latter sailing from New York Nov. 29 and passing Algiers the 12th of May, just a month later than the *Humboldt*.

In October 1882, the ship *Humboldt*, under Reynolds' command, sailed again, this time from Boston to China. In the autumn of 1883, the vessel left Shanghai on a return trip to New York, but soon after leaving port, a storm came up and gale force winds forced Reynolds' ship off course. The ship had passed through the Formosa Channel but the captain was unable to take any navigational observations in the fog. The *Humboldt* struck a reef in the China Sea and began to leak badly. By midnight, waves were breaking over the ship and the vessel lay on her side. The crew clung to the wreckage until 4 A.M. when they decided to swim to the reef's shore. The *Humboldt's* cargo, largely straw goods and bales of tea, also floated to the island and reached it even before the men.

Thirteen survivors made a shelter of these bales to offer some protection from the storm. They were unsure where they had landed or whether there was any food or water; they had no shoes and very little clothing. In the light of morning, they saw four more men struggling through the waves and helped them ashore. One of them was Captain Reynolds. In the words of the mate, "It proved to be my captain, but if I had not been looking for him, I should never have taken him for Captain Reynolds. He was as white as a ghost, and his feet and legs were badly cut."

Reynolds and the other three survivors had clung to the wreck until daylight and had assumed all the others had drowned. As they fought their way ashore and spotted the rag-tag band of men on the land, they wondered who they were and what kind of reception they would receive. The mutual surprise of both parties of survivors soon gave way to relief as the captain was helped to the shelter of the bales, covered with straw mats, and left to rest.

The crew's initial search of the small island was for water because they only had two kegs which had washed ashore along with some provisions, bales of freight, clothing, and parts of the ship. The stern was found a quarter mile away and the beach was strewn with debris for a distance of two miles. A tent was made of the sails and straw bales were opened for beds. Their first sparse supper consisted of four cans of preserved meat and a few bottles of whiskey which had washed ashore.

The next day, a search party located a small lake with plenty of fresh, useable water and the survivors began to feel better. Shelter and water were assured, clothes were designed from straw hats and rags, and soon their explorations yielded more clothing, three barrels of pork and beef, two bales of tobacco, two hams, two oil cans, a binnacle lamp with the bull's eye still intact, three barrels of dry flour, two hatchets, a frying pan, a pair of scissors and a razor. With a slow match which had been found and the bull's eye which made a good sun glass, a fire was started. The fire was watched by night to keep it bright as a signal of distress while flags signalled by day.

The mate's account details the living conditions:

> Two men volunteered to do the cooking. By knocking one end off the oil cans and boiling out the oil, we had two splendid kettles, one for tea and one for soup. The ship had 650 chests of tea which had washed ashore and, after drying, we had a very good article. We soon had a dozen boobies killed and boiling, and mixing some flour and water together, we had a flapjack apiece. (The boobies were web-footed birds that came up on the beach to roost in the bushes and could be knocked off and caught). Shell fish were abundant. About 2 o'clock that afternoon everything being all ready, I sat down to one of the best meals I ever ate in my life.

For supper, they had the soup with dumplings made from the flour. They made pipes of bamboo and ate their soup from fine china bowls in the cargo.

But even though their daily needs had been met, the crew knew they had wandered at least fifty miles outside the normal path of ships' traffic and could only depend on chance or providence to save them. They began building a raft from the timbers of the *Humboldt*.

Captain Reynolds and three others planned to set out aboard a raft and try to find help. While they were building the raft, they caught an immense turtle. There were 148 eggs in her, each as large as pigeons. The men dined on eggs for breakfast and turtle soup for supper with dumplings and onions and salted beef.

More than half of the ship's cargo had been straw hats, Captain Reynolds estimated about 500,000. They sold in China for a quarter cent but could be resold in the United States for five cents apiece. The beach and the bushes for over a mile were covered with these hats.

First Mate Frank Powers of Salem wrote:

> After getting back from the wreck I took a Bible and lay down to read. After reading a few chapters I sat up and looked out to sea, wondering how or when we would get away from here. What worried me most was it would be such a long time before we should be missed. After a while I lay down to wait for supper time to come, for I was hungry and faint, and thinking how much I would like to be just where I was a year ago–at home in Salem–when all at once men outside the tent began running round and shouting "We are saved! We are saved! There's a steamer coming toward the island." And sure enough there was a steamer quite near with flags flying. She came in as near as she dared, lowered a boat which started for the beach. The men, with difficulty, swam out to her and were soon aboard. She proved to be the *Gordon Castle*, Captain Waring, bound for Hong Kong.
>
> We were a hard looking lot of men, with our feet tied up in straw hats, with scanty clothing on. The first thing I said was I am glad there are no ladies aboard. Every attention was paid, as warm clothing and comfortable quarters were furnished. At supper that night Captain Waring told us he was quite provoked at noon that day to find his ship fifty miles to the westward of where he supposed her to be, right in the midst of shoals and reefs. He had traded in China all his days and had never been caught there before, but he was very glad now, as things had turned out. We were landed at Hong Kong. So ends a true account of the loss of the good ship *Humboldt* and the sufferings of her crew.

After the loss of the *Humboldt*, Captain Reynolds commanded the barque *Cheshire* for several years, running between New York and Manila.

Finally, Benjamin Reynolds captained the Dover Navigation Company's schooner *Jonathan Sawyer* for twenty-one years from 1886 to 1907. He died May 28, 1923 in the Snug Harbor, New York Sailors Home.

Captain Washington W. Hardy (1838-1916)

Washington Hardy, born in Chesterfield, New Hampshire on March 15, 1838, was the son of Thomas and Sarah Folsom Hardy. The family moved to Dover when Washington was a small boy and he attended local schools and the Franklin Academy.

In 1854, he began his seafaring life, shipping out on the *Sea Duck* from New York to Havana, the West Indies, London, and back to Boston. When he was only eighteen, he commanded the *Sea Duck* on a voyage from Boston to the West Indies for a cargo of sugar. Another of Hardy's early trips was to Japan to deliver a vessel, the *Matthew Luce,* which had been sold to the Japanese government.

Among the many vessels which Captain Hardy commanded were the *Cleopatra*, the *Winfield Scott*, the *Horatio*, the *Game Cock*, and the *W. W. Crapo*, all owned by Francis Hathaway of New Bedford, for whom Hardy named his only son. The ships were mainly engaged in trade with China and Japan.

The *Horatio* had been a whaler in New Bedford until the 1870s when Hardy began sailing the vessel to faraway ports. The *Dover Enquirer*, keeping tabs on local captains' journeys, reported on March 23, 1871 that Hardy "arrived at New York from Yokohama on Saturday last," and on August 22, 1872 offered the reassuring news that the *Horatio* had "arrived safely at Hong Kong previous to August 14." The paper noted on May 7, 1874 that the captain had landed in New York "from Foo Chow, a passage of 104 days. He reached his home in this city of Dover on Wednesday."

In 1875, during his second trip to Shanghai while accompanied by his wife, the former Elizabeth Bickford, Hardy's ship was docked in the harbor with a load of kerosene oil. The kerosene had been stored in five gallon cases, some of which leaked and ignited the cargo. Captain and Mrs. Hardy and the first mate were eating dinner in the cabin when the blaze was discovered. In no time, the ship was engulfed. Mrs. Hardy was rushed to one of the lifeboats and taken ashore while the captain and mate went back to rescue the ship's papers. They became trapped by flames in the cabin and were forced to jump overboard. Both were taken, badly burned, to a hospital where the mate soon died. Captain Hardy, after several weeks recuperation, was released and was able to return home.

The *Game Cock*, a famous clipper, was disabled off Cape of Good Hope. The April 22, 1880 *Dover Enquirer* says,

> Captain W. W. Hardy arrived home Wednesday of last week by way of London, looking hale and hearty. It will be recollected

that his vessel the *Game Cock* sprang a leak in December last and he put into Cape Town where the vessel was condemned as unseaworthy and was sold for the benefit of the underwriters.

Another barque commanded by Washington Hardy, the *William W. Crapo*, 1573 tons and built in Bath, was in almost constant use, traveling the globe from 1880 through 1895.

The *Dover Enquirer* regularly reported on the comings and goings of this adventurous captain, noting his arrivals and departures from such ports as San Francisco, Seattle, and Tacoma on the west coast, Philadelphia, New York and Boston on the east, Yokohama, Hong Kong, and Philippines in the Far East, and LeHavre, France and Liverpool, England in Europe.

The *Crapo* was destroyed by fire on July 2, 1895, but this time the blaze was set by crew members. The ship was anchored off the coast of Chile when the arsonists ignited the sodium nitrate (gunpowder) on board. Mrs. Hardy, who was along for this ill-fated voyage too, lost all her wedding silver and good china when the vessel exploded and sunk. The Hardys returned home by way of Panama.

Captain Hardy seemed to have an abrupt way of dealing with the sailors in his crews. In 1883, he had been arrested in Boston for forcing a man named Sweeney to go to sea against his will. Eventually, the charges were dropped, but Hardy did in fact have to always guard against mutinous shiphands.

The captain's last trip was in the steamer *Guy C. Goss*. The steamer's regular captain had to remain ashore for a time, so Hardy consented to take the *Goss* to San Francisco. Two days out of harbor, while Hardy was relieving one of the officers at the wheel, the steering mechanism broke and the spokes hit Hardy, badly crushing his arm. He spent several weeks in a hospital on the west coast.

Captain Hardy's career at sea spanned over forty-six years, thirty of those as captain. He circumnavigated the globe thirteen times, eleven as captain. He retired in 1901 and died April 19, 1916.

Captain Redford Sargeant (1844-1902)

Redford Webster Sargeant, son of Amos and Julia Hanscom Sargent, was born January 28, 1844 in the Captain Varney house on Portland Street in Dover. He attended Franklin Academy and paid his tuition by ringing the bell and tending the fires. Later he worked in the *Dover Gazette* office under editor John T. Gibbs.

Redford's first voyage in 1859 was as an apprentice boy aboard the *Orion* sailing from Boston to San Francisco. His mother's cousin,

Henry Libbey, was captain of the vessel and his uncle, George Hanscom, was first mate. The trip took over four months and when the *Orion* finally anchored in San Francisco harbor, Redford was greeted by a Dover native, Albert Canney. Canney, in search of the California gold fields, had made his journey west aboard the ship *Iconium* in 1858.

From San Francisco, the *Orion* and Redford Sargeant traveled to Puget Sound for a cargo of lumber bound for Sydney, Australia. From Sydney, the ship made for Calcutta, India with a cargo of wheat. When the *Orion* was within five miles of the wharf at Calcutta, the two apprentice boys, Webb and Sargeant, decided to swim the remaining distance. Webb reached the dock easily, but Redford was not as fortunate. Although he did manage to reach the port safely, the boy spent the next ten weeks recuperating in the local hospital, and if not for the fact that his relatives commanded the vessel, Sargeant probably would have been left in India to die. But when the *Orion* sailed, he was taken aboard in a still quite serious condition. In fact, a hogshead of tar (for immersing dead bodies) was put aboard just in case the boy did not live through the voyage. His companion, Webb, went on to become a famous English Channel swimmer.

The *Orion* sailed back to New York in ninety-three days. Sargeant came by train to Boston and to Kittery where it took several years to regain his good health. He eventually returned to the sea and worked for two years as a sailor on a vessel traveling between Portland, Maine and Havana, Cuba, with raw sugar to be refined. He then worked as second mate on the *Nera* running between Bombay, India and the Suez and carrying fruit and hemp.

Sargeant then came home and got a job with the American Steamship Company as second mate on the *S. S. Olin*. He was soon promoted to first mate and then captain of the *S. S. Abbotsfor*d traveling from Liverpool to Philadelphia. This vessel ran aground and was lost in 1877. Sargent then served as first mate once again on the *Olin* and eventually as captain of the *Indiana* in the employ of the Cramp Ship Company of Philadelphia. In 1900, he was made a supervisory captain in the U. S. Navy, navigating the trial trips of the new men-of-war vessels, and served in this capacity until his death in 1902. Captain Redford Sargeant was buried in Kittery.

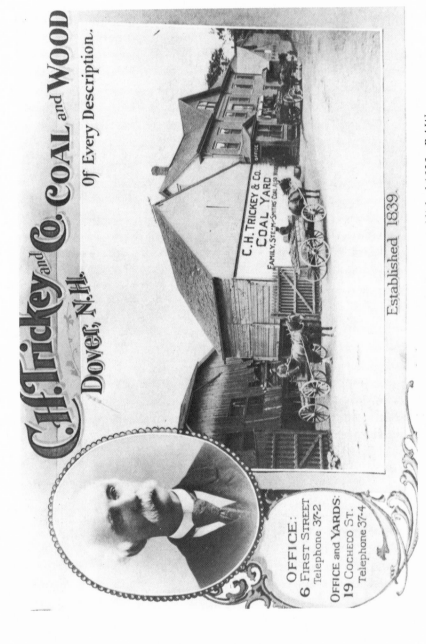

C.H. Trickey and Company office and yards, 19 Cochecho Street, established 1839. RAW

106

VII   The Renaissance Years, 1870-1896

THE PORT OF DOVER, whose maritime business interests had steadily declined since the Boston and Maine Railroad had come to town in 1842 and which had further suffered when all attention was focused on the War of the Rebellion, experienced an exuberant renaissance following the close of that Civil War. As early as 1865, signs of dissatisfaction in the lack of activity at the waterfront and the lack of convenience of the rails began to appear:

> Freight has a roundabout way of getting from Dover to Lawrence....Brick is being transported from Dover Point to the railroad in (Portsmouth) and thence via Manchester to Lawrence, Mass. Several hundred thousand are being sent by this new route.[1]

Surely someone could devise a less roundabout route than this. The newspaper prodded further in 1868:

> The river below the dam is clear of ice and the schooner *Hattie Lewis*, Captain Trefethen, and the packet *Factory Girl*, Captain Drew, and *Z. S. Wallingford*, Captain Rand, have commenced their trips. This branch of business ought to be increased, and could be with profit if men of enterprise would take hold of the matter.[2]

That same spring the Dover City Council appointed a committee to look into the expense of "clearing out the obstructions in the river at (the Gas Company) wharf."[3] Enterprising businessmen

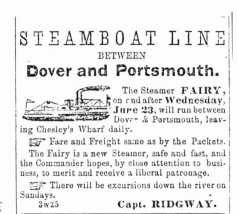

*Steamboat Line,
Capt. Ridgeway DE*

were beginning to see that if private industry and municipal government worked together, the Cochecho River could once again be a vital part of Dover's commercial growth. Federal dredging funds were once again secured during 1871 and the port was reborn.

In 1869, a Captain Ridgway advertised Sunday excursions aboard his forty-two foot steamboat, the *Fairy*, between Dover and Portsmouth. The *Dover Enquirer* heartily endorsed the venture and encouraged its longevity:

> This new, safe, and fast little steamer is to make daily trips between Dover and Portsmouth for the accommodation of the traveling and business public. She is not an old hulk, unsafe to use anywhere else, but has never been run before. There ought to be business enough to secure the permanancy of this boat, and will be if our businessmen patronize it as they ought to.[4]

By 1870 the turn back to the river, for both business and pleasure, was evident. A survey of the Cochecho by United States Government engineers was underway and this, it was hoped, would make Dover's inland port more navigable and accessible for bigger schooners. More steamboats carried more passengers on pleasure trips to Portsmouth, York Beach, and the Isles of Shoals. These steamers became the favorites of church, social, and civic groups, who planned to hold their annual outings aboard and had picnics and musical entertainment by live bands along the way. These vessels were also used as tug boats to guide heavily loaded large schooners and gundalows into Dover. They drew very little water and were quite dependable and maneuverable. The tugs *Mystic*, *Ann*, *Cocheco* and *Hamilton Mathes*, varying from fifty to seventy-seven feet in length, were well-known, reliable craft in Dover waters. As dredging

Dover Gas Light and Electric Company on Cochecho Street. Note the coal on the right. RAW

in the river continued year after year and conditions improved, business at Dover Landing also flourished.

D. Foss and Son's factory was started in 1874 on Portland Street at the site of an old flax mill. Dennis Foss and his son, A. Melvin, came

Looking from the river side of the Dover Gas Light and Electric Company, the tower for unloading coal can be seen on the left. There were six such towers on the Dover Landing at one time. DPL

to Dover from Strafford and originally manufactured wooden boxes and dealt in grain. Gradually, they added the manufacture of doors, sashes, blinds, stair posts, rails, bobbins, and spools, and by 1900, seventy-five people were employed in the three story plant providing packing cases for all the cotton cloth and shoes being exported out of Dover.

Valentine Mathes was a hustling businessman who dealt in flour, grain, groceries, coal, wood, shingles, clapboards, hay, and straw from his retail store which he began on Folsom Street in 1879. In 1881, Mathes bought land and wharfage on the river and built a fifty-foot coal pocket on Cochecho Street to which came many loaded schooners. He employed fifteen people there until his retirement at the turn of the century.

The Dover Gas Light Company was organized in 1850 and located its gasworks at the Landing. In 1891 the company was leased for twenty years to the United Gas and Electric Company. In 1905 they became known as the Interstate Gas and Electric Company and merged in 1909 with Twin State Gas and Electric. In 1914 Twin State advertised that "having absorbed all previous light and power interests in the City," they were the monopoly in town. The foundation of the gas works can still be seen on Cochecho Street and Public Service Company of New Hampshire still occupies the old power plant there.

Another business that benefited greatly from the improvements at the Landing was a lumber yard, started in 1874, and originally called Converse and Blaisdell (Joshua A. and Edward W., founders). Located opposite the gas works at 17 Cochecho Street, the firm carried a large line of lumber, lime, cement, plastering hair, and pipe. In 1878 they became Converse and Hobbs, in 1883 Converse and Wood, and in 1884 Converse and Hammond. In 1889, A. C. Place became the partner of Moses Hammond when Joshua Converse retired, and by 1891, Place was sole owner. It was not until 1898, however, that the name of the business changed from Converse and Hammond to A. Converse Place Lumber Company. By that time, the business was immense with an annual output of between four and five million feet of lumber each year, fifty employees, and wharfage covering six acres at the Landing. A. Converse Place additionally sold stone, slate, fire brick, decorative interior mantels, guano and fertilizers, and dried bone.

The frenzied activity at the Landing cannot be described without mentioning the Charles H. Trickey Coal Company, whose volume of business kept dozens of schooners sailing up the Cochecho for thirty years. Trickey's location at the Landing could store 4000 tons of coal and the firm sold annually about 10,000 tons imported to Dover from New Jersey and Pennsylvania. Charles Trickey originally bought the

Wiggin & Stevens Sand Paper and Glue Company, Est. 1858. OBHS

business in 1872 from Moses D. Page, and by 1876 had enlarged the coal sheds at the Landing and expanded to six pockets there. The company did all of the hauling for the Cocheco Manufacturing Company and employed about twenty men and sixteen horses. Mr. Trickey himself was one of the founders of the Dover Navigation Company and was an active promoter of business on the Cochecho. Russell B. Wiggin and William S. Stevens established a sandpaper and glue-making factory at 89 Cochecho Street in 1858. Wiggin and Stevens imported large quantities of sand, flint and quartz during the company's early years, and most of these raw materials came by schooners to their wharves near the Gulf. By 1890 only glue, (some sixty tons per year), was manufactured in Dover. The glue was then shipped to a Malden, Massachusetts sister factory for use in making emery, sand, and match papers. Eight people worked at the Dover branch of Wiggin and Stevens.

The most important business that depended on the schooners coming up river however, was still the Cocheco Manufacturing Company. Not only did the river serve as a channel for importing raw materials for mill spindles and exporting finished goods, but also served to keep these other Dover businesses thriving at the port. D. Foss made their packing crates, Mathes perhaps serviced mill employees' grocery needs, the gas and electric companies supplied Cocheco Manufacturing with power, Converse Place gave it the lumber to build with and the mortar which held its brick factories together, and C. H. Trickey fed mill boilers with 20,000 tons of coal each year. Without the gargantuan demands of the Cocheco Manufacturing Company, there would be no need for these suppliers' large inventories or services. Each business, although profitable on its own, was inherently dependent on the other for mutual survival. It is no surprise therefore that several of these companies' founders: Foss, Place, and Stevens, were Dover mayors and that their interests were city interests.

The Cocheco Manufacturing Company, by 1890, employed 2000 people, operated 130,000 spindles and 2800 looms, and produced over sixty-five million yards of printed cloth each year at the Print Works. The mills were Dover's heart and the Cochecho River pumped their lifesblood.

The newspapers of the last quarter of the nineteenth century present a remarkable story of the events, sometimes humorous, sometimes mundane, that took place at Dover Landing. They reflect the interests of the citizenry of Dover who were, it seems, always curious about the comings and goings of the schooners, their sizes and their cargoes, the voyages of the deep water sea captains who traveled around the world, the progress of the dredging operations and the technical details of how the work was done, the commercial success of the Dover Navigation Company's ten vessels, tales of accidents, fires, and criminal activities at the river, and even the dates of the river's "icing in" and "icing out."

Pointed editorializing abounded and the newspapers of that time were certainly not averse to giving their opinions about the shipping industry in Dover. Occasionally self-congratulatory and at other times satirical and derogatory, the papers were quick both to praise and to condemn. In order to fully comprehend the great volume and diversity of activities at Dover Landing from the renaissance in 1870 to the port's final demise following the terrible flood of 1896, the following chronological log is presented. Read as a story, this chronology presents the world of the Landing in the best way possible, in the words of the people who were there at the time. (The excerpts following were taken from the *Dover Enquirer* unless otherwise cited. Specifications for most of the individually named vessels will be found in the Appendix.)

1870

January 13—On the 4th inst. Messrs. Chas. F. Ham and Wm. H. Hill, of this city, sailed down the river to Dover Point in Captain J. Rand's packet, *Z. S. Wallingford*, and pedestrianated the distance home, six miles, in one hour and forty-two minutes—a feat not often to be accomplished at this season of the year.

March 31—The ice broke up in the river between Dover and Portsmouth from the heavy winds and rain on Monday last, and Captains Dame, Drew and other navigators of our river, expect to commence their regular trips to old "Strawberry Bank" by the first of next week.

April 21—Tommy Lyons, son of Mrs. Kate Lyons, on the Landing, had his left hand badly torn to pieces on Monday last by the accidental discharge of a pistol, with which he was playing. Dr. Stackpole dressed the wound, and is in hopes to save the hand, although in a damaged condition.

The copious descent of the "elements" on Monday and Tuesday caused a rapid rise in the "sweet rolling Cocheco," which, as usual, brought out "Jesse" and his spear to collect the valuable truant debris. The water was higher in our river on Wednesday morning than it has been with one exception for upwards of twenty years.

June 30—On Saturday last the Cushing Steam Mill and machinery were sold at auction. The buildings, the land adjoining and one-half of the Clements wharf, were knocked off to Benjamin Collins for $1,650. The engine, boilers and machinery were purchased by

NOTICE.

COCHECHO STEAM MILL

HAVING lately put in one of the most improved Machines for *Bending Wheel Rims,* I am now prepared to fill any orders that may come. Those that wish to furnish their own stock can do so. I also keep Rims and Stock for the same on hand at all times. **WHEELS** built to order,

——ALSO——

Plows, Harrows, Cultivators & Hay Cutters

constantly on hand and for sale.

I am also prepared to do *Plaining and Matching Boards, Turning and Grinding.*

Shop Work done to order. *Doors and Sash* constantly on hand. *Lumber* of all kinds. *Frames* got out to order. *Shoe and Cloth Boxes* made to order

T. H. CUSHING Proprietor.

Dover, Feb. 26, 1863.   41

*Notice, Cocheco
Steam Mill DE*

Wilson & Co. of Boston and Collins of Dover, the aggregate of the sales amounting to about $4,000.

July 28—Plum Moulton has placed a single scull in the waters of the Cocheco which is attracting much attention. It is so ticklish that the oarsman has to keep his eyes straight to the front and part his hair in the middle to keep it balanced.

The steamer *Favorite*, which is to ply between Dover and Portsmouth, is to take the members of the Printers' Convention to the Shoals, to the Navy Yard &c., on Thursday.

August 4—Ho for the Shoals—The Dover Cornet Band is getting up an excursion party for the Shoals in the steamer *Favorite*. The trip will be made on Friday next, leaving Pierce's Wharf at 7:30 A.M. This will afford a fine opportunity to all who wish to get a sniff of sea air, have a day of recreation, enjoy a fine sail, and visit this popular summer resort. We hope they will receive liberal encouragement in their efforts.

We were glad to meet that well-tried seaman, Captain William Drew, of this city, as Pilot of the steamer *Favorite* on her trip at the Printers' Convention. He thoroughly understands our river and coast, and parties may feel perfectly safe in his care.

August 11—The excursion of the Dover Cornet Band, on Friday last, was in every respect a grand affair. The day was pleasant, the party large, numbering 300, the playing of the band excellent, and everybody entirely satisfied. They landed on Star Island, enjoyed with a relish dinners at the hotels or upon the rocks as they chose, rambled, bathed, inhaled the pure and cool sea breeze, and returned at night invigorated and delighted.

The steamer *Favorite* found plenty of business during her stay with us. Between four and five hundred enjoyed the moonlight

excursion; but some on board were not satisfied until they had done mischief by pitching about two dozen stools overboard. Some one will have an eye to such chaps hereafter, and the one detected will have to pay for all that may have been lost.

A rescue—On Saturday evening last as the crowds were embarking on the steamer *Favorite* for the moonlight excursion, and other crowds were standing upon an adjoining wharf looking on, a splash was heard and presently the cry, "a child overboard!" Mr. Andrew J. Roberts was standing a few feet from the water, but as soon as he comprehended the situation, rushed through the crowd, plunged into the river and rescued a little daughter of John Scanlan, age about eight years, just as she was going down the second time in about twelve feet of water. Several men were standing close to the water's edge, but through cowardice or want of presence of mind failed to render assistance till the child was lifted by Mr. Roberts to them from the river. While it is unquestionably every man's duty to do under the circumstances just as Mr. R. did, yet not every man has the pluck and presence of mind to do it, and hence he deserves the thanks not only of the parents but the entire community for his heroic conduct. We all feel safer with such men among us.

August 25—The Washington Street Sabbath School, in connection with portions of the Charles Street and Methodist Schools, took their annual picnic down the river on Tuesday last, accompanied by the Dover Cornet Band, but not in Elliott [sic], as proposed, because there was no suitable wharf there to land upon; so the party were brought back and landed upon the abutment of the old Piscataqua Bridge in Newington, and held their picnic in a grove near by. A very pleasant time was enjoyed in strolling in the woods and upon the shore of Great Bay, in boating, swinging, sociability, listening to the sweet strains of the band &c. But as clouds often follow the beautiful sunshine, this happy occasion was destined to have its share of shading. Captain Davidson of the steamer *Favorite* had failed to make his usual trip to the Shoals on account of the party not being able to land where it was designed and threatened not to move a peg until he had been paid $150 for the use of his boat for the day, instead of the twenty cents each, the price at which he offered to the party to Elliott and back. The managers thought the price exorbitant, as he had charged only $100 per day to other parties in Dover for the use of his boat, and offered him the $100. This he obstinately refused to take, and for two hours the parleying went on, —many of the women becoming anxious and excited and some of the children frightened. The managers contended that, instead of laying at the wharf nearly seven hours, the Captain might have made his trip to the Shoals, making a shorter stop than usual, carrying passengers to Portsmouth, and those to the Shoals who wished to stop there; also carrying the mail and freight, and bringing back those from there who wished to return. And this being the fact, thought the $100 ample pay for his boat. The managers then offered him $125, which he took, and the party started for home.

We had intended to make some comments, but instead will give this bit of advice to all: When making arrangements with a steamboat captain, get his figures in black and white when he tells you he must have pay for his boat if certain matters are not as you expect to find them, and not take it for granted that he means to pay for his boat what he has charged other parties in the city for a greater service than you are requiring; then no advantage can be taken of embarrassing circumstances.

Picnic at Fox Point, Newington, showing one end of the old Piscataqua Bridge of 1794-1855. WI

September 22—The project of buying a steamboat to run upon our river is agitated. A boat nearly new and every way adapted to this business is offered for sale, and we hope there is enterprise enough in Dover to purchase it. There is no reason why our citizens should not or could not clear a thousand dollars a month, as well as allow the steamer *Favorite* to come here and do it.

December 8—The packets discontinued their regular trips to Portsmouth on Saturday last, although the river is not yet frozen over.

December 29—The valuable glass for making observations recently stolen from the vessel of Captain John Smith while lying at a wharf in this city, was recently found, with some overalls, by the side of the track of the Great Falls & Conway Railroad and forwarded to Marshal Abbott of this city, who returned it to the family of Captain S.

1871

February 2—Fire—The machine shop of Richard Rothwell, located on the landing next to the old jute mill, was destroyed by fire on Monday morning last, at 2 o'clock. The fire originated in a small ell attached to the front of the main building, in which there had been no fire, and communicated with the other building, which was nearly consumed. Mr. Rothwell estimates his loss in tools, engine, machinery, and work nearly or quite completed, at $3000; insured for $1000. The prompt and efficient efforts of the fire department saved the large building located but a few feet from the one destroyed. The Tigers (Fire Co.) played the first water, followed quickly by the factory hose. The Tigers will have to look well to their laurels or the Cocheco Hose Company will soon come in ahead. Mr. Rothwell is burnt out but not discouraged for he immediately commenced fitting up a shop near the old one, and will be at work again in a few days. The building burned belonged to Captain John Riley of New York City.

March 9—The schooner building at the yard of Messrs. Tobey and Littlefield of Portsmouth, for parties in Dover and Portsmouth, is to be a center-board vessel, built of New Hampshire pasture oak, with a length on deck of seventy-five feet, breadth of beam twenty-two feet, depth of hold five feet, and measuring seventy-five tons. She is intended for general freighting business, will carry a heavy cargo on a very light draft of water, and will be commanded by Captain Thomas C. Coleman of this city. (Schooner *G. W. Raitt*)

March 16—Captain Dunn brought his packet, the *Eagle*, from Portsmouth on Saturday last, and expects to commence his regular trips on Monday next, which is some two weeks earlier than navigation commenced last year, and earlier than for the past fifteen years. By his close attention to business and his promptness in his engagements, Captain D. is receiving a liberal share of the business done between this city and Portsmouth.

April 13—General Thom visited Dover on Monday last to take measures toward clearing out the river. He will probably advertise for proposals, and if acceptable let the work out by contract. If not, he will put on a gang of men and expend the appropriation under his own immediate supervision. It is thought that he will commence at the Narrows and work up the river.

March 23—At a meeting of the Board of Trade held on Friday evening last, John Bracewell, William S. Stevens and Moses D. Page were appointed by a committee to attend to the expenditure of the $10,000 voted by Congress to improve our river.

May 18—Schooner *Arcola*, arrived on Tuesday from Bath, Me. with a load of lumber consigned to Dr. Murphy and E. C. Kinnear, Esq., to be used in the construction of their new houses.

On Saturday last Captain Dunn was hoisting molasses from his packet, by some mishap the apparatus got out of gear he caught hold of a rope going at a tremendous velocity, which took all the skin off from the inside of the hands and in some places badly mangling the fingers. He is able to attend to his business and keep his packet running, although not able to do any work.

July 6—The first trip to the Isle of Shoals will be made by the schooner *G. W. Raitt*, on Wednesday of next week. This vessel is new, having been launched this spring, is a good sailor, and the trip will doubtless be very delightful.

A slight altercation occurred between Michael Agnew and a friend of his on the Landing on Tuesday evening last, and as a consequence Michael received a scalp wound from an axe in the hand of his friend. It was a clean cut to the skull of about an inch and a half long, and was dressed by Dr. Ham.

July 13—Saturday we noticed the schooner *Village*, from Gloucester, loaded with mackerel and dried fish; schooner *Ceres* from Philadelphia, loaded with coal for Page & Vickery; and schooner *G. W. Raitt,* from Boston, loaded with merchandise. She ships a load of gas pipe from the Dover Iron Foundry for Dorchester, Mass.

December 7—The ice blockade stopped navigation on our lower river on Wednesday night of last week, closing in several vessels that are usually wintered in ever open water.

1872

April 11—The ice in the lower river took its departure on Wednesday, 10th, and Captain Dunn informs us that he expects to be making his usual trips to Portsmouth by next Monday.

We are glad to announce that the Steam Mill at the Gulf is partly occupied for manufacturing purposes. Captain Hiram F. Snow is manufacturing a Chemical Paint there, and another portion of the building is used for barrel making.

May 10—Large quantities of tubs and pails have recently been brought from the factory of F. P. Trickey, in Barrington, to be shipped to New York in the schooner *Ceres*. This schooner arrived here last week with the first cargo of coal of the season, for C. H. Trickey & Co., successors to Page & Vickery. C. H. Trickey & Co., will be able to offer the best Lakawana for $8.50 per ton, which is fifty cents less than it has been retailing for, and which will probably be the ruling price during the season.

June 6—The Steam Mill of Mr. J. A. Glidden on the Landing, is a most lively place of business, as any one will find upon a visit to it. Planing, sawing, jointing, matching, turning, etc., is done; boxes, doors, blinds, windows, etc. are made, and everything in the lumber line is offered for sale. Schedule frames are furnished, as well as everything else in his line. Mr. G. is one of our most enterprising young men, and is well deserving the liberal encouragement he is receiving.

Capt. T. K. LANE,

Of Saco, would inform the public that he will, with his fine Steamer, "Clipper," make Regular Trips between Portsmouth and Dover, commencing the first of the coming week. He would also announce that he is prepared to take

Excursion Parties,

Of any size, landing at any point along the River or outside of Portsmouth harbor. The Steamer is in first-class running order, having been newly repaired and painted, is of about 65 tons burthen, and of so light Draft (2 feet) as to be almost independent of tide. He can promise all who may see fit to patronize him ample accommodation and polite attention. ☞ See Posters.

Capt. T.K. Lane DE   Dover, July 18, 1872.   29tf

June 27—Business has been lively at our wharves for a short time just past. The schooner *G. W. Raitt*, arrived the 19th with an assorted cargo, and reloaded with nearly 100 tons of gas pipe for Dorchester, Mass. The *Hattie Lewis* arrived on the 23rd, with a cargo of lime for D. Trefethen. The schooner *Casco* from Bath, with a cargo of lumber for F. A. & J. Sawyer. And on Saturday night the schooner *Ceres*, with a cargo of coal for C. H. Trickey & Co.

July 18—Captain Dunn had a piece of his sail taken out by the gale on Friday about twelve by twenty feet square while coming up the river.

We ask particular attention to the advertisement of Captain Lane, to be found in another column. We can assure all of the gentlemanly manners of the Captain– That he comes here especially to afford us an opportunity of enjoying the delightful trip between here and Portsmouth, calls for encouragement on our part. We want to see the *Clipper* crowded every day.

July 25—Schooner *G. W. Raitt* arrived Monday last with 500 casks of cement for Captain Daniel Trefethen. The schooner *Hattie Lewis,* also arrived Monday with 650 casks of lime for Captain Trefethen.

August 15—Captain T. K. Lane, of the steamer *Clipper*, has discontinued his regular trips to Portsmouth, but is prepared to make engagements to take parties down the river at reasonable rates.

August 22—The many friends of Captain Washington W. Hardy of the ship *Horatio*, will be pleased to learn that he safely arrived at Hong Kong previous to Aug. 14.

October 24—Schooner *Ceres*, arrived here on Thursday with a cargo of coal for C. H. Trickey & Co. She made the trip from here to

Fourth of July DE

Newburg, N.J., and return, about 500 miles, in twelve days. The schooner *G. W. Raitt*, arrived on the 15th, loaded with merchandise.

November 4—Schooner *G. W. Raitt*, arrived from Boston on Monday last freighted with merchandise.

November 21—Schooner *Hattie Lewis*, arrived on Friday last with a cargo of lime and cement and the *G. W. Raitt*, arrived on Monday last with a similar cargo, also for Captain D. Trefethen.

December 5—The ice in the river had become sufficiently thick on Saturday last to stop navigation.

1873

April 17—The first trip of the season from Portsmouth to Dover, was made by the gundalow *Flying Cloud*, Captain J. Butler, with a cargo of cement and plaster for Captain Trefethen. Time, three hours, with a great pressure of fresh water, and wind northeast.

May 29—Schooner *Ceres* has arrived with her second cargo of coal this season for C. H. Trickey & Co.

Hunt & Blaisdell have opened a lumber yard on the wharf on Cochecho street recently occupied by the late A. C. Chesley. Mr. Hunt is an extensive lumber dealer from Bath, Me. and Mr. Edward Blaisdell, the junior partner, is a well-known business man in this city. Mr. Hunt will give his whole attention to the lumber business, while Mr. Blaisdell will continue to attend to drafting and building as heretofore in connection with this new enterprise. He has an office in the brick building on the wharf.

June 5—Schooner *Hattie Lewis*, arrived with a cargo of lime for Captain Dan'l Trefethen, from Rockland, Me.

July 3—Captain James Butler will run his boat, *Ben Butler*, between this city and Portsmouth on the Fourth of July, as will be seen by his advertisement.

Destructive Fire: The extensive Sand Paper Manufactory of Wiggin & Stevens was destroyed by fire on Tuesday morning last. At about one o'clock the engineer discovered fire in the quartz crushing room, and immediately set to work to operate the force pumps, but the material was so combustible that his efforts were futile, and he immediately gave the alarm. The fire department were promptly on hand, considering the distance, but the fire had made such progress that it was impossible to save the Sand Paper Manufactory, and they tried only to save the neighboring buildings, which they succeeded in doing, notwithstanding some of them were several times on fire. The building burned was 120 feet long by thirty feet wide, three stories high, and was filled with valuable machinery and stock. The loss is estimated at between $40,000 and $50,000, while the insurance amounts to about $35,000. The loss is great to the city, and throws about thirty hands out of employ. We hope, however, that it will be rebuilt as speedily as possible that the ability and enterprise of this well known firm may not be long lost to Dover. The Tigers played the first stream on the fire, and the entire department worked with a will. The new Board of Engineers managed this their first fire with much skill. The fire is supposed to have been caused by spontaneous combustion or to have been the work of an incendiary.

The coffer dam at the Gulf is completed, and Captain George Dunn's packet will hereafter make her regular trips to Portsmouth.

We are glad to see our friend Captain Benjamin Reynolds still in town, notwithstanding the report that he has sailed for Manila on a long cruise. He is waiting for the completion of a new and much larger ship than he has heretofore commanded.

September 18—Wiggin & Stevens are to enlarge their glue business here by the erection of a new building on the site of their sand paper mill.

October 9—The Flax Mill property on the Landing has been purchased by Dennis Foss Jr., and Alonzo M. Foss, of Strafford. It is reported that they are to put in a grist mill and other machinery and intend to make business lively in that locality.

October 23—The schooner *George Edwards*, from this city for Boston, on going down the river, ran against the pier near the railroad bridge in Portsmouth and had her foremast carried away.

November 8—The truss at Dover Point will be ready to be swung into position, should the workmen be favored with good weather. It is an immense structure, about 200 feet long, forty feet wide, and twenty-five feet high, and thousands are anxious to see the task performed of moving it into position.

December 18—The immense truss in the Dover Point bridge was placed in position in the morning between five and six o'clock. The time occupied in the work was about twenty-eight minutes. The schooners

Dover Point bridge with its 200-foot long truss. Dover Point House is on the right; the railroad was the Portsmouth and Dover Railroad. DLW

G. W. Raitt and *Rough & Ready* were used in floating the truss to its place, and the force to move the mass, two steam tug boats, worked to a charm. The work was under the immediate direction of Captain James Card, who unfortunately met with an accident by falling and striking upon a long iron rod. The job was a grand success, and large numbers were present to witness it. Miss Emma Bean of Newington was the first lady who had the honor to cross over the truss, who was assisted by B. A. Ford Esq., and others. J. W. Ford was the first man who walked across the truss and others quickly followed.

1874

March 30—The first gundalow of the season came up the river with coal for C. H. Trickey.

April 8—The first arrival of any vessel since the river opened was the schooner *Hattie Lewis*, with lime for Captain Daniel Trefethen.

The schooner *Ceres*, arrived in our river with a cargo of coal for C.H. Trickey & Co., after a passage of only four days from New York. Quick time.

May 21—The Dover Gas Light Company have constructed a bridge over Cochecho street from the Gas Works to the wharf, to enable them to get coal from vessels to their works with greater ease.

Nov. 5—A schooner has been loading at our wharves during the past week with apples to be shipped away down east.

1875

March 18—The steamer *Major* has been chartered by the Eastern Railroad Company to break up the great fields of ice in the Piscataqua river above the railroad bridge at Dover Point. Nitroglycerine and explosive agents are to be used.

April 15—The ice took its departure from the lower river on Friday, and now vessels can come again to our wharves.

June 24—Joshua Converse has purchased one half of the wharf property on Portland street belonging to the late A.C. Chesley. It is a fine location for certain kinds of business, and we hope it will soon be improved to the best advantage.

Sept. 9—Workmen in deepening the river channel excavated from two feet below the bed of the river an oak log forty feet long, two feet in diameter, and perfectly sound. General Thom was in the city last week, and accepted the work of deepening the channel of the river. He was the guest of the Board of Trade.

Sept. 23—The contractors for dredging our river have arrived with their apparatus and have commenced operations.

1876

Feb. 17—The schooner *Ceres*, of this city, is reported as driven ashore off Gloucester, probably by the gale of Tuesday evening.

Feb. 24—The schooner *Ceres*, ashore near Gloucester, was got off from Pavillion Beach, where she struck, the next afternoon, with but slight damage. The packet *Zimri S. Wallingford*, which went ashore at the same time and place, was considerably damaged.

May 18—Captain M. J. Clark and Captain C. A. Drew have chartered a steamboat, the *Moses Taylor*, to be used upon our river during the coming season, in towing vessels up and down the river, taking excursion parties to the Shoals, or to any point down the river or along the coast. It has double decks, the upper one covered with canvas, will carry from two to four hundred passengers, and is provided with life preservers, and has good accommodations every way. It is expected to be here about the 15th of June.

The schooner *E. A. Staples* arrived from Rockport with cargo of 800 barrels of lime for Converse Blaisdell.

June 29—The schooner *Hattie Lewis* arrived here with a cargo of new lime for Captain Daniel Trefethen.

The new and fast sailing steamer *Mystic* will make an excursion to the Isles of Shoals on Sunday next, leaving here at 9 o'clock A.M. Fare for the round trip $1.00.

The steam propeller *Mystic* is now in Portsmouth being painted and fixed up in good shape for excursions to the Shoals and other points along the coast, as well as doing other business on the river. She is stoutly built, entirely seaworthy, being nearly new, is a fast sailor, and has a capacity of carrying several hundred passengers. Benevolent organizations, churches, and societies of various kinds, will now have a grand chance for excursions to the Shoals.

A schooner laden with coal struck the Portsmouth & Dover railroad bridge across the river at Dover Point on Friday afternoon last, breaking timbers, throwing the track out of line, and doing other damage to the amount of several hundred dollars.

The Eastern Railroad have again commenced giving those delightful and cheap ocean trips which our citizens have heretofore so much enjoyed excursions from Dover to the Isles of Shoals. Parties can leave Dover on Tuesday, Thursday, and Saturday, and go either on steamer *Appledore* to Appledore Island, or steamer *Major* to Star Island, and return for the small sum of $1.15. Saturday tickets good only to return on Monday. This trip is not only pleasant, but must prove beneficial to the health, as nothing can be more invigorating during the heated term than frequent and short trips upon the ocean.

Schooner *Eliza A. Anderson,* of 240 tons, is expected this Wednesday evening. Schooners *Planter* and *Fleetwing* are at mouth of the harbor, all bringing coal for these dealers, who have their large coal sheds completed, and are prepared for a most extensive business.

The steam propeller *Mystic*, M. J. Clark, Captain, took a party of nearly one hundred from Dover to the Isles of Shoals, on Saturday last, stopping a short time at Portsmouth. The steamer is a staunch craft, running smoothly and as steadily as any could wish. She has been thoroughly fitted up for carrying pleasure parties, has a neatly finished and furnished cabin, with a fine awning over the upper deck. The party left here about nine in the forenoon, and after stopping at Portsmouth an hour, reached Appledore Island at 12 o'clock, and the steamer could have made much better time if there had been need of haste. After a most excellent dinner at the Appledore, some of the party employed the time in strolling over the rocks, while others took a trip among the islands, landing upon Smutty Nose and visiting the scene of the Wagner murder. At four o'clock the party started on the return trip and everything passed as satisfactorily as could be desired, until about the time of entering the Piscataqua, when the pump that forces the water into the boiler refused to work, which made it not quite safe to continue farther, and Captain Clark landed them at Newcastle, from which place they went to Portsmouth and took the cars for home. Measures are to be taken that will prevent the recurrence of a similar mishap in the future.

July 27—Hussey Brothers have been loading one of the large schooners lying at the wharf of Converse & Blaisdell with ice to be shipped to Philadelphia. They are sending off about two hundred tons. We hope this is but the beginning of an extensive business in this line, as the best ice in the world can be obtained from our river, and a little enterprise only is needed to make it a successful business.

December 14—The schooner *Ceres*, Captain Garland, struck the Portsmouth bridge as she was being towed through the draw on Thursday last, receiving such injury as to cause her to sink. She had on board 155 tons of coal for C. H. Trickey & Co., which was insured,

Cocheco Print Works coal sheds, now Henry Law Park, showing the arrival of a coal-laden gundalow. Also visible are the Belknap Church, and City Hall on the site of the present Masonic Building at Central Square. OBHS

but there was no insurance on the vessel. The Captain saved his chronometer and charts, and the crew saved themselves by climbing upon the bridge. The vessel was owned by C. H. Trickey, Moses D. Page, and others of this city. *Ceres* was a staunch vessel, and would probably have sustained but little injury from striking the bridge, but for a projecting timber which stove a hole in her, which may render the bridge company liable.

1877

April 5—The river below the dam was open for navigation this year on Saturday, March 24.

May 17—Captain Joseph S. Abbott, who has the contract for building the river wall on the Landing for the Cocheco Mfg. Co., came near meeting with a fatal accident on Saturday evening last as he and his men were hoisting stone from a gundalow upon the wharf, the iron dogs slipped from the heavy stone; this sudden force caused the block to become unhooked from the derrick, and in falling the rope became coiled around his neck and body in such a way as to force him fifteen or twenty feet into the river, where it was considerably over his head. Being an excellent swimmer, he was soon at the surface and after clearing his mouth and throat of water, and taking his bearings, struck out for the gundalow, and by the help of his men, clambered up the side of it and was soon all right again for work.

May 24—C. H. Trickey & Co. have become the owners of the steamer *Mystic*, and she is being put in the most thorough repair, the iron work being done by the Swampscott Machine Co. She is to be commanded by Captain C. A. Drew, a most careful and skilled commander. Coal for C. H. Trickey & Co. and the Cocheco Mfg. Co. is to be shipped to Portsmouth in large vessels and transferred to gundalows and towed up the river by the steamer *Mystic*. She also has other contracts for towing vessels and gundalows to other points, and during the season will probably be a most useful boat. She can also be chartered for pleasure parties. (Dover's first tug).

Gundalow *Paul*, belonging to Captain Butler of this city, struck against a schooner as she was leaving her wharf in Portsmouth on Tuesday loaded with coal, which stove a hole in her. She filled with water and capsized, dumping about forty tons of coal belonging to the Cocheco Mfg. Co. into the river.

The last of the old landmarks on the Landing is being torn down, the building known as the Hale store. It was built in 1783, taking the place of the one carried away by a freshet the year previous. It was purchased by Hales in 1806, when it was sold to the Cocheco Mfg. Co. It was the headquarters of Hon. William Hale for fifty years. In 1877 sold at auction to Israel P. Church who bought the Hale store for $42.50. It is being taken down and will be so reconstructed as to make two houses, with additions.

July 26—One of the largest and handsomest blocks of granite ever brought to this city was unloaded from a gundalow at Butterfield's stone yard. It was quarried by Captain Joseph S. Abbott from his quarry in Durham, and is for the base of the Soldiers' Monument. It weighs about ten tons.

August 9—Samuel Hussey is shipping ice to Philadelphia and is now loading a schooner which is to take 175 tons.

The Boston divers are now confident that they will be able to raise the wrecked schooner *Ceres*, which lies near Portsmouth bridge. They have succeeded in moving her about 200 feet towards flats near the Kittery side, where it is proposed to place her.

November 29—Captain Joseph S. Abbott is putting in a splendid granite wall for a wharf on the south side of the river. It is about eighty feet front, and is upon land purchased of the city for a coal yard for the Cocheco Print Works.

Steamer James Sampson, *built in Dover 1878. DLW*

December 6—The dredging of our river has been discontinued for this fall, and the boats and machinery have been moved down to Portsmouth.

1878

January 17—Eugene Smart is having a new yacht built down near the steam mill, to take the place of the one sold to the Leighton brothers at the Isles of Shoals. It is to be a propeller, fifty-two feet long, fourteen feet wide, with cabin capacity for 100 persons. She will be named in honor of an old and well known resident, James Sampson. It is to be ready to launch in March.

March 7—The Cocheco Mfg. Co. are making arrangements to erect immense coal sheds upon their wharf at the city farm. A railway is to be built from these sheds to connect with the new mill and Printery, which will be a very convenient arrangement.

March 14—The lower Cochecho opened on Friday, March 8 which is unusually early.

April 4—Wiggins & Collins have about 700 tons of ice stored on the wharf near the steam mill, which they have placed there for shipping to New York and Philadelphia, unless they find a purchaser nearer home.

April 11—Charles C. Trickey & Co. already have four cargoes of coal on the way to this city, and the Cocheco Co. one. This is certainly a good beginning of the business upon our river for the season.

April 25—Four schooners, loaded with coal arrived at the coal yard of C. H. Trickey & Co. during last week, and discharged their cargoes. Also three for the Cocheco Mfg. Co. Seven vessels in one week makes quite a shipping business for Dover.

May 2—A schooner load of new lime, 800 casks and a second schooner with 400 casks of cement were received last week by Daniel Trefethen.

May 23—The new steamer *James Sampson*, made a trial trip out to sea. She steams fast, and everything works admirably.

June 13—The schooner *Ceres*, which was sunk last season at the Portsmouth bridge, arrived at our wharves with a load of coal for C. H. Trickey & Co. She still retains the dirt color which came from her long stay at the bottom of the river.

Michael Howley of the Landing, was before the Police Court on two complaints, one for keeping a disorderly house, and the other for keeping open saloon on Sunday. On the first complaint he was discharged, on the latter fined five dollars and costs, from which he appealed to the Supreme Court.

About 20,000 shingles intended for the roof of the new coal shed of the Cocheco Mfg. Co. have been stolen, the thieves carrying them away by means of a boat. Several crafts have been overhauled, yet no trace of the missing property has yet been discovered.

July 18—Six schooners were in our river with cargoes of coal. A contrast with business at our wharves before the improvements in our river when only one or two schooners were seen then at a time, and sometimes none.

August 29—The Cocheco Mfg. Co. are making active preparations to connect their immense coal shed on the city farm by iron rail with their new mill and the printery. The ground is all graded for the tracks, and the derrick is set to build the abutments on the opposite side of the river. The two iron bridges necessary to cross the river are made and subject to their order.

1879

April 9—The Cochecho River below the falls was open and the steamer *Mystic* came up to her wharf on Wednesday of last week.

April 24—The schooner *Louella* arrived with a cargo of Cobb's Celebrated Heavy Filled Lime for Converse & Hobbs, also fifty tons of

Tug Ann, *Dover's second tug, belonging to C.H. Trickey and Company. OBHS*

Schooner Hattie Lewis *, also used as a brick schooner. DLW*

fine ground plaster. Those wanting either of the above will do well to call, as they are selling at bottom prices.

May 8—C. H. Trickey & Company have purchased the steam tug *Ann*, to take the place of the *Mystic* in towing vessels up the river. (Dover's second tug). She brought up the schooner *John Bracewell* with a cargo of coal for C. H. Trickey & Company. The *Mystic* will either be sold or let for pleasure parties, as she is not built right for towing purposes.

June 19—The schooner *Dauntless*, from St. John, N. B., arrived with a load of cedar shingles and cedar posts for Converse & Hobbs. Their stock of lumber at this time is immense.

Aug. 14—The schooner *Hattie Lewis*, Captain Garland sailed from this port on Sunday morning, with a pleasure party of twenty-one young men of Dover for a sea voyage of two weeks. They were off in fine spirits, neatly uniformed, and bound to have a good time. Some of them had never before been upon the briny deep, and some of them have before this learned something of the effort of the whale to dispose of Jonah, and the trip to sea is more romantic in anticipation than in reality. The following are the names of the twenty-one brave young men who started on this novel voyage.

Clarence W. Wendell, Charles E. Wendell, Herbert Hansom, David W. Madock, Fred Sawyer, Frank Rollins of Concord, Byron E. Hayes, H. D. Everett, Theodore Everett, John L. Kingman, Frank Worthen, William Kimball, Alvah Place, Charles G. Foster, John Cressey, Isaac Brooks, Halder P. Young, Arthur Freeman, Michael Gallagan, Frank W. Hanson, Harry Snow. Dr. Kingman is the medicine man, and as rumor hath it the vessel had hardly taken the salt sea breeze before all but three had an attack of the qualms, which made a lively demand upon the doctor who unfortunately was similarly affected. The results were that the first night they put in at Boar's Head, which probably gave things a chance to settle and on Monday morning bright and early, they again set sail.

Aug. 28—John W. Trefethen is making arrangements for another excursion to Portland and down the harbor about the 10th of September. Fare for the round trip $1.15 for adults and 55 cents for children.

Sept. 11—Schooner *Louella* arrived from Bangor with a full cargo of lumber, mostly laths and shingles, for Converse & Hobbs.

Mr. James Drew, toll keeper at the Dover Point bridge, gives the following statistics: During the month of August, ninety vessels passed through the draw, which was opened seventy times. Amount of money taken in August: $172.32. The largest number of crafts passing through the draw in any one month since the bridge was built was in the month of June 1877: 210.

Oct. 23—About 20,000 tons will make the sum total of coal that has been and will be brought up the Cochecho this season consigned to C. H. Trickey & Company, Cocheco Manufacturing Company, and the Dover Gas Light Company.

Oct. 30—It was fortunate that both the schooner *John Bracewell* and schooner *C. H. Trickey* were in our river when the gale of Tuesday night came on.

1880

Jan. 10—The schooner *Louella*, which used to discharge lime at Trefethen's wharf during the past summer, has just left Portsmouth for Boston with 500 bbls. of apples, which have been consigned by Samuel Dixon of Eliot to a Liverpool fruit dealer. New England apples are in great demand just now in the English market.

March 25—Business on our river has already commenced in earnest. The steam tug *Ann* towed two vessels, loaded with coal, up the river, one for C. H. Trickey & Company and the other for the Cocheco Manufacturing Company. This is earlier than usual.

April 15—It would seem that all the vessels in which our citizens are interested are doing a splendid business. The schooner *John Bracewell* is on its way to this city with a cargo of coal, and will take a return cargo of ice from the house of Hussey Brothers for Baltimore. The schooners *C. H. Trickey* and *B. F. Nealley* will both load with ice on the Kennebec, one for Newport and the other for New Haven, rate of freight for the *Trickey* and *Nealley* is $1.50 per ton, which is much higher than it was one year ago. Converse & Hobbs received two cargos of lumber of all kinds, and will be constantly receiving it, so as to meet the active demand that will grow out of the large amount of building in Dover this season.

April 22—The schooner *John Bracewell* arrived with about 300 tons of coal for C. H. Trickey & Co.

May 27—Something novel in navigation business upon our river was the arrival of the schooner *City of Green Bay* from New Orleans, with 1,211 bales of cotton for the Cocheco Manufacturing Company. The vessel is the largest that ever came up the river, as she is capable of carrying 675 tons of coal. Captain J. B. Hall, an experienced officer, is the commander. She made the voyage in little less than four weeks, which is good sailing. We understand this to be an experiment, and if cotton can be brought cheaper by water, including extra insurance, much of the cotton for this company may be brought that way.

July 29—The threatening weather of Thursday morning prevented a large party from going to Haverhill and down the river on

Steamer City of Haverhill *came to the port of Dover July 29, 1880. DWL*

the steamer *City of Haverhill,* but those who did go speak of it as one of the finest excursions to be had in this section. The sail on the large and commodious steamer is splendid, and the scenery at Black Rocks and Salisbury Beach is magnificent.

Aug. 5—Since March 10, there have been brought up the river 3,558 1/2 tons of coal, mostly for the Cocheco Manufacturing Company and C. H. Trickey & Company.

Aug. 12—Up to Saturday morning, there have arrived at this port this season, 100 vessels.

Aug. 26—Patrick McMann was struck upon the head by a coal bucket at Dover Gas Company wharf. A flesh wound was inflicted about one and one-half inches long.

Schooner *C. H. Trickey,* anchored off the Gas Company's wharf, loaded with 365 tons of gas coal. The remarkable part of the business is this: she came up to the Gas Company's wharf without lighting an ounce, though drawing over ten feet of water; this is without parallel, as there is surely only nine feet of water at high tide.

Aug. 29—Schooner *Laura E. Roberson,* loaded and ready for sea, unable to get down the river and out. The schooner *B. F. Nealley* was ashore in the Cochecho River and blocking the channel.

Sept. 2—The schooner *C. H. Trickey* is proving to be a very fast sailor. She left Philadelphia August 12, and at midnight on the 18th was anchored off the Dover Gas Company wharf. Went down river at noon August 21, arriving at Richmond, Maine where she was loaded with ice and left on the 25th; August 27 she dropped anchor at New Haven, Conn.

Sept. 23—Schooner *C. H. Trickey* arrived with 355 tons of coal for C. H. Trickey & Co.

Nov. 11—Messrs. Goss, Sawyer and Packard of Bath, Maine who have built several fine schooners for the Dover Navigation Company successfully launched at their yard a fine Barque of 1750 tons named the *W. W. Crapo*, and to be commanded by Captain Washington W. Hardy of this city. A large party witnessed the launch including a number from Dover. She is intended for the general freighting business.

1881

March 11—The schooner *Bracewell* has sailed from Boston to Boothbay Me., where she will load with ice for Atlantic City, N.J. at $1.50 per ton.

April 7—The first cargo for this port for this year, was for Converse and Hobbs. It was a load of lime and cement, and arrived in the schooner *G. W. Raitt*.

April 28—The schooner *John Bracewell*, cleared from Baltimore April 20, with 300 tons of gas coal for Galveston, Texas. She will come back to Pensacola, Florida and load with dimension lumber for New Haven, Conn. The distance covered on this trip will be about 5500 miles.

The schooner *B. F. Nealley*, arrived at Boston, from Baltimore, with 300 tons of pitch, and fifty tons of brick and gas retorts.

The schooner *C. H. Trickey*, from Penobscot River with a cargo of granite for Washington, D. C. and will load coal at Georgetown for some eastern port.

May 12—Captain J. S. Abbott is building a wharf for the Dover Gas Light Company adjoining their present wharf. He also has the contract to build a wharf for Joseph Hayes, near the above, upon which a storehouse is to be erected.

May 26—Valentine Mathes has purchased a wharf of Joseph Hayes, upon which he is to erect extensive coal sheds, so that he can have coal come by rail or vessel. His sales have been so large during the past winter that he has got to largely increase his facilities to meet the demands of his increasing business.

June 30—B. F. Nealley of this city has been presented by Captain John Handy with a beautiful oil painting of the schooner *B. F. Nealley*, of which he is master. She is represented under full sail, passing Boston Light. The picture is 24x36 inches, and was painted by Stubbs of New Bedford. Captain Handy is proud of his craft, as is Mr. Nealley and all the stock holders, for she is a noble vessel.

The captain of the schooner *B. Frank Nealley* has contracted to carry 350 tons of ice from Kennebec to Annapolis, where she will take another load of coal for Dover.

Valentine Mathes' coal pocket is approaching completion. It will be fifty feet square when finished, which is to be located on the wharf he has just completed on Cochecho Street.

July 28—Captain Washington W. Hardy of this city arrived in San Francisco in his new barque *William W. Crapo*, in 120 days from Liverpool, which is considered a remarkably good passage. His vessel has been chartered to load with grain for Liverpool.

Aug. 18—There were nine schooners moored at one time in the lower Cochecho recently. A grand sight, prophetic of the brilliant future awaiting Dover as a port of entry.

The Cushing steam mill property located on the lower Cochecho has been purchased by the Cocheco Manufacturing Company. The present buildings are to be removed and a store house for cotton at once erected thereon.

The owners of the schooner *T. B. Garland* who visited the vessel, while she lay at her moorings in Saco express themselves as having been highly pleased with the appearance of the craft and all join in the opinion that it is the finest of the fleet owned in Dover. With a capacity of 448 tons burden, she has the proud distinction of having, on her initial trip, brought to the city of Saco the largest cargo ever landed there by any schooner. The qualities for fast sailing which she has already exhibited, the perfect ease with which she can be handled, and the great conveniences to be found upon, and beneath her decks, are features distinguishing first class schooners, under which class she will hereafter sail on "The Dark Blue Sea."

The party visiting the schooner *T. B. Garland* was composed of her namesake, with Rev. John B. Richmond and wife, John J. Hanson and wife, B. Frank Nealley and sister, Miss Deering of Saco, John Holland, Superintendent of the Cocheco Manufacturing Company, and J. T. W. Ham. They stopped at Old Orchard and dined at Lane's Restaurant where for a half dollar each, they were served with a dinner of whose virtues they continue to speak in the most glowing terms.

Oct. 6—Schooner *G. W. Raitt* discharged a cargo of lime for Converse & Hobbs recently, and is to load with brick for Boston, after which she will go to Rockland for another load of lime for the same parties.

Dec. 1—The three-masted schooner *Sallie M. Evans* arrived at this port with coal. She was towed from Portsmouth bridge by the tug *Ann*, which took her up river to Dover.

The river above Dover Point is now being liable to be closed by ice any day.

1882

Feb. 9—Our schooner abroad, schooner *C. H. Trickey* has cleared Philadelphia for Allyns Point, Conn. with 356 tons of coal. The schooner *John Bracewell* is now at Norfolk, Va., loading with railroad ties for New York, at "lump sum" of $700. The schooner *T.B. Garland* arrived at Weymouth, Mass. with cargo of coal for Philadelphia. The ship *Crapo*, Captain Hardy of this city, arrived in Le Havre, France, on the 28th instant accomplishing the voyage from Wilmington, California in 120 days. Considering the ship was loaded heavily with wheat, the passage was a remarkably quick one.

April 13—Schooner *T. B. Garland* arrived in Newport with coal from Richmond, Virginia. The schooner *C. H. Trickey* cleared Philadelphia for Boston with 362 tons coal.

April 20—Captain Hardy received cordial greetings from many friends upon his arrival home from his long and prosperous sea voyage. He is looking finely.

June 1—*Daily Republican*: Shipping Notes:

Schooner *C. H. Trickey* of this port, cleared from Lanesville, Massachussetts with paving stone for Philadelphia.

Schooner *T. B. Garland* cleared Boston for Philadelphia seeking business.

Schooner *B. Frank Nealley* of this port cleared Cape Ann with paving stones for Baltimore, Maryland.

The schooners *Mary B. Rogers*, *Nellie E. Gray* and *Mary A. Rice* arrived at the wharves in this city today, and the *James Henry* was brought up to the lightering point, all on one tide by the tug *Ann*. The *Peirce* and *R. B. P. Smith* were towed down river by tug.

The schooner *Harry Percy*, from Port Johnson to this city with a load of coal for the Cocheco Manufacturing Company when in Long Island Sound on May 27, sprang a leak, and the captain headed her for Long Island Shore, but when off Rocky Point near East Marion, she sank in five fathoms of water. The crew, three in number, had entered their yaulboat and put in their personal effects. Captain Hincky remained at the wheel until the water on deck was knee-high, when he sprang into the boat and the vessel went down almost immediately.

June 29—Henry Boss of Portsmouth, employed as fireman on the steam tug *Ann*, while bathing at Clement's Wharf near the gas house Monday night at about 10:30 was taken with cramp and drowned. It seems that a party wanted to go in bathing and asked him to join them. He, fearing cramps, refused to go, but the party kept teasing him till he consented. Upon entering the water he was immediately attacked and instantly sank, and never rose. The body was recovered at 11:30 and was carried to Glidden's undertaking rooms, and afterwards to Portsmouth. Mr. Boss was twenty-two years of age and engaged to be married soon.

Aug. 15—There are five vessels in the lower harbor, three of which are expected up tonight.

Aug. 23—A new lighter *G. W. Avery*, has arrived and went into commission today, her first work being to lighten the schooner *John Bracewell*.

1883

April—Eight masts, each ninety feet long and of large diameter, came down from New Durham and went on their way to Bath, Maine.

Schooner *C. H. Trickey* cleared from the Kennebeck River, for Philadelphia with a load of feldspar.

The schooner *Mary E. Whorf* has just arrived with a cargo of fresh oysters from Virginia for Henry D. Freeman.

Schooner *B. Frank Nealley* arrived as far up the river as Clement's Wharf, near the glue factory, where it had to be partially unloaded.

April 3—Schooner *Helen* was detained in the Cochecho River twenty-four hours, by a strip of ice 1000 feet long, stretching out from the Watson Shore. Captain Drew with the tug *Ann* broke it up.

Schooner *Cyprus* came up the river with a load of lumber for Converse & Hobbs.

April—*Daily Republican*: The following are the schooners which will be engaged in carrying brick from the yards along the Cochecho this season: The schooners *Triton*, *Hattie Lewis*, *George W. Raitt*, schooners *Chilion*, *Satellite*, and schooner *H. Prescott*.

May 24—Among the freight engagements to this port reported last week were those of two schooners from Port Johnson with coal at $1.20 per ton and one from Hoboken at $1.15 per ton.

June 5—Dover schooner *C. H. Trickey* went ashore at Nantucket Shoals but was got off by wreckers at a cost of $240. It was on its way from Philadelphia to Boston with coal.

June 6—The schooner *John Bracewell* arrived at the lightering place last night and came up to the wharf today.

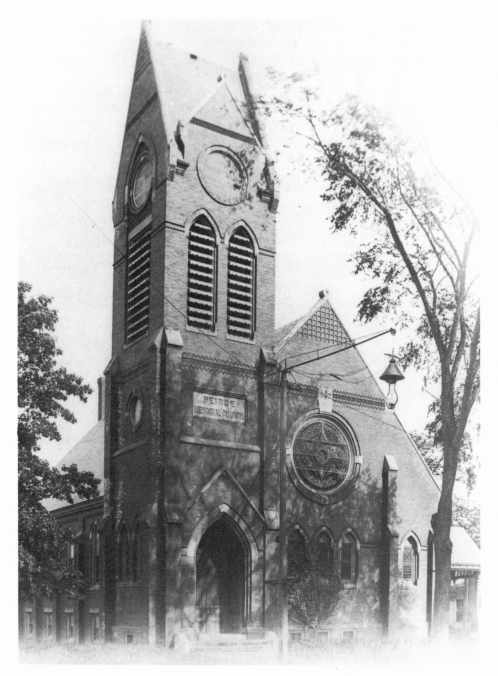

The Peirce Memorial Church, donated to the city of Dover in 1883 by Col. Thomas W. Peirce in honor of his deceased parents. The Peirce family controlled the Dover to Boston packet line during the 1830's and 1840's. DPL

June 14—Schooner *Fleet-Wing* arrived at the Cocheco Company wharf with coal. This was the first schooner owned out of town to bring coal here; it first came in July 1866, consigned to C. H. Trickey and has made several trips to this city since.

July 12—Captain W. W. Hardy of this city arrived in Boston on the 4th with his vessel, the barque *William W. Crapo*. He sailed from Port Townsend on February 22 with spars to order, vessel to *M. F. Pickering*.

July 18—Captain W. W. Hardy spent the Sabbath in this city. He is in fine health and good spirits, and his numerous friends were glad to see him safe returned from his voyage round Cape Horn.

Aug. 1—One hundred and fifty tons of coal were brought up the river in two gundalows by the tug *Ann* for the Cocheco Manufacturing Company.

Aug. 5—*Daily Republican*: Colonel Thomas W. Peirce yesterday concluded his brief visit to Dover and returned to Boston in his yacht *Marion Wentworth*. Early in the morning he was taken in charge by Mayor Lothrop and other prominent citizens who gave him a drive around the city to show him the growth and improvements since his last visit here forty years ago.

He called upon Mrs. John P. Hale and then returned to his yacht where he held a reception for a few hours...visited by hundreds of our citizens. Two boats were employed in taking persons from the wharf to the yacht which was anchored out in the river.to shake the hand of a man who by his ability and enterprise, had achieved such success in business, and who has generously disposed of some of his wealth in building a church that is not only an ornament to Dover but a credit to the donor. He remarked that this church in honor of his revered parents had formed a new and increased attraction for his native town....

Aug 31—Schooner *Julia A. Berkele* has been discharged and has sailed for the east. Schooner *Mary A. Rice* went east. Schooner *Iva Bell* was towed up today. Schooner *C. H. Trickey* was towed to the lightering place.

Sept 12—*Daily Republican*: Schooner *T. B. Garland*, Tenant's harbor for New York City, to reload coal for C. H. Trickey & Co. of this city. Schooner *B. Frank Nealley* arrived in Boston with sand and is discharging. Schooner *Nealley* on way from Baltimore to Boston. Schooner *Z. S. Wallingford* is charted from Albany to Petersburg, Va. with lumber.

Sept. 25—The coal at the Cocheco wharf coal shed is still burning and a large number of workmen are engaged in shoveling over the enormous mass which is stored there.

Sept. 29—Schooner *T. B. Garland* is at the lighting station, being lightered.

Oct. 11—Schooner *Rosa Ada* arrived at C. H. Trickey & Co.'s wharf and is discharging.

Oct. 15—*Daily Republican*: Schooner *C. H. Trickey* put in to Gloucester harbor on account of fog. It was on its way from Clark's Island, Me. to Philadelphia, where after being discharged it will reload with coal for C. H. Trickey & Co. of this city.

Dec. 20—The lower river froze up Saturday; it has been open about eight and one half months.

1884

Jan. 11—Captain Drew took the tug *Ann*, from Mathes wharf two miles down the river with the intention of getting through the ice to Portsmouth to bring a schooner up from Portsmouth lower harbor. The ice was found to be six inches in thickness and the tug returned without accomplishing its purpose that day anyhow.

April 21—The schooner *Mary E. Whorf*, with a cargo of oysters for Henry D. Freeman had been discharged at the oyster grounds down the river and all were nicely planted for spring and summer business. This method, it is said, assured their perfect freshness in the warmest weather, and Mr. Freeman could serve his customers as well in July as January. They were taken out fresh every day and served to suit all testes of his patrons.

April 23—The tug *Ann* had a tandem tow down the river, of schooners *Lillie*, *J. Chester Wood*, *Emily A. Staple*s, and *Hattie Lewis*, all loaded with brick for Boston.

June 13—Two gundalows are being used between Major J. S. Abbott's stone quarry in Durham and Portsmouth, carrying stone for Jones' new buildings there.

Aug. 8—Harrison Haley of Dover while on the wharf at Portsmouth had his gold watch stolen from him by some thief.

Dec. 12—Captain Hardy starts on a voyage this week; his family will remain in this city during the winter.

Schooner *C. H. Trickey* is laid up at Portsmouth, the *B. F. Nealley* at Cotuit, Mass., the *T. B. Garland* at New Bedford; the *John Bracewell* is at New York discharging stone; *Z. S. Wallingford* is at Jacksonville, Fla.

Dec. 19—Navigation on the Cochecho is closed for the winter; no more schooners till spring.

1885

April 3—Captain Stevens has taken 1,002 tons of coal from Baltimore for New Bedford in the schooner *J. J. Hanson*.

April 10—Schooner *John Bracewell* arrived at Trickey's dock with coal, will next go to Boothbay, to be caulked; this vessel is now seven years old.

April 24—The schooner *J. J. Hanson* arrived at Newport News and is landing with coal for Portsmouth. Schooner *Ira R. Sturgis* from Weehauken for Dover, passed through Hell's Gates.

May 9—Colonel A. T. Peirce has a fine picture of the schooner *J. J. Hanson* painted by the artist W. B. Stubbs. In the picture is Highland Light off Boston Harbor.

The Cocheco Mfg. Co. are building a large addition to their coal pocket and will begin filling it about July 1st.

July 17—W. M. Courser's schooner, the *Estella*, arrived down the harbor. She is loading brick at Courser's yard for Boston. William keeps things moving on land and sea.

Sept. 11— *Z. S. Wallingford* is in the river with coal for the Cocheco Mfg. Co.

Oct. 30—Captain Jonathan E. Kelley of the schooner *C. H. Trickey*, is at home sick and during the last trip out and back the vessel left here for Hoboken, N.J. stopping at Portsmouth, for Mr. Benson to take out his papers as captain, loaded at Hoboken, and arrived in river again last night, notwithstanding the severe storm last week and the calm during the last three days, making a trip of which Mr. Benson may well feel proud.

Dec. 11—The river is reported frozen over down as far as Dover Point. The schooner *Bracewell* is at Portsmouth with cargo of coal for C. H. Trickey & Co., the schooner *Z. S. Wallingford* and schooner *Golden Rule* will soon arrive with cargoes for the same firm. The coal will have to be brought up by rail from Portsmouth.

Dec. 25—The schooner *Golden Rule* and *Z. S. Wallingford* will finish unloading and go down river tomorrow, which will close navigation on the Cochecho for the season.

1886

Jan. 20—The schooner *J. J. Hanson* arrived at Providence, from Baltimore with nine hundred tons of coal. During the gale of last week it was in Chesapeake Bay and rode out the gale in fine shape. The cargo on the schooner would make five train of cars, thirty cars to a train, each carrying six tons.

Feb. 19—Captain W. W. Hardy and wife will be on a voyage about 1st March, when the captain takes command of his ship.

April 9—The tug *Ann* went to Portsmouth this afternoon to take the place of the tug *Bateman* for a few days.

April 16—The tug *Ann* towed up a large lighter with coal for the Cocheco Mfg. Co., the first arrival of the season.

Two schooners with coal for Cocheco Mfg. Co. are daily expected.

May —The steamer *May Queen*, took a party of excursionists to the Isles of Shoals. The steamer left Clements wharf at 7 a.m. and returned at 5:50. A very pleasant time was reported.

May 14—There are eight schooners upon the water loaded with coal for this city, four for the Cocheco Mfg. Co., two for C. H. Trickey & Co., one for Mathes and one for Converse & Hammond.

The schooner *Orion* which was run into at Vineyard Sound on the 7th by the schooner *Marshall Perrin*, was loaded with coal for C. H. Trickey & Co. of this city and was insured for its full value. The schooner will be along with its cargo all right, by and by.

May 28—The steamer *May Queen* of Newburyport lays in the river opposite the old steam mill, and is being painted and fixed up ready for excursion parties during the season.

June 4—A remarkable thing occurred last night showing high tides, once in a while in the Cochecho river. The schooner *C. H. Trickey* came up to the Cocheco dock without being lightered, at midnight, and is now being discharged.

June 11—W. M. Courser sent a crew of men to Dover Point at midnight last night to launch a gundalow that he has had built for him there; he will put the gundalow into active service at once as he has a contract to deliver a lot of brick at South Berwick. Mr. Courser keeps business lively where ever he takes hold.

June 18—A small schooner loaded with 100 tons of pebbles for H. F. Snow has arrived in the lower harbor.

July 23—The tug *Ann* went down the river and reached the lower harbor just as the schooner *Z. S. Wallingford* arrived and was preparing to cast anchor, so it took the schooner in tow and brought it up to the lightering place at an early hour; the schooner contained 432 tons for the Cocheco Mfg. Co. Ninety tons of it was taken off and the schooner arrived at wharf at 1 A.M.; Quick work.

Aug. 20—It has always been supposed that a person must be very smart to "set the river on fire." It seems that the feat was done last night; somebody on the Landing was smart enough to set the Cochecho on fire. The fire on the river was very dangerous to shipping. The schooner *C. H. Trickey* was expected at the wharf at high tide last night, but did not arrive; had it arrived it would have been burned, without doubt.

Aug. 27—The total tonnage of all the schooners of the Dover Navigation Co. is 2506 tons. Schooner *John Bracewell* 225 tons, schooner *C. H. Trickey* 281 tons, schooner *B. Frank Nealley* 275 tons, schooner *Thomas B. Garland* 319 tons, the schooner *Z. S. Wallingford* 295 tons, schooner *J. Chester Wood* 55 tons, schooner *John J. Hanson* 656 tons, and the schooner *Jonathan Sawyer* 400 tons.

Sept. 3—The brick schooner *J. Chester Wood*, schooner *Triton*, schooner *Hattie Lewis* and schooner *Lillie* arrived at Portsmouth from Boston and proceeded up river to load.

Oct. 22—Schooner *Abbie H. Green* with coal for the Cocheco Mfg. Co. arrived in the river. Several more schooners with coal for both the Cocheco and C. H. Trickey & Co. are on the way.

Nov. 19—The new schooner *Lizzie J. Call*, was launched at Portsmouth. A large gathering was present to see her slip into the water, which she did very prettily, bringing up to one anchor, she will load at once at Appledore wharf with apples for a Baltimore firm. (Launched at Freeman's Point.)

Dec. 3—The Government contract for widening and deepening the Cochecho river in this city has been awarded to Captain Thomas Symonds of Leominster, Mass. Work will be commenced in April 1887.

Dec. 17—Schooner *Jonathan Sawyer*, Captain Reynolds, is in the lower harbor on her way from an eastern port for Baltimore. She is to have iron plates put on her bow to protect her planking from the ice.

Dec. 24—The schooner *C. H. Trickey*, containing 350 tons of coal, which had such a struggle breaking its way through the ice of the Cochecho river, has discharged its cargo, and has been towed to Portsmouth for the winter. Lighters have been employed in conveying the coal from the mouth of the river to the coal houses and to accomplish the work so expeditiously were obliged to work all last night.

1887

Jan. 14—The River and Harbor Bill drafted during the recess of Congress by the sub-committee of the Appropriation Committee. $7,500 is allowed for the improvement of the Portsmouth Harbor, $2,000 for the Cochecho river.

Jan 21—The schooner *Thomas B. Garland*, with a cargo of coal for Weymouth, is lying at Simpson's wharf, East Boston, to wait for the going out of the ice so she can reach her destination.

Mar. 25—The ice went out of the Cochecho river Sunday, at 9 o'clock, up as far as the wharves, so that boats can come up now when they please. Messrs. Converse and Hammond will have some coal come up in course of a few weeks.

April 1—W. M. Courser has the first vessel on the river this season; she is loading with brick at his yard at Dover Point for Boston.

Schooner *Cora A. Kennard* came up the river with lime for

Tug Cocheco *on an excursion trip from Dover to the Isles of Shoals. The tug was built in 1887 at Bath, Maine for C.H. Trickey's coal company and was Dover's third tugboat. JPA*

Converse & Hammond. This is the first schooner to plow the waters of the Cochecho since the river was frozen over last fall.

Schooner *C. H. Trickey* has been chartered to carry stone from Cape Ann to Philadelphia.

The schooner *Susan E. Nash*, built at Westerly, R.I. in 1868, and until recently owned there, will be put in the brick carrying trade between Dover and Boston.

April 29—C. H. Trickey & Co.'s new tug, which is now being built at Bath, Me., is now framed, and will be sealed up immediately. The delay and general rub will come in making the machinery which will be of entirely new design. (Dover's third tug, the *Cocheco*)

The schooner *Clara B. Kennard* has arrived at this port from Rockland with lime for Converse & Hammond. The schooner *B. F. Nealley* left Greenwich, Penn. bound for Dover loaded with 377 tons of coal.

June 17—Schooner *Cottingham* started for sea this morning and schooner *Dick Williams* on the way from New York for Dover Gas Light Co.

June 24—With water works on Garrison Hill and whiskey works on the Landing, the city ought to be well supplied with fluids.

The schooner *John J. Hanson* arrived in Baltimore from Boston. Schooner *Dick Williams* for the Cocheco Mfg. Co. is expected from Philadelphia hourly. The schooner *Ivy Bell* from Elizabethport, arrived at the wharf this noon with coal for Dover Gas Light Co.

Captain W. W. Hardy and wife arrived home last week from their long and prosperous voyage. Their numerous friends here gave them a hearty greeting.

July 1—Schooner *John J. Hanson* sailed from Baltimore with 950 tons of coal for the Boston & Maine Railroad.

July 22—The Burned Tug:

It was with a feeling of disappointment that the Dover people record the new of the destruction of the new tug *Cocheco* by fire at Bath, Maine. It was about eleven o'clock in the forenoon that fire was discovered in the oakum loft. Immediately it was all ablaze. Flying about like so much tinder, the oakum spread the fire wide over the yard, igniting the dry chips in many places at once. The wind, the dryness of everything about the yard, and the difficulty of getting the engines to work aided the fire. So rapid was the spread of the flames that the whole north end of the city was threatened. Dispatches for help were sent to Brunswick, Lewiston, and Portland. A change of wind at a critical moment saved the river front and business portion of Bath from threatened destruction. Nearly one hundred thousand dollars worth of property was destroyed. For building wooden vessels this yard is the largest in the world. Maine builds most of the wooden ships that sail on the seas. Before the fire started the scene in the yard was one such as could not, it is safe to say, have been witnessed anywhere else in the United States, very likely nowhere else in the world.

The tug *Cocheco*, building for C. H. Trickey of this city, and ready for launching, was entirely destroyed. The loss is about $5,000. As the machinery had not been put in the loss is considerably below the value of the tug, which when finished, would have been valued at $10,000.

It was about one o'clock when the fire was controlled, but it was late in the evening when the flames were completely subdued. There is very little insurance on any of the property. As the boat had not been delivered to Mr. Trickey it is thought he will not be obliged to sustain the loss. The directors held a meeting shortly after the fire and voted to replace the vessels burned.

The Dover Navigation Co. had no interest in the tug *Cocheco* and lose nothing by the Bath fire.

The tug *Cocheco* at Bath will be immediately rebuilt and the lumber has already been ordered. It is thought that the tug will be completed by the middle of September. C.H. Trickey of this city sustains no loss whatever by the conflagration.

July 29—Captain W. W. Hardy is waiting for his ship to be loaded at Philadelphia, whence he will soon sail for Japan, a long voyage of six months.

Aug. 5—At a meeting of the stockholders of the New England Ship Building Co. at Bath, it was unanimously voted to subscribe the amount necessary to cover the loss by the recent fire at the company's yard.

Sept. 6—Boston Mass: Explosion, Dover Vessel Blown to Pieces—Fire broke out this forenoon on board the schooner *War Eagle*, lying at Cunningham's wharf in East Boston. The schooner *War Eagle* was loaded with 350 iron tanks of naptha. The fire commenced in one of these tanks and a terrible explosion followed. Henry O'Donnell of 417 Chelsea Street, who was on the vessel, was blown into the air and instantly killed. The cook, Henry Moran, was also killed. The captain and three of the crew were covered by blazing fluid and badly burned. The flames of the burning naptha instantly wrapped the wharf. Rapidly spreading they soon enveloped the wharf and the buildings on it. At this juncture the fire engines arrived. After an hour's struggle they succeeded in getting the flames under control. The *War Eagle* was literally blown to pieces. The only injuries so far as learned are those above reported. The injured have been taken to the Chelsea Marine Hospital. The entire loss will be about thirty thousand dollars. The vessel was owned by Foss & Wentworth of Dover, N.H. and was valued at two thousand dollars and was not insured. The captain's name was Philpot. He is a young man of about twenty and belongs in Dover. He was burned about the head and arms. His injuries while serious are not dangerous.

The schooner *War Eagle* was built at Portsmouth Navy Yard, and was purchased some years ago by J. W. Foss, dealer in second-hand furniture, and Chas. E. Wentworth, of the firm of Geo. B. Wentworth & Son, shoe manufacturers of this city, the balance of the stock being held by Portsmouth parties. John W. Foss was agent. Messrs. Foss and Wentworth were informed of the affair by a representative of the *Daily Republican*, and will start immediately for the scene of the disaster. We are informed by Mr. Foss that, so far as he knows, the crew contained no Dover persons.

Sept. 16—The new tug *Cocheco* built for C. H. Trickey was launched at Bath last Saturday, and the work of putting in the machinery is now going on.

Sept. 23—Captain Symonds will complete the job of deepening the Cochecho river this week.

Oct. 7—Schooner *Jonathan Sawyer* cleared Saco to Philadelphia, where she reloads with coal for the York corporation.

Schooner *B. F. Nealley* is at Saco with coal from Philadelphia.

Tug Cocheco *at Dover Point on its way to Dover Landing. This tug moved hundreds of schooners up and down the river to the port of Dover. OBHS*

Oct. 14—The schooner *Willard Sauisbury* has arrived at the wharf from Hoboken and is discharging coal for C. H. Trickey & Co.

The schooner *Z. S. Wallingford* arrived at Portsmouth and was expected to come to the Dover wharf today. She is chartered to load with stone from Carver's Harbor to New York.

The schooner *City of Ellsworth* cleared Dover this morning.

The schooner *T. B. Garland* is in Boston with coal.

The schooner *C. H. Trickey* is at Cambridgeport.

The schooner *John Bracewell* is now loading with stone at Carver's Harbor.

Nov. 18—The new tug *Cocheco* left Bath this morning 7:15, and will probably arrive here some time tonight.

The C. H. Trickey & Co. have applied to the U. S. Government for a license for their new tug boat, which will probably be called the *Cocheco*. Without this license they could not carry any passengers in their tug, which will however be generally used as a tow boat. Occasionally she may be devoted to the uses of an excursion party.–*Dover Daily Times*

The schooner *Lizzie J. Call* arrived inside Whale's Back Light this morning and later was taken up to Portsmouth. She is loaded

Schooner Lizzie Call *at Freeman Point, Portsmouth. This vessel came to Dover August 5, 1886 with coal. JPA*

with coal for C. H. Trickey & Co. and will be brought up to this city when the storm subsides. Mr. Trickey has three other schooners on the way to this port loaded with coal. The schooner *Lizzie J. Call* has arrived at the Dover wharf late today from New York.

Dec. 16—The schooner *B. Frank Nealley* arrived at the lightering place with coal from New York for C. H. Trickey & Co.

Dec. 23—The schooner *Warren B. Potter* from Hoboken arrived at the wharf with 440 tons of coal for C. H. Trickey. They unloaded till midnight and will continue until the same hour tonight in order to get out before the river freezes.

The schooner *C. H. Trickey* has hauled up for the winter at Green's wharf, East Boston.

Mr. C. H. Trickey felt happy today and probably every load of coal that went out contained several pieces of coal in excess. It is a Boy and weighs nine pounds.

1888

Jan.—Where the schooners are: schooner *T B. Garland* at Hyannis, schooner *Jonathan Sawyer* at Boston, schooner *J. J. Hanson* at Providence, schooner *John Bracewell* at Round Pond, Maine, schooner *Z. S. Wallingford* at Jersey City, schooner *B. F. Nealley* at New York City, schooner *C. H. Trickey* at Boston, laid up there.

Jan. 13—The Dover steam tugs *Cocheco* and *Ann* towed the four-masted schooner *T. A. Lambert*, now discharging coal for J. Albert Walker at Portsmouth. It is the largest vessel of her class in the world; she is 257 feet long, forty-seven feet beam, has a depth hold of twenty-two feet, and carries easily 2,600 tons of coal. It requires ten days to discharge this schooner.

March—The schooner *Z. S. Wallingford* is down the river with coal for the Cocheco Mfg. Co.

Seventeen tons of leather arrived in Dover for Hurd's shoe factory.

March 30—The River and Harbor Committee have completed their bill. In it are the following appropriations: Portsmouth Harbor $15,000; Little Harbor $10,000; and Cochecho river $9,000.

The schooner *Kate E. Rich* arrived with coal from Philadelphia to Dover.

April 3—The schooner *C. H. Trickey* is expected at any time now. She will be the first schooner to come up the river this season. She has a cargo of coal for the Cocheco Co.

April 14—The steamer *James Sampson* which was built here in Dover, is said to have towed over 9000 tons of coal to Exeter, South Newmarket and Newmarket. Friday morning she found herself frozen in at South Newmarket and was obliged to cut her way through the ice an inch and a half thick nearly down to Great Bay.

May 4—Three of the schooners of the Dover Navigation Co. have been chartered to bring coal here during the season for the Cocheco Mfg. Co. They are the schooner *B. Frank Nealley*, schooner *C. H. Trickey* and *Z. S. Wallingford*. The schooner *Jonathan Sawyer* has been chartered to carry coal to Saco for the season.

May 11—The schooner *John J. Hanson* arrived at Norfolk, Va. on the 4th of May. She was all loaded and sailed for New Haven again on the 5th; Quick work that.

The schooner *B. F. Nealley* has come up to the lightering place with coal for the Cocheco Mfg. Co. from Philadelphia.

May 12—Schooner *B. Frank Nealley* cleared Dover for Cape Ann to load paving stones for Philadelphia, there to load back with coal for the Cocheco Mfg. Co.

May 14—Last night a merry party of thirty-four went down the river in the steamer *George B. Smart* to Fort Constitution, where lobster nets were set and a good catch was the result. Only two fish were taken, one by Miss Fannie Grant and the other by Mrs. Wyman E. Brown. The lobsters taken were boiled on the steamer and a fine supper was enjoyed. The party returned home at 2 o'clock this morning. All were pleased with the trip and determined to go again.

Frank Varney of Dover Point, owner of the schooner *Triton*, which is now laid up at the eastern pier of the Portsmouth bridge, according to the *Portsmouth Chronicle*, is having a new main mast got out for his vessel. Mr. Varney and Captain Amee of the *Triton* have just hauled from Newburyport to Kittery Depot a large spar about seventy-five long and two feet through of Georgia Pine, which men commenced to work down to the right dimensions.

May 21—The schooner *Katie G. Robinson* is at the Cocheco Co.'s dock discharging. The schooner *C. H. Trickey* is in lower harbor with coal for Cocheco Co. and schooner *Dick Williams* with coal for C.H. Trickey, all from Philadelphia.

May 25—The schooner *Jonathan Sawyer* run upon the bar at the mouth of the Saco river last Thursday and remained all night.

June 1—There were several schooners on their way with cargoes of coal and pipe, but bad weather has kept them back.

Another pipe schooner with a mile of sixteen-inch pipe for Central Avenue is expected by any tide.

Included in the cargo that was shipped on the tug *Cocheco* this morning there were three kegs of lager beer marked "City of Dover." The members of the city government and a lot of other good fellows are down the river today and probably out at sea on the tug boat *Cocheco*. The party left the wharf at a little after 7 o'clock. They had Dan Bradley on board to serve as caterer.

The steamer *Dione*, owned by Messrs. Foss and Wentworth of this city, carried a party of fifteen to the Isles of Shoals Sunday and very successful they were, for they caught one hundred pounds of elegant cod.

The schooner *Maine*, schooner *B. Frank Nealley*, schooner *Fannie and Edith*, are in the river discharging. Schooner *Mary Day* is expected at any tide with coal for C. H. Trickey & Co.

Eliot is quite an apple country. S. Dixon of that town has shipped 700 barrels of a No. 1 Baldwins from there in the schooner *Arthur A. Hall*.

The pipe schooner is unloading at Mathes' wharf. There are four schooners in the river unloading.

The schooner *A. Benton*, 206 tons of pipe, four, six, eight, and twelve inch size, for the Dover Public Water Works, arrived at Mathes' wharf last night and is being discharged and tested today. If they have good luck it will be out by Wednesday. Speaking of the public water works, it was odd that the superintendent should choose just this time to shut off the water. Yesterday when not a drop of the critter could be bought, the water was turned off and the people who have been drinking the Dover Landing water had to go dry.

Schooner *Z. S. Wallingford*, after being cleared of her cargo at C. H. Trickey & Co.'s, was towed down to Portsmouth, from there she took a cargo of 3000 barrels of apples to New York.

The schooner *Maine*, with 260 tons of pipe, arrived from Camden, New Jersey and the pipe is being discharged on Mathes' wharf today. Marine Notes:

Schooner *Samuel L. Russell* is at Cocheco Mfg. Co. wharf discharging.

Schooner *Z. S. Wallingford* is at the lightering place with coal for C. M. Co.

Schooner *B. Frank Nealley* is on her way here with coal for C. M. Co.

Schooner *John J. Hanson* is discharging at J. Albert Walker's wharf at Portsmouth.

Schooner *Jonathan Sawyer* is on way with coal for Saco.

Schooner *John Bracewell* is at Boston with cargo of sand from New York.

Schooner *C. H. Trickey* passed Hyannis on the 3rd loading with paving stones for Philadelphia.

Schooner *T. B. Garland* has arrived at Providence, R.I. with a cargo of wood from the James River.

Schooner *Willard Sauisbury* is on the way from Hoboken with coal for C. H. Trickey & Co.Captain W. W. Hardy of this city, master of the barque *W. W. Crapo*, arrived in San Francisco from the Philippines with a cargo of sugar.

June 29—The latest addition to the handsome fleet of the Dover Navigation Co., the schooner *J. Frank Seavey*, will be launched at Bath, Me. July 1. A number of the stockholders will be present at that time.

July 8—Sawyer's will hold their second annual excursion on the steamer *Cocheco*. A general good time is expected: music and refreshments. Tickets 25 cents each, can be obtained at Varney's Drug store.

July 27—The pipe schooner is expected every day. If she doesn't arrive this week there will be a pipe famine on the north side of the river and the work will be transferred to the south side of the river.

Aug. 1—The schooner *Mary Brewster* is on the way from Port Johnson N.Y. for this city with cement for Converse & Hammond, and a Portland packet is enroute from Red Beach, Me. for the same parties with lumber.

The schooner *Nathaniel Lank* which arrived at Trickey's wharf this morning about 1:30 o'clock, drew eleven feet two inches of water and was not obliged to lighten a pound. This beat the record.

Aug. 3—The steamer *James Sampson* came up from Portsmouth and took on board a party of about fifty. They went down river and outside on a fishing trip, returning home in the evening.

The schooner *B. Frank Nealley* sailed from Philadelphia on Saturday with coal for Cocheco Mfg. Co. and the schooner *Jonathan Sawyer* also sailed for Saco.

Aug. 16—*Daily Republican*: Six schooners in the river. Schooner *Eva D. Rose* arrived at Mathes' last night, with a cargo of pipe for the Water Works.

Oct. 1—There are five schooners in the river today, which with the dredger and small boats give the appearance of quite a shipping port to the Cochecho.

Oct. 5—The dredger of Captain Symonds has been brought up the river and he has commenced the work of dredging out the channel.

Dover Daily Times: The schooner *E. F. Gandy* which arrived at the Cocheco Company's dock brought 401 tons of coal without lightening.

Nov. 20—The schooner *John Bracewell* has just made one of the fastest trips on record to New York. She went down the river Tuesday afternoon and sailed from Portsmouth at 4 o'clock. C. H. Trickey received a telegram early this morning, announcing her arrival at City Island in New York Harbor. She made the trip in about thirty-six hours.

The tug *Cocheco* towed the schooner *T B. Garland* down the river yesterday afternoon, and she was anchored at Dover Point in front of the Point House, it being too dark to take her to Portsmouth. During the heavy gale last night she tugged at her anchor fearfully, and there was some danger of her going ashore.

Dec. 7—The schooner *J. Frank Seavey* arrived at Portsmouth this noon, with 600 tons of coal from Philadelphia. The schooner came up without lightering a pound of coal, and is the largest cargo ever brought here by any vessel.

The schooner *G. W. Raitt* was hauled up at Portsmouth and most of the Brickers have been, or soon will be, moored in their winter quarters.

Dec. 14—Captain Symonds has left the river with his dredging machine, scow and house boats, and will haul up at Portsmouth for the winter. The schooner *Luella* is discharging lumber at Converse & Hammond Co., Dover.

Work on the new gundalow being built at Freeman's Point by William Fernald for Captain Cheney of South Berwick is progressing rapidly.

Dec. 29—*Dover Daily Republican*: The river froze over last night, hard enough to bear up any person's weight with safety. In the Cochecho at the wharf of V. Mathes this morning was moored the schooner *C. H. Trickey* all ready to be towed out. Ice formed around her and it looked to the observer as though she was there to stay. The old

Tug Hamilton A. Mathes *at Dover Point draw. Buildings in the background are brickyards. The one over the center of the tug is the location of Newick's today. JPA*

tug *Ann* came up with her prow encased in an ice cutter and succeeded in breaking through the ice to Mathes wharf. The schooner *C. H. Trickey* was towed out of the river and will be hauled up at Portsmouth.

1889

Jan.—New steamboat: The fleet of the Piscataqua is to have an addition next spring, without doubt, in the shape of a new towboat. Mr. H. A. Mathes of Durham, the enterprising Brick Manufacturer, and Valentine Mathes of this city, are making arrangements to have a new tug built for them, to be used in towing their barges and vessels. The parties have been to Bath, Me., but could not make satisfactory terms there, and have been negotiating with builders in Biddeford. Captain John C. Coleman of Dover Point will be the pilot of the new tug. (Dover's fourth tug).

Jan. 18—G. W. Horne has about half a million of brick at his yard on Cochecho street.

The schooner *J. Frank Seavey* arrived in Baltimore, loaded with stone from Red Beach, Me. She will return with Gas Retorts, for Boston, for $1000.

Feb. 1—The schooner *Z. S. Wallingford* has arrived in Palatka, Fla. from the Penobscot River, Me.

Schooner *John J. Hanson* arrived at Bull River, N.C. and will load with Phosphate rock for the north.

The *Jonathan Sawyer* is on her way to Galveston, Texas from Philadelphia.

March 15—Schooner *Clara B. Kennard* sailed for Boston with 60,000 bricks from Clements and Henderson yard, Dover Point.

March 22—Schooner *John Bracewell* is bound north from Philadelphia, with a cargo of coal for C. H. Trickey & Co.

The roaring of the sea could be plainly heard all day at Dover Point yesterday. The coasters are lying in the river and harbor unable to go out.

March 29—Schooner *T. B. Garland* is loading with ships timber at Williams Ferry for Waldoboro, Me.

The schooner *J. Chester Wood* went out with a load of brick from the yard of H. A. Mathes, for Boston; her first trip.

The schooner *Bracewell* came up river; it beat two other schooners which started from Philadelphia at the same time; the *Bracewell* is a fast sailer.

Captain W. W. Hardy lost his pocket book on the sidewalk yesterday afternoon, and did not miss it until his attention was called to it by a man who saw him drop it in front of Jenness hardware store. He started in pursuit of the man who picked it up and overtook him on Locust Street and demanded his pocket book. The man claimed he did not know any thing about it, but when Captain Hardy pressed the matter further he admitted the fact and unwillingly turned over his treasure to the rightful owner.

April 5—Captain Symonds is at Portsmouth now getting ready to come up the river the last of this week and begin work on the Cochecho where he left off last fall.

April 12—The Cocheco Mfg. Co. are laying a line of six-inch water pipe from Washington Street bridge to the coal sheds on the City Farm. They are having a hydrant put in to be used in case of fire.

Steamer *Geo. A. Smart* was launched this afternoon at 3 o'clock near the old steam mill.

May 3—Captain Willett took his schooner, the *Wallingford*, down the river and will sail to Lanesville and load with stone for Philadelphia.

May 4—The schooner *B. F. Nealley* and *H. E. Russell* will go down the river and sail for Lanesville.

May 9—Captain B. O. Reynolds arrived in this city last evening; his schooner, the *Jonathan Sawyer*, is at Saco.

May 24—The schooner *Empress* has discharged its load of coal and sailed for Rockland, Me. In six and three quarter hours yesterday, four men, Brown, Walker, Williams, and Haley, unloaded from the vessel 173 tons of coal at Trickey's dock. That was lively work.

Two new towers are being erected at the Cocheco Company's coal sheds on the City Farm, saving the company demurrage on vessels having to wait. They intend to have two tracks to the coal shed, instead of one as at the present time, so that they will be able to discharge a vessel in half the time.

June 28—Inward bound vessel reports whales as being unusually numerous on the coast. Captain Ingraham of the schooner *Penobscot* says that during one day it looked as if his vessel was running into a bed of rocks over which the sea was breaking. The animals were resting on the water apparently unconscious of the nearness of the boat.

July 4—The schooner *Abbie Bursley*, a two-masted schooner of 315 tons register which arrived at this port June 25th with a cargo of 425 tons of coal for Dover, had a somewhat dilapidated look on arrival. On the 22nd, when off Cape Cod she was run into by a large three-masted schooner whose name is unknown, as she refused to answer to a hail, and kept on her course without stopping to see whether the vessel went down or not. The schooner *Abbie Bursley* was close-hauled at the time of the collision, while the other vessel was running free. The schooner *Bursley* had her bowsprit broken and the stump driven inboard, her windlass and one cathead carried away, rail smashed and deck beams broken as far back as the foremast, the damage amounting to $700 or $800. A jury bow-sprit was rigged, and the vessel arrived near the Isles of Shoals on the 25th, and was towed in by the tug *Clara Bateman* —*Chronicle.*

July 11—Dover Point. The vessels of the brick fleet are not very busy just at present, having cleared out pretty thoroughly last season's stock of brick. The schooner *J. Chester Wood* is hauled up at the Dover Point house where Captain Sanders is giving her a coat of paint. The schooner *Hattie Lewis* is loading at the R. A. Pinkham yard. The schooner *Chilion* has been loaded at John Coleman's yard. Schooner *Wilson* and schooner *Willard* are out with a cargo from Thomas Parle's yard. The schooner *Addie*, schooner *Delia*, and schooner *George W. Raitt* are in Durham.Present indications are that there will be a little more activity in the brick market for the next few weeks. Good paving bricks are selling in Boston at fair prices with a good demand.–*Daily Republican.*

July 19—That excursion to Black Rocks will be Sunday; the party will go down the Piscataqua river in the tug *Cocheco*, instead of going to Haverhill and down the Merrimac river. This will be a spendid trip and afford a view of the beaches and seacoast from Portsmouth to Ipswich. Councilman Wentworth and Daniel Bradley have charge of the affair; $1.00 for the round trip.

Aug. 9—The navigation on the river is slowly but surely increasing, of scows and gundalows. A new gundalow, launched this week by the Adams brothers in Great Bay, has made her first trip; this boat is about sixty tons burden, and will be engaged in the coal freighting business.

Captain Reynolds and Mate Benson left for Saco to join their schooner *Jonathan Sawyer* which is discharging coal there.

Sept. 6—Schooner *Z. S. Wallingford* sailed from Philadelphia with coal for Cocheco Mfg. Co.

Sept. 20—The tug *Cocheco* was lying off the harbor when the tug *Oceanic* came in by Whales-Back on Saturday, with the Appledore staging in tow, and Captain Drew very generously ran out a line and helped tow the landing to its place of winter quarters at the north end.

Sept. 28—Captain E.Y. Oliver of the schooner *B. Frank Nealley*, mailed a postal to B. Frank Nealley, treasurer of the Dover Navigation Co., from Monmouth, New Jersey that he had laid in Sandy Hook all through the last great storm and is all right. He hailed some parties digging clams, so was enabled to send this report. The storm lasted four days and he has not had the chance to proceed to destination.

Oct. 4—Schooner *B. Frank Nealley* left Philadelphia on the 26th with coal for the Cocheco Mfg. Co. and arrived in the lower harbor Tuesday afternoon. Quick trip.

Nov. 8—The schooner *John Bracewell* arrived at the lower harbor.

Tug *Cocheco* left for Cape Ann to tow Captain S. Symonds fleet of dredgers round there.

Captain Reynold's schooner *Jonathan Sawyer* is discharged; he will leave here for the south where he will pass the winter, first going to Frankfort, Me. to load with stone; hence he will sail and not return with his ship till spring.

The barque *W. W. Crapo*, Captain W. W. Hardy of this city, Master, sailed from Hiogo Japan, Sept. 27, for Seattle and Tacoma, to load spars for Boston.

Nov. 15—The tug *Cocheco* which went to Salem to take Captain Symond's fleet of dredgers to that port, returned. She reports a rough return trip.

Steamer *G. A. Smart* has been engaged for the past ten days in towing schooners to Newmarket Mfg. Co. having taken some 2500 tons up there. She completed her duties and arrived at her wharf and will be put on the flats near the Cocheco Mfg. Co. coal shed and housed for the winter.

Dec. 6—Schooner *City of Ellsworth*, lumber laden from Bangor to Plymouth, Mass., hard and fast on reef at Boon Island. Crew saved. Vessel may be brought off all right.

Dec. 27—A letter received by C. H. Trickey from Captain Monroe of the schooner *John Bracewell*, dated Weymouth, Mass., Dec. 20, states that he is discharging at that port and will sail at once for Liberton, R.I.

1890

Jan. 10—The schooner *Jonathan Sawyer* arrived at Savannah, Ga. from Philadelphia, after experiencing a very rough passage.

Jan. 24—Barque *William W. Crapo*, Captain W. W. Hardy, 1573 tons left Puget Sound, January 7, bound to Boston with a cargo of Oregon pine spars, which will be used in new vessels which are to be built in New England.

The schooner *Empress* went ashore on Handkerchief Shoal. She was aided with the assistance of wreckers, and proceeded to her destination, which is this city.

Jan. 25—Our Dover schooners earned $18,393.42 during the year 1889. The Dover Navigation Company declared a six percent dividend the first six months and seven and three quarter cents the last.

Jan. 31—Captain Reynolds of the schooner *Jonathan Sawyer*, which has arrived at Mobile, is expected to sail for Nicaragua, Central America.

Feb. 2—The Dover Navigation Company is considerably interested in the bill before Congress to do away with compulsory pilotage about the waters of Maryland and Virginia. C. H. Trickey has been invited to appear before the committee at Washington.

Feb. 5—The six schooners of the Dover Navigation Company are all running this winter and doing a good business.

Feb. 6—The draw at the Dover Point Bridge on the upper Piscataqua, was opened 934 times during 1889, and 1,314 vessels passed through, of which 413 were steamers, 245 schooners, 589 gundalows, and miscellaneous small craft, forty-nine. The reason this up-river bridge had to open its draw so many more times than was the case with the Portsmouth bridge, through which everything which goes up or down the river must pass, while none of the traffic to Dover or South Berwick goes through the Dover Point bridge, is that the Dover Point bridge is much lower than the Portsmouth bridge, so that the draw has to be opened for the gundalows in river parlance–the stump mast of which enables them to pass under the Portsmouth bridge without the opening of the draw when the huge lateen sails are lowered.

Feb. 7—The large four-masted schooner *King Philip*, which ran into the lower harbor off Fort Constitution and dropped anchor, was

Dover Point bridge and draw; Dover Point House is on the right. DLW

towed up to the north end coal pocket in Portsmouth by the tug *Cocheco* of Dover. She brought nearly 2,000 tons of coal for J. Albert Walker.

Feb. 28—Schooner *J. F. Seavey* is reported to have passed Chatham Mass. in company with a large fleet of vessels bound for Newburyport.

The large five-masted schooner *Gov. Ames* which arrived in Portsmouth with 2,860 tons of coal for Walker Co. was towed from the lower harbor to Portsmouth and docked all right by the tug *Cocheco* of Dover. This is the first time that she has ever been hauled by our tug.

March 1—*Evening Star*: The schooner *J. Frank Seavey* arrived at Newburyport from Satilla River, Ga. with a cargo of hard pine for George E. Currier. She was thirty-two days on the voyage; when nine days she encountered a heavy gale, which carried away her sails, and she was obliged to put in to Beaufort, N.C. for repairs.

March 2—The schooner *Z. S. Wallingford* arrived at Baltimore from Savannah, Georgia.

March 6—There has not been enough ice in the river since last Friday to stop the tug *Cocheco* from coming up.

March 21—Mayor Nealley has received a letter from Captain Reynolds of the schooner *Jonathan Sawyer*. She is unloading at Nicaragua, Central America.

March 28—Schooner *T. B. Garland* of the Dover Navigation Co. passed through Hell's Gate on the 21st inst., loaded with ships timber from Washington for Bath.

April 4—The first vessel up the river this season arrived with 1000 barrels of cement for Converse & Hammond.

The schooner *John Bracewell* is on its way from Round Pond, Maine.

April 12—There are four schooners on the way here with coal for Cocheco Mfg. Co.

April 18—The tug *Cocheco* came up the river with the schooner *Rival* in tow with coal for C.H. Trickey & Co.

A model of the schooner *John Holland*, five feet long, beautifully carved etc. was placed in the show window of Dover Clothing Co. It will be built by New England Ship Building Co., Bath Me. The dimensions are as follows: keel 182 feet long, beam forty feet, depth seventeen and one-half feet. On the stern is the name, *John Holland*.

May 2—The schooner *John Bracewell* cleared from Portsmouth for Blue Hill; when off Boon Island she was obliged to return owing to threatening weather.

June 20—Captain Hardy brought back a boat from China which he had built for his children. It lies at Gould's wharf and is quite a curiosity as it is entirely different from our idea of naval architecture. Captain W. W. Hardy of the barque *W. W. Crapo* expects to sail from Boston on an extended voyage in a few days.

June 26—The schooner *Bertha Louise* which was here the other day was one of the finest proportioned boats that has ever been here. She is 117 1/2 feet keel, twenty-eight and one-half feet beam and is registered at 230 government tonnage.

June 28—*Daily Republican*: The first excursion down the river takes place when the steamer *Cocheco* will go down the river on a pleasure and fishing trip to York Beach. A string band of six pieces will be on board and plenty of lines and bait. Tickets only seventy-five cents. The steamer will leave Mathes wharf at 9 A.M.

June 30—The schooner *Wm. F. Collins* will go to sea tomorrow.

July 12—*Daily Democrat*: Mrs. Charles H. Trickey and a party of twenty-three relatives and friends went down the river on the tug *Cocheco* for a pleasure trip. After a brief visit to Portsmouth, the party set off for the Isles of Shoals where they landed on Star Island. They examined the old Church, the cemetery, old records, and the monument to Captain John Smith, and collected momentos before returning to Portsmouth. Since there was no schooner ready to tow up river, the tug remained there. The party came home by train.

July 16—John Holland has presented C. H. Trickey with two large photographs of the new schooner *John Holland*, now in process of construction at Bath Maine.

July 19—The Shoals steamer is crowded on each of her trips these sweltering days.

The sides of the schooner *John Holland* have been planked and the boat will be ready for launching August 5. There is no doubt but that a large party will go to Bath on that date to see the big boat go into the water.

July 25—Captain W. W. Hardy and wife and their son Hathaway left for Boston on the 2:26 train, thence they will go to New York and soon sail from that port for Japan. Mrs. Hardy and son will accompany him.

Oct. 31—Schooner *John Holland* bound from Baltimore to Portsmouth is wind bound, but will arrive in a few hours when it shifts.

Dec. 19—The schooner *T. B. Garland* succeeded in working her way up the Cochecho to Trickey's wharf last night, notwithstanding the ice in the lower river and is now discharging. This, we understand, is a feat unprecedented in the navigable waters in this section.

1891

Feb. 20—The barque *W. W. Crapo,* Captain Hardy of this city, arrived in Yokohama, Japan Feb. 12, all well.

March 13—The schooner *T. B. Garland* sailed from Pool's landing March 1 and was reported off New York March 4. She arrived at Cape Charles City, Va. March 8 loaded with ice. She lost her cabin windows in a blow but otherwise is all right and tight.

The schooner *John Holland* sailed from Norfolk for Providence, R.I.

Navigation on the Cochecho river will soon begin as the ice is well out.

The schooner *Wallingford* sailed from Wilmington for Philadelphia.

The schooner *Lucy*, belonging to C. H. Trickey & Co., is loading coal at Hoboben, N.J. for that company and will arrive here soon.

April 3—Schooner *John Holland* put into Hampton Roads. She is bound for Providence, R.I. The schooner *Warren B. Potter* is on its way from Philadelphia here with coal for the Cocheco Mfg. Co. This is the first cargo of the season.

April 10—The gundalow *Tippecanoe*, Captain Philpot of Dover, brought a load of bricks down river and discharged them at Broughton's wharf, Portsmouth.

April 17—Captain Drew of the tug *Cocheco* is making trips from Portsmouth to this city, towing the arrivals bound here. He feels his way up the narrow and tortuous passages on the darkest nights. He has had so much experience that he knows the way with only six inches of water under the keel.

May 8—The gundalow *Tippecanoe* is to be converted into a steam lighter by having a small engine placed aboard to furnish motive power.

May 15—Captain Drew expects that the repairs on the tug *Cocheco* will be made so fast that she will return to Portsmouth the first of the coming week.

Schooner *John Bracewell* left the wharf, light, for Philadelphia to load back with coal for the Cocheco Co.

The schooner *Z. S. Wallingford* arrived at the Cocheco Mfg. Co.'s wharf this afternoon.

The schooner *John Holland* left Norfolk, Va. for Boston May 16th. She had 1742 tons of coal aboard.

July 17—Schooner *Ira E. Wright* was discharged and sailed for Rockland, Maine.

The dredger has arrived in the Cochecho and will commence widening the channel. They will excavate to the depth of seven feet of water at low tide, and the channel will be seventy feet wide.

Aug. 7—The Cochecho river near the Cocheco Mfg. Co. coal sheds presented a busy appearance. The New England Dredging Co.'s large dredger, with a fleet of six scows, the tug *Ocean Queen*, schooner *Abbie S. Walker*, steam tug *Iva*, and several smaller crafts were laying at anchor there.

Aug.14—The Leighton brothers of the Isles of Shoals have chartered the steamer *Iva*, owned by Eugene Smart of Dover, for the accommodation of their guests at the different hotels on Appledore and Star Island for the season.

The work of dredging in the lower Cochecho river will not be completed this season, notwithstanding Captain Clark, who has charge, is making good headway.

Aug. 21—Captain Reynolds entertained a party of Dover people on board the schooner *Jonathan Sawyer* at Saco, where his vessel is discharging.

Aug. 28—The schooner *T. B. Garland* sailed for Gardner, Me. to load ice for Philadelphia; she will return with coal for Dover.

Sept. 4—At Bar Harbor, this week, the steam yacht *Now Then* was the winner in three races with the fastest yachts on the Atlantic Coast; it will be remembered that George A. Hussey, a Dover boy, is the engineer of this boat, which is said to be the fastest pleasure craft in the world.

Oct. 2—It is reported that Captain Trefethen contemplates giving a free excursion and a "Spread" of good things when the steamer *Mystic* is ready to run on the river.

Nov. 20—The brick schooners *Hattie Lewis*, schooner *J. Chester Wood*, schooner *Satellite*, schooner *G. W. Raitt*, and schooner *Clara Kennard* are down river receiving cargoes of brick.

Schooner *John Bracewell* is unloaded and will go down river where her deck will be caulked before going to sea.

Brickyards of Elbridge Gage on the Bellamy River near what today is the location of the Spaulding Turnpike toll booths. OBHS

The schooner *John Holland* was in Vineyard Haven and is probably now in Boston, for which port she is bound.

Dec. 4—C. H. Trickey & Co. have had 1,000 tons of stove coal on the way to their dock in vessels at one time, and they have kept them pretty busy receiving it. They have only one more cargo for this season and that is on the way.

Dec. 25—Schooner *Z. S. Wallingford* sailed from Norfolk, Va. on the 16th for New Haven loaded with coal.

1892

Jan. 22—The schooner loaded with coal for C. H. Trickey & Co. is a long time on her trip to this port and it is feared she will be unable to get up here on account of ice, though the river is free from it at present.

Jan. 29—The accounts of the schooner *Hattie Lewis* were balanced and a thirty percent dividend was declared to her owners. Captain O. A. Clark has shown one of the best records made by any of the brickers that sailed from this port last season, having made thirty-three trips. Charles H. Carrett is her agent.—*Portsmouth Times*.

The schooner *Agnes Chamberlain* is to be unloaded in Portsmouth and her cargo of coal shipped to C. H. Trickey & Co., of this city by rail, as the ice is too thick in the Cochecho to allow her to come to this port. Captain L. J. Stevens of the schooner *John Holland* and Captain William B. Crosby of the schooner *T. B. Garland* were in town over night, and were the guest of Mr. C. H. Trickey. They attended the meeting of the Dover Navigation Co.

Feb. 12—The tug *Cocheco* is not tied up for the winter as has been reported but is ready for business if there is any, so says Captain Drew.—*Portsmouth Post*.

Captain Hardy of the barque *W. W. Crapo* left this city for Philadelphia, where the vessel is receiving a merchandise cargo and will sail for San Francisco in a few days.

The schooner *John Paul's* cargo of coal got on fire during her trip from Norfolk to Providence the first of this week, and although the vessel reached Providence, she was sunk in her dock. Captain Harry Philpot, who is well known in Dover, is master of the vessel and his friends here will be sorry to learn of the mishap.

April 1—The schooner *John Holland* sailed on the 23rd inst. from Norfolk, Va. to New Haven, Conn.

The schooner *Z. S. Wallingford* is up the James River in Virginia loading with lumber for New Haven.

April 8—The first vessel to come way up the river to Dover this spring is the schooner *Mary S. Newton* which was towed up by tug

Cocheco. She is now discharging her cargo of plaster at Converse and Hammond's wharf.

The schooner *Jonathan Sawyer* has arrived at Galveston, Texas with a cargo of coal. The first schooner to sail for the Cochecho with coal for the Cocheco Mfg. Co. this year is the *W. L. Elkins,* which cleared Philadelphia March 25 bound for Dover.

Captain Harry Philpot, late of the schooner *John Paul,* has been in town today visiting friends. He is to take charge of another schooner shortly.

April 22—Schooner *John Holland* made a remarkably quick run from New Haven, Conn. to Norfolk, Va., arriving on the 13th after a passage lasting but fifty-two hours. She sailed for Providence on the 14th.

Converse & Hammond are making extensive improvements at their lumber yard. A new building is to be erected on the site of the old pipe factory.

May 13—Steamer *Iva* towed the schooner *Granville* down the river this morning.

The schooner *Emily S. Baymore* arrived at the Cocheco Mfg. Co. loaded with coal.

Schooner *Z. S. Wallingford* and schooner *W. B. Potter* are on their way to this city with coal for C. H. Trickey & Co.

Schooner *Emma B. Shaw* came up river loaded with coal for C.H. Trickey & Co.

The tug *Cocheco* has been chartered to take a party of twenty Ladies and Gentlemen to the Isles of Shoals this evening.

May 20—The schooner *Warren B. Potter* went aground near the Powder House while being towed up the river. She will be taken off at high tide this afternoon or pulled off at high tide Tuesday night after being lightened.

Schooner *Veto* was towed down the river by the tug *Cocheco.* The schooner *Maggie Miller* and schooner *J. M. Kennedy* arrived with lime and cement for Converse and Hammond. The *Kennedy* with 1500 barrels of cement; also the schooner *Miller* with a million and a half of shingles from New Brunswick.

May 27—The trial of the Piscataqua Navigation Co's new tug *Hamilton A. Mathes,* will be held Wednesday.

Schooner *Z. S. Wallingford* and schooner *Maggie Miller* were towed down the river last night.

June 1—Schooner *Index* is on the way loaded with coal for Cocheco Mfg. Co.

A pile driver was set to work at the river wharf of Converse & Hammond and piles are being rapidly driven for the new structure.

June 17—Fire was set this morning to the first kiln of brick at Horne's Brickyard on Cochecho Street.

The idea of purchasing a new tug boat for use on the Cochecho has been abandoned by the Dover Navigation Co.

C. H. Trickey & Co. are making an addition to their coal shed on Cochecho Street, which will give them additional space for the reception of the Black Diamonds.

The work of planking over the new wharf of Converse & Hammond was begun today and this substantial piece of work will be completed in a few days. The pile driver is now at work on the opposite side of the river near the Cocheco Mfg. Co. coal shed.

June 24—The tug *Cocheco* and steamer *Sam Butterfield* collided at Portsmouth, lightly damaging the latter.

Schooner *Emily S. Baymore* is in with coal consigned to C. H. Trickey & Co. Captain H. L. Philpot leaves tonight for Bath, Me. where he will personally superintend the rigging out the new schooner *Mary E.H.G. Dow*, which he is to command. The new schooner *Mary E.H.G. Dow* has been chartered to take a load of ice from Bath to Baltimore on the maiden trip. Quite a number of Dover people go to Bath this week to see the new craft.

(The schooner *Mary E. H. G. Dow* was named for Mrs. Mary Edna Hill Gray Dow who became famous as the president of the Dover Horse Railroad Company.)

July 8—The tug *Cocheco* towed down river the schooner *J. A. Warr* and schooner *Marcus Edwards*. The former sailed for Calais to load shooks for Jacksonville, Florida, and the latter to Kennebec, to load ice for a southern port.

The schooner *Fostina*, with 250 tons of coal for R. Haley of Dover, arrived at Portsmouth and is discharging at the Boston & Maine wharf.

Schooner *Abel W. Parker* floated the National Colors yesterday. She is discharging at C. H. Trickey & Co. dock.

The brick schooner *Sadie A. Kimball* with 50,000 bricks from the Thomas Parle's yard, and the schooner *Clara B. Kennard* with 60,000 bricks from Eldridge Gage yard, sailed for Boston.

July 22—The water in the lower Cochecho is very low at high tide at the present time; and coal laden schooners are compelled to unload a part of their cargo at Gilman's point.

Schooner *Amelia P. Schmidt* arrived with coal for the Cocheco Mfg. Co.

July 29—A huge rat was caught in the Cochecho waste house this noon by Mr. George W. Caswell in a steel trap; he weighed two pounds and was sixteen inches long. This is one of the largest ever caught in this city; he was evidently very old, "as gray as a rat," and as savage as a bear.

Officer Stevens arrested Richard Philpot this noon in a drunken condition. Philpot came into town with a yoke of oxen and

Schooner MARY E. H. G. DOW. 1196 Tons. H. L. PHILPOTT, Master.

Built by W. T. DONNELL, Bath, Me.   Launched April 13, 1892.

LENGTH 203   DEPTH 19.5
BREADTH 39.0

Schooner Mary E.H.G. Dow, *named for Mrs. Mary Edna Hill Gray Dow, a Dover resident who became famous as president of the Dover Horse Railroad Company. Mrs. Dow had 4/64 ownership of the schooner. MMM*

left them standing on Cochecho Street all day without food or water. The oxen were put up at a stable.

The U. S. Harbor & River Inspector, Peter A. Hains and son, accompanied by Chas. H. Trickey, John Holland and J. Frank Seavey made a trip down the river on the tug *Cocheco*.

Aug. 5—The steamer *Cocheco* goes to Portsmouth to haul out and have her bottom cleaned and be repainted. Other repairs and alterations to the boat will be made, including adding another length to the smokestack.

Aug. 19—Mrs. M.E.H.G. Dow, son and daughter, and Rev. Hovey and daughter, left Portland today on the schooner *M.E.H.G. Dow* for Bangor.

The schooner *John Bracewell* arrived at the Cocheco Mfg. Co. dock.

Schooner *H. T. Hedges* sailed for Philadelphia light, to load with coal for the Cocheco Mfg. Co.

Schooner *J. L. Molloy* was towed down the river by tug *Cocheco*.

It is stated in navigation circles that the Piscataqua Co. have offered Captain Horace Barns, now of the schooner *Sadie Kimball*, the position of captain on their smaller tow boat, the *H. A. Mathes*.

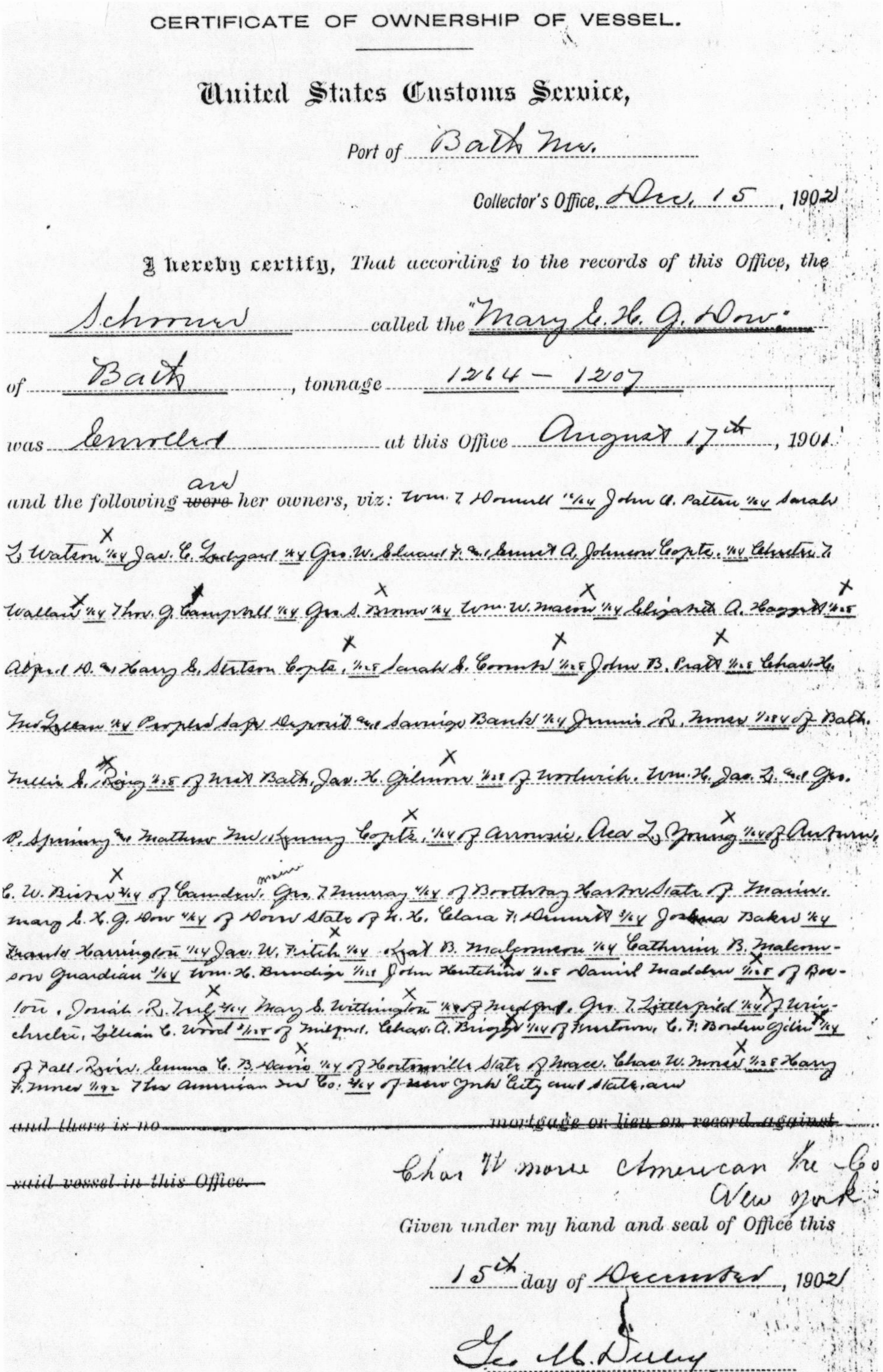

CERTIFICATE OF OWNERSHIP OF VESSEL.

United States Customs Service,

Port of Bath Me.

Collector's Office, Dec. 15, 1902

I hereby certify, *That according to the records of this Office, the*

Schooner called the "Mary E. H. G. Dow"

of Bath, *tonnage* 1264 – 1207

was Enrolled *at this Office* August 17th, 1901

and the following ~~were~~ are *her owners, viz:* Wm. F. Hounell 1/64 John A. Patten 1/64 Sarah L. Watson 1/64 Jas. E. Ledyard 1/64 Geo. W. Edward F. and Emmet A. Johnson Copts. 1/64 Chester T. Wallace 1/64 Thos. G. Campbell 1/64 Geo. S. Brown 1/64 Wm. W. Mason 1/64 Elizabeth A. Haggett 1/128 Alfred H. and Harry E. Stetson Copts. 1/128 Sarah S. Combs 1/128 John B. Pratt 1/128 Chas. H. McLellan 1/64 Peoples Safe Deposit and Savings Bank 1/64 Jennie R. Innes 1/384 of Bath. Nellie E. Ring 1/128 of West Bath, Jas. H. Gilmore 1/128 of Woolwich. Wm. H. Jas. L. and Geo. P. Spinney and Mathew McKenney Copts. 1/64 of Arrowsic. Ada L. Young 1/64 of Auburn. C. W. Bisbee 1/64 of Camden. Geo. T. Murray 1/64 of Boothbay Harbor State of Maine. Mary E. H. G. Dow 1/64 of Dover State of N. H. Clara F. Dennett 1/64 Joshua Baker 1/64 Frank Harrington 1/64 Jas. W. Fitch 1/64 Fred B. Malcomson 1/64 Catherine B. Malcomson Guardian 1/64 Wm. H. Brandige 1/128 John Hutchins 1/128 Daniel Madden 1/128 of Boston. Josiah R. Teel 1/64 Mary E. Withington 1/64 of Medford. Geo. T. Littlefield 1/64 of Winchester. Lillian C. Wood 1/128 of Milford. Chas. A. Briggs 1/64 of Newton. C. F. Borden Giles 1/64 of Fall River. Emma C. B. Davis 1/64 of Hortonville State of Mass. Chas. W. Innes 1/128 Harry F. Innes 1/192 The American Ice Co. 1/64 of New York City and State are

~~and there is no mortgage or lien on record against said vessel in this Office.~~

Chas W. Morse American Ice Co New York

Given under my hand and seal of Office this 15th *day of* December, 1902

Geo. M. Duley
Depy Collector.

2—4245

Aug. 26—Schooner *William Thomas* cleared this morning.

The schooner *Hattie Lewis* narrowly escaped being cut in two by the steamer *Portland*, while working along in a heavy fog off Cape Ann. Schooner *Mary Brewster* has discharged a cargo of lumber at Converse & Hammond dock and cleared today.

Schooner *Annie V. Lawton* left Philadelphia for Dover.

Schooner *E. P. Kimball* is on way to this city with coal for C. H. Trickey & Co.

Schooner *Mary E. H. G. Dow* left Kennebunkport last Monday, arriving at Baltimore Saturday morning; a pretty quick run.

Captain Hardy has arrived at San Francisco, a little late but all right, as his friends and family here have learned by a telegram from him this week.

Sept. 23—The schooner *M. E. H. G. Dow* arrived in Portsmouth this morning with passengers all well. No accidents have happened to the schooner or passengers; the latter will come to this city this afternoon. The schooner will remain at Portsmouth until the middle of next week and any one desiring to see it can do so by going there.

Sept. 30—Schooner *Warren Edwards* arrived with coal for the Cocheco Mfg. Co.

Oct. 21—Schooner *John Holland*, coal laden, is on her way to Portsmouth.

Oct. 28—The tug *Cocheco* arrived from Portland after undergoing extensive repairs.

Nov. 4—Schooner *Nevada* is discharging a cargo of lime at the wharf of Converse & Hammond.

Schooner *T. B. Garland* was towed up river this afternoon by the *Cocheco*.

Nov. 18—The schooner *Clara B. Kennard* has made thirty-two trips from Dover Point to Boston with brick so far this season. The schooner *J. G. Morse, Jr.* is in the lower river with a cargo for C. H. Trickey & Co. She went aground while coming up the river near the Glue Factory Point, she will be hauled off at high tide.

Nov. 19—Schooner *Morse* is still aground, all efforts to haul her off having proven futile. The rain will cause a high tide late this afternoon, when vessel will be hauled off by the tug *Cocheco*.

1893

Jan. 13—Messrs. Converse & Hammond are to erect an immense lumber shed at their yard on Cochecho Street. The new building will be twenty-three wide by 150 feet in length.

Jan. 20—The bricking transportation season up river is now closed for the season. The schooner *Clara B. Kennard* has made

Converse & Hammond lumberyard, Dover Landing. WI

thirty-two trips, the leading number; the schooner *Sadie A. Kimball* thirty; schooner *Hattie Lewis* twenty-nine; schooner *G. W. Raitt* and *Chilion* twenty-four each; and the schooner *Willard and Wilson* twenty-three.

Jan. 27—Shipping Summary: During the year 1892 the number of vessels arriving in the lower river was ninety-three, of these, seventy-eight brought coal, fifteen lumber and lime. Four firms or corporations receiving the entire ninety-three cargoes. The total amount of coal brought up river was 27,000 tons. The shipping business is increasing year by year and has already developed into considerable importance. (Four firms: Cocheco Mfg. Co., C. H. Trickey & Co., Converse & Hammond Co., and V. Mathes Co.)

The annual meeting of the Dover Navigation Company was held at the Cocheco Hose Rooms and the following officers elected for the ensuing year. President Thos. B. Garland, Sec. & Treas, B. F. Nealley. Managing Committee, T. B. Garland, B. F. Nealley, Chas. H. Trickey, J. Frank Seavey, John Holland, John J. Hanson, Chas. H. Sawyer. Auditors - J. T. W. Ham, Benj. Brierley.

The fleet of schooners owned by the company now numbers seven. The average annual dividend has been ten percent. The company was organized in 1877 with a capital stock of $13,121.92.

Port of Dover about 1890. Left to right: D. Foss & Son's mill, Converse & Hammond lumberyard at Dover Landing, Dover Gas Light Company coal tower, C.H. Trickey's coal tower, the tug Cocheco and Valentine Mathes' wharf. OBHS

The capital stock of the present time is $181,374.36. Dividends have been paid amounting to $193.894.92.

Feb. 10—The schooner *Jonathan Sawyer* arrived at Mobile, Ala. from Cuba.

The schooner *John Holland* arrived in New London, having left Norfolk, Va. Feb. 2nd; a remarkable quick trip and all safe.

The schooner *Chilion*, which was wrecked near Dover Point while coming down the river several weeks ago, will be repaired by William F. Fernald, the well-known ship carpenter and builder. The vessel will be taken to the shipyard at Freeman's Point as soon as the weather permits.

March 10—The schooner *Wallingford* has arrived at Norfolk and will load with lumber for Philadelphia.

The schooner *John Bracewell* is at Bridgeport, Conn. Captain Benson is in this city and says that there is half a mile of ice, six inches thick, between the vessel and clear water, hence they are unable to get out.

Schooner *Thomas B. Garland* arrived at Provincetown on the 16th inst. from Rockport, bound to New York.

Schooner *John Holland* left Norfolk on the 15th inst. on the way to Boston.

The tug *Cocheco* is engaged in towing in Portsmouth Harbor at present.

April 7—The tug *Cocheco* has returned from Portland where she has been undergoing repairs. A new chime whistle has also been put on in place of the hoarse-sounding affair formerly used.

April 14—Schooner *John Bracewell* and *T. B. Garland* are on their way to the city loaded with coal for the Cocheco Mfg. Co.

The schooner *Jonathan Sawyer* arrived at Biddeford with a cargo of coal from Philadelphia

During the high wind last night a part of the old steam mill on Cochecho Street owned by the Cocheco Mfg. Co. was blown down.

May 5—Brick manufacturers have come to the conclusion that shipping by barge is the proper method and the day of the schooners is past, although there are several still carrying from yards in this vicinity to Boston.

Regular steamboat trips between Dover and the sea have long been needed on this river during the summer and the advent of the new boat will be hailed with a general murmur of approval.

We are pleased to learn that the new steamer line from Dover to York Beach is going to materialize beyond doubt. The steamer is expected this week and is said to be a fine one in every respect. The steamer *Jeannette* should be made to pay handsomely during the summer, and as York is the favorite beach of Dover people, they could

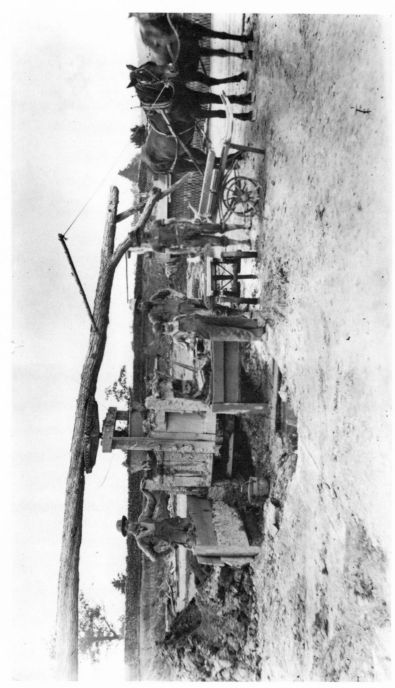

Elbridge Gage's plug mill used at his brickyard for mixing clay. OBHS

find no pleasanter method of reaching that watering place than by the lovely Piscataqua and a bit of Ocean thrown in.

The steamer is to stop at the Point House each trip, and many will avail themselves of the opportunity of moonlight rides to and from that popular resort. As the boat will probably return to Dover in the evening, people can come down on a hot day at 6:40 by train and enjoy a few hours on the Point House lawn and take in the cool breezes before returning by boat. The wharf here is in good condition for a steamer landing and would delay a boat but a few minutes.

May 26—Schooner *Wallingford* is unloading a cargo of coal at the Cocheco Mfg. Co. dock.

Schooner *C. H. Trickey* arrived at the Cocheco Mfg. Co. dock with a cargo of coal.

Tug *Cocheco* brought the schooner *R. T. Randlett* up the river. The vessel has a cargo of coal for C. H. Trickey & Co.

June 9—Schooner *B. W. Pierce* is discharging a cargo of coal at Cocheco Mfg. dock, also schooner *Z. D. Walker*.

Schooner *Thomas B. Garland* is discharging a cargo of coal at dock of C. H. Trickey & Co.

Captain C. W. Howard has arrived at Portland with the steamer which will run between this city and York Beach this summer. The furnishings are now being put in and the boat will arrive here about the middle of June.

June 16—The schooner *Jonathan Sawyer* which ran on the Saco Bar was worked off and is all right.

Schooner *Mary E. Crosby* is discharging a cargo of coal at the dock of Valentine Mathes.

Schooner *Marcus Edwards* which arrived at the dock of Valentine Mathes with coal, lost her fore-topmast in a gale on her trip to this city.

Schooner *Jennie Simmons* arrived with coal for Cocheco Mfg. Co. A Narrow Escape: The tug *Cocheco* went on a sunken ledge off Blue Cove, at the Shoals, and came very near staying there. The ledge is a smooth, turtle back rock and the steamer sustained no damage.

Schooner *Frank McDonnell* is discharging a cargo of coal at Cocheco Mfg. Co.'s dock.

June 23—Schooner *Z. S. Wallingford* is discharging a cargo of coal at the dock of Cocheco Mfg. Co.

Schooner *Abner Parker* has arrived with coal for Cocheco Mfg. Co.

Schooner *E. W. Perry* cargo of coal for Cocheco Mfg. Co.

Schooner *Luella* arrived with cargo of lime for Converse & Hammond.

Schooner *H. T. Hedges* is on way to this city from Philadelphia, loaded with coal.

Dover Point House, now Hilton Park. DLW

Schooner *T. B. Garland* was brought up to the Cocheco Mfg. Co.

June 23—Schooner *Jonathan Sawyer* is unloading a cargo of coal at Saco.

Schooner *Emily S. Baymore* is unloading a cargo of coal at the Cocheco Mfg. Co.

The steamer tug *Cocheco* has been chartered by a private party who will witness the trial of the new cruiser, *New York.*

June 30—Schooner *Clare Rankin* with coal for Cocheco Mfg.

The schooner *Iva May* is on the way with coal for C. H. Trickey.

On Friday the tug *Hamilton A. Mathes*, while towing a loaded brick barge through the wide arch in the Portsmouth bridge, bumped the barge, against the bridge with such force as to start a plank. Seeing that the barge was sinking the captain of the tug ran for the flats, where the craft was beached and repaired.

July 7—The schooner *S. J. Watts* arrived from Perth Amboy with coal for C. H. Trickey & Co.

July 14—Schooner *Lucy* sailed for Cape Ann to load stone for Philadelphia.

Schooner *J. S. Davis* arrived at the lightering place with coal for Cocheco Mfg. Co.

The schooner *R. T. Randlett* arrived at the Cocheco dock with coal.

July 21—The schooner *Willard Sauisbury* from Perth Amboy for this port with coal.

Schooner *Frank McDonald* from Philadelphia at Cocheco Mfg. Co. dock.

Schooner *J. E. Simmons* is at the lightering place and the schooner *Z. S. Wallingford* is in lower harbor both for Cocheco Mfg. Co.

The schooner *C. H. Trickey* arrived at the dock with coal for C. H. Trickey & Co.

July 28—The draw bridge at Dover Point was opened 104 times during the month of June. The total number of vessels passing through was 139, classed as follows; steamers sixty-three, gundalows sixty-six, schooners six, barges three.

The schooner *Emily Baymore* is at the Cocheco Mfg. Co. dock with coal.

The schooner *Sadie A. Kimball*, with 50,000 bricks from Parle's yard, sailed for Boston yesterday.

The steam gundalow *Fanny P.*, Captain Langley, with eighty tons of coal for Newmarket passed up the river.

The gundalow *Fannie M.*, Captain Adams, came down river yesterday with twenty-five cords of hard wood for John Mathes brick yard, Eliot. Messrs. Gage and Blackwood have recently finished burning a large kiln of bricks at their yard on the banks of the Cochecho.

E. Oscar Pinkham is burning a kiln of sixteen arches, 300,000 brick this week.

Aug. 11—The steamer *Jeannette* expects to complete her term of service between Portsmouth and the Shoals about the latter part of next week; Captain Howard has decided to remain in this section the balance of the season but will run his boat only on charter.

During the month of July, the draw of the bridge was opened 113 times, the number of vessels passing through was 154, classed as follows, gundalows sixty-four, steamers seventy-five, schooners ten, barges one.

The gundalow *Fannie M.* came down river yesterday with twenty-five cords of hard wood for J. Wesley Clement's yard.

The steam gundalow, *Fanny P.*, with eighty tons of coal for Newmarket, went up river this morning.

Aug. 18—Captain W. W. Hardy went to Boston and took his ship around to New York, where the bottom will be recoppered and the whole vessel put in thorough repair, ready for loading for another trip abroad.

Aug. 25—Schooner *Frank McDonald* arrived at the wharf with coal for Cocheco Mfg. Co.

Sept. 1—Schooners Collide: The morning despatches contain the intelligence that the schooner *Charles H. Trickey*, Captain Fickett from Baltimore for Dover, with a cargo of coal, and schooner *Governor*, of Castine, Me., Captain Low, from Sargentville, Me. for New York, with a cargo of paving stone, collided about 7 o'clock Friday evening when about ten miles north-northeast from Nausett, Cape Cod, during a fresh westerly wind. The *Trickey* lost her jibboom with all the rigging attached, carried away cutwater and foretop mast, damaged her stern and received other damage. The *Governor* was struck just aft of the main rigging on the port side, and was cut down and sank almost instantly in twelve fathoms of water. The captain and crew succeeded in getting on board the *Trickey*, just as the vessel went down.

The *Trickey* was taken in tow by steam tug *Triton*, from Boston for New York, with barge *Moon Beam* in tow, and arrived at Vineyard Haven, Saturday.

The schooner *Trickey* is leaking, but one pump keeps her free. The *Governor's* mast heads are out of water and the wreck is a dangerous obstruction to navigation. Her crew saved nothing. The schooner *Trickey* was formerly of the Dover Navigation line, but was sold in 1888.

Schooner *R. T. Randlett* arrived in the lower harbor from Baltimore with cargo of coal for Cocheco Mfg. Co.

Sept. 15—The schooner *Jonathan Sawyer* has arrived at Philadelphia, from Rockport, and the schooner Bracewell at Saco.

The schooner *C. H. Trickey* has finished discharging at the Cocheco Mfg. Co's dock and will sail for Portland at once and be hauled up for repairs.

Sept. 29—The schooner *Z. S. Wallingford* arrived at Crisfield, Md.

Oct. 13—The schooner *T. B. Garland* has just started from Vineyard Haven for New York with paving.

Oct. 27—Schooner *Abbie S. Walker* arrived at the Cocheco Mfg. Co. with coal from Philadelphia. Another Scare: It looked like an attempt to burn Converse & Hammond's lumber sheds. John Wesley, who lives on Portland Street, summonded the police last night to investigate what appeared to be an incendiary attempt to burn up Converse & Hammond's store house on the Landing. Wesley discovered a suspicious character hovering around the premises and attempted to frighten him away by discharging a revolver, but the weapon failed to operate. He then called officers Fody Sterling and Assistant Marshall Robinson, and a systematic search was at once inaugurated. The man in the meantime made his escape, but a bottle of oil, matches, and a large ball of waste was found, also a brown dip hat.

After taking precautions against further attempts to set the premises on fire Asst. Marshall Robinson started on his return to the

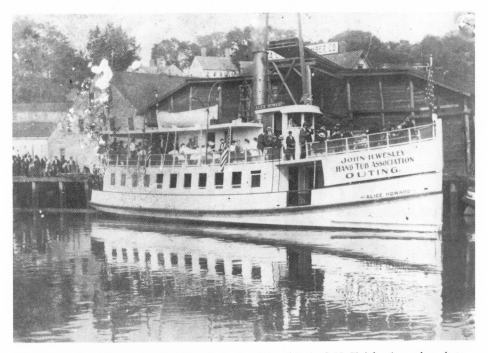

Steamer Alice Howard. *Building in back of the ship is C.H. Trickey's coal pockets. To the left is A. Converse Place's lumberyard. EH*

central part of the city. On the way up Main Street he discovered a drunken man under some steps and took him to the station. The man was bareheaded and his clothes were covered with mud. It was found later that the man had lost a brown dip hat. A warrant will be in readiness for his retention on the charge of attempting to set fire.

The schooner *C. H. Trickey* arrived at C. H. Trickey's & Co. wharf last evening with coal.

Schooner *John Bracewell* at Philadelphia, loading with coal for C. H. Trickey & Co.

Nov. 17—The schooner *Z. S. Wallingford* is at New York.

Schooner *H. G. Hedges* has finished discharging and sailed for New York to return with cargo of coal for C. H. Trickey & Co.

Dec. 1—The schooner *H.T. Hedges* is discharging at C. H. Trickey & Co. wharf today. It is probable that the river business for the present season will be completed with the departure of the schooner *Z. S. Wallingford*, which is now discharging at the Cocheco Mfg. Co. dock.

Dec. 15—The schooner *Fleetwing*, which is well known in these waters, went ashore abreast of coast life saving station. At last accounts the vessel was leaking, her cargo was on fire, and in all probability the vessel and cargo will prove a total loss. The captain and crew reached a place of safety in their own boats.

1894

Jan. 26—The tug *Cocheco* is preparing to lay off for the winter. During the tie up the steamer will have a new boiler put in.

Feb. 2—Schooner *Jonathan Sawyer* arrived at Delaware breakwater from Cieafuga, Cuba and will await orders. The passage was a quick one, the distance being made in seventeen days. The cargo consisted of 3300 bags of sugar.

March 30—The tug *Hamilton A. Mathes* was put in commission and in charge of Captain Drew, went below to tow up a couple of coal vessels.

April 6—The River and Harbor Bill carries the following appropriations for New Hampshire: Cochecho river $15,000; Bellamy river, $7,500, Little Harbor $10,000.

April 27—The schooner *T. B. Garland* was run into while at anchor in Boston Harbor, by a barge in tow of a tug, and had all her headgear carried away, including the bow sprit. She was from Philadelphia bound for Lynn, and will probably be repaired in Boston.

May 4—The factory of D. Foss & Son was shut down for the purpose of putting in a new engine. The present one is too small for the work, and they were obliged to have a larger one as their business is increasing every day. They now employ between sixty and seventy men and are working over time. Men are paid off Saturday afternoon at 5 o'clock, our reporter was present last Saturday afternoon and witnessed the men receiving their pay. It did not take over ten minutes to do this as they receive an envelope with the amount due them enclosed.

May 8—The tug *Piscataqua* went from Portsmouth to Dover Point and towed the barge *York and Berwick* down to the lower harbor. She then took a three-masted schooner and a large lighter to Dover from the lower harbor.

May 18—There was an accident on the steam tug *Cocheco*, as she was near Flagg's wharf some part of the boiler that had been repaired temporarily blew out, so that she was unable to proceed. There is a new boiler being made for her in Boston and she will be towed there today. The steamer tug *Mathes* will take her place until she returns.

The schooner *Z. S. Wallingford* loaded with phosphorus rock arrived at Richmond, Va. from Charleston, S.C. only being seventy-four hours on the passage from dock to dock. The passage was made in extraordinary time and the Dover Navigation Company to which she belongs feel well pleased with the achievement.

D. Foss and Son's factory, Dover Landing. RAW

May 25—The schooner *John Bracewell* will arrive at the dock this afternoon with coal for the Cocheco Mfg. Co.

June 1—The tug boat *Cocheco* is expected to arrive here Monday. She has been in Boston for several months having new boilers put in and other necessary repairs and is now in fine condition.

June 8—The schooner *Bracewell* cleared at West Sullivan, Me. for Philadelphia with paving stones.

June 15—The schooner *Jonathan Sawyer* is discharging coal at Newburyport, and will clear for Sullivan, Maine. where she will leave with paving stones for Boston.

June 29—The schooner *Alice T. Boardman* cleared for Calais, Me. Schooner *F. H. Hedges*, schooner *Veto*, schooner *H. H. Chamberlain* and schooner *C. H. Trickey* are in the lower harbor.

July 6—Schooner *Bracewell* cleared for Sullivan, Me., where she will load with paving stones for Philadelphia.

July 13—Schooner *Mary E. H. G. Dow* has arrived in Boston from Newport News.

Aug. 3—The schooner *J. J. Hanson* has arrived at Philadelphia from Kennebec and loaded with ice.

Aug. 16—The steamer *Iva* towed the gundalow *Alice*, with ninety tons of coal to Exeter.

Tug Piscataqua, *built in Boston 1891; 78 feet long. DLW*

The steamer *Lester L.* went up to Newmarket, having in tow the gundalow *Fanny P.* with ninety tons of coal.

Aug. 17—The Dover Navigation Company schooner *Jonathan Sawyer* is discharging a cargo of stone at Philadelphia.

Schooner *J. J. Hanson* is discharging a cargo of coal from Philadelphia at Boston.

Sept. 21—J. Wesley Clements of Dover Point has sold 7,000,000 bricks to Boston parties and has engaged the schooner *Sadie A. Kimball* to freight them.

Schooner *John Bracewell* and schooner *H. H. Chamberlain* have arrived loaded with coal for Cocheco Mfg. Co.

The schooner *Trickey* has arrived at the lighting place. The schooner *Sophia*, schooner *Godfrey* and schooner *Franconia* have arrived in port with coal for the Cocheco Mfg. Co.

Oct. 5—The schooner *A. E. Stevens* has finished discharging at the Cocheco dock.

Oct. 25—The Wiggin & Stevens Glue Factory on the Gulf road has been started up for the winter's run.

Oct. 26—The schooner *Delaware* came up with a cargo of Franklin coal for C. H. Trickey.

Nov. 2—Six vessels are on the way to this port with cargoes of coal. The schooners *Wallingford* and *Bracewell* of this number are for C. H. Trickey & Co.

Nov. 6—Schooner *C. H. Trickey* arrived in port with cargo of soft coal for C. H. Trickey & Co.

Nov. 23—Schooner *St. Elmo* came up today with coal for C. H. Trickey.

Schooner *Florida* ran up high and dry near Mathes coal wharf, the captain thinking he could work down river without a pilot. She came off at high water and the tug *Cocheco* towed her down river.

Schooner *Franconia* and schooner *Bessie C. Beach* are on the way here with coal for Cocheco Mfg. Co.

Schooner *Benj. T. Briggs* from Perth Amboy and schooner *Lucy* from Philadelphia are on way to this port with cargoes of coal.

A master to appraise the value of wrecked schooner *John Holland* will probably be appointed on December 15. In the meantime, the stockholders of the Dover Navigation Company are not uneasy as the interest upon the value of the vessel is going on all the time and at a higher rate percent than can ordinarily be invested elsewhere.

Dec. 7—The work of dredging out the rock in the Cochecho Narrows is nearly completed by Captain Symonds's fleet.

Dec. 14—Schooner *C. H. Trickey* was towed down river today.

Schooner *A. H. Stevens* has arrived at the mouth of the river and will wait a better tide to come in.

Schooner *Lucy* was towed from this port to Portsmouth where she is to be hauled up for the winter.

The Schooner *C. R. Flint* came upriver in tow of the tug *Cocheco* and was anchored at the lightering place.

The dredging fleet has finished work in the Cochecho and has been towed out of the river.

Dover Landing about 1895 with Young's Storehouse, Foss mill, Converse &
Hammond, Dover Gas Light Company, and C.H. Trickey and Company. OBHS

1895

Jan. 4—Captain B. O. Reynolds is loading his schooner, the
Jonathan Sawyer, with coal at Philadelphia for the West India
Islands; he will load with sugar for the return voyage.

Jan. 18—B. Frank Nealley has received a check for $39,000
which will be divided among the stockholders of the sunken schooner
John Holland.

March 8—The tug *Cocheco* is to be hauled out at Portsmouth to
receive a coat of paint.

The Dover Navigation Company will start their Brick Barges next
week; E. S. Gage of Dover Point will begin to ship to Boston at once.

April 6—Navigation will soon be open to this port and there
are now three schooners, *E. W. Perry*, schooner *Katie G. Roberson* and
schooner *Marcus Edwards* on their way here with coal for the Cocheco
Mfg. Co.

C. H. Trickey Co. will also have cargoes come in very soon.

April 12—Captain B. O. Reynolds of schooner *Jonathan
Sawyer* was in town over night. His vessel is now in Portsmouth
discharging a cargo of sewer pipe for Manchester.

The Alice Howard *from Portsmouth, ca. 1892. The building is D. Foss & Son's Mill where blinds, wooden boxes, stairposts, bobbins, and spools were manufactured.*

Schooner *Sadie A. Kimball* is in port with lime for Converse & Hammond.

The steam tug *Iva* is undergoing repairs and receiving a coat of paint, and will soon begin operations upon the river.

Schooner *Katie G. Roberson*, with soft coal for the Cocheco Mfg. Co., arrived at the lightering place.

April 19—The barque *W. W. Crapo*, Captain Hardy, has arrived at Iquique, Peru with all well on board.

Lobsters are dropping in price but are at present seventeen cents per pound.

May 3—The schooner *Jennie E. Simmons* has discharged her coal at C. H. Trickey's wharf.

The tug boat *H. A. Mathes* has been charted by Dover parties to take them outside next Sunday.

The schooner *Samuel Caster, Jr.* of Boston was placed on the Marine Railway at Portland to have a bad hole in her bottom repaired. The damage was sustained by striking a rock while being towed up the river to this Port. Several vessels have met with similar accidents during the past few years at the same place.

Dover Landing 1895; coal tower, schooner Silver Spray (77 feet long), and St. John's Methodist Church in the background. JPA

June 21—Schooner *Emily S. Baymore*, with a cargo of 336 tons of coal for Cocheco Mfg. Co., also schooner *R. S. Corson* with 396 tons, both from Philadelphia.

June 28—Schooner *R. T. Randlett* with coal for Cocheco Mfg. Co. arrived Thursday, left Saturday. Schooner *Sophia Godfrey* on her way here with coal for Cocheco Mfg. Co. from Philadelphia.

July 5—Schooner *C. H. Trickey* is loading at New York with coal for this city.

Another vessel which leaves today is the schooner *Abbie S. Walker* of Vinal Haven, Me. She is a three-masted schooner. Her register is 181 tons and she loaded with coal at Philadelphia for C. H. Trickey & Co. She unloaded and on leaving the harbor here will load stone for Philadelphia. The *Abbie Walker* made a trip here last year and is likely to make a second visit to Dover.

July 12—News has been received from Captain W. W. Hardy that his ship was burned just as they were sailing out of port, and that no lives were lost. The ship and cargo were a total loss.

Schooner *John Bracewell* and schooner *Jennie Simmons* arrived from Philadelphia with coal for Cocheco Mfg. Co.

July 19—Schooner *Marcus Edwards* was tugged up river by tug *Cocheco* to the Cocheco dock with coal.

Schooner *Annie A. Booth* arrived at the lightering place last evening.

The *Cocheco* tugged schooner *Ned P. Walker* and schooner *Sophia Godfrey* down the river and out to sea.

July 21—Schooner *Jonathan Sawyer* is at Saco loading with stone for Delaware Breakwater.

July 26—Dredging is being steadily carried on in the lower river.

The horse drawing Joe Darvill's baker cart ran away on the Landing this morning and food for the hungry was scattered in every direction.

Aug. 2—Of the Dover Navigation Company's ships: The *J. J. Hanson* is on the Kennebec loading ice for the south, and the schooner *Bracewell* is sailing from Sullivan, Me. with stone for New York City.

Aug. 23—C. H. Trickey & Co. have received about 5000 tons of coal this far this year. As much more will be stored away for winter use.

Aug. 30—The schooner *Anna M. Lamson* of Philadelphia has finished unloading and will be towed down the Piscataqua as soon as the tug *Cocheco* arrives from Portsmouth. She is a three-masted schooner and registers 300 tons loaded. She arrived with about 500 tons of coal for the Cocheco Mfg. Co. From here she will go to Portland where she will load with ice for Wilmington, Delaware. The vessel has not been here for two years; she is engaged in the coast carrying trade, and is one of the largest schooners that have visited this port.

Sept. 13—The schooner *James L. Molloy* is in Portsmouth Harbor with coal for Dover Gas Company.

Schooner *Baymore* and schooner *Lucy* have reported with coal for the Cocheco Mfg. Co.

Sept. 27—The tug *Cocheco* brought two three-masted schooners to this city and took two down in the afternoon.

Nov. 1—There are no vessels in port and they are so scarce that none are on the way, although Dover companies are still in need of coal which must come by water.

The schooner *Lilly* sinks: The *Lilly*, the brick schooner, Captain Thomas Coleman of 34 Atkinson Street, was run into by a fishing vessel in Long Sound, Boston Harbor, last night at about one o'clock and sank in less than three minutes. The crew of four men and the captain barely had time to escape but did so in the ship's boat, leaving the schooner and its cargo of brick in the bottom of the sea. Not a thing outside the clothing they had on was saved in the few minutes allowed them to escape.

The *Lilly* was loaded with brick from one of the Dover Point yards, which cargo it was carrying to Boston when the collision occurred. There was no insurance on the vessel, so the loss will be a great one to Captain Coleman. He came home this morning and was inquired for this afternoon but did not care to talk.

Captain Thomas C. Coleman tells the story of his vessel's destruction and gave more facts about the sinking of the *Lilly* in Broad Sound near Long Island in Boston Harbor.

The *Lilly* was loaded with 50,000 bricks worth $150 from Charles Morang's yard at Dover Point and cleared Portsmouth bridge at 1 o'clock Wednesday afternoon bound for Boston where the cargo was to be delivered to Henry Craft's Sons of Albany Street who were in a hurry for the brick. John Ham and George Young of Dover Neck and Wm. Parker of Kittery with Captain Coleman made up the crew.

They had a good trip and were going head on to the wind which was north west by north Thursday at 1 o'clock when the red light of a fishing schooner was seen by Captain Coleman who was then guiding his ship up Broad Sound at a place about half a mile from Deer Island Point. After porting his wheel as it drew near he luffed up expecting the captain of the other schooner would keep to the right according to the law among seamen, but instead, with sails spread and coming down with the wind, he put his wheel to the starboard and ran into the *Lilly*, driving the bow sprit right through the forecastle making a big gap. Captain Coleman ran forward and looking down an open hatchway saw the water coming in and then he knew the ship was sinking.

Ham and Young, who were asleep, were aroused by the shock and at the captain's order they lowered the boat getting it loose just as the schooner went under and entirely out of sight. The captain had time to get some money from the cabin but nothing else.

The other schooner was the *William Cross*, ninety tons burden, of Gloucester, in command of a Dutchman, managed to get clear and waiting round took Captain Coleman on board where he stayed for fifteen minutes. The Dutchman said Captain Coleman should have gone to the starboard but as that was contrary to law Captain Coleman failed to see why he should have done so and on this ground he has a good case against the Dutchman.

Leaving the schooner *William Cross*, he and his three mates, in a choppy sea, against the wind rowed up to Boston, a distance of eight and one-half miles in three hours and were nearly exhausted by the effort. Reporting at the Custom House he was given a blank and told to report the loss at the Portsmouth Custom House within five days, as the law reads, or pay a penalty of $100.

Captain Coleman did not own a share in the *Lilly*. He says that the case against the other boat is good and that one of the *Lilly* owners, Thomas Rider of Portsmouth, a sea lawyer, may bring suit for the owners.

This is his first serious accident in forty years of service and his men certainly had a narrow escape.

Nov. 8—The schooner *Jonathan Sawyer*, Captain B. O. Reynolds, has cleared west Sullivan, Me. with stone for Philadelphia. Captain Reynolds will make a southern trip this winter.

Dec. 20—Schooner *C. R. Flint,* which has been discharging coal at C. H. Trickey Co., was towed out to sea today by the tug *Cocheco.*

Dec. 27—Schooner *Lizzie B. Small* arrived from New York loaded with coal for C. H. Trickey and Co.

1896

Jan. 3—The tug *Piscataqua* has been hauled up for a month for lack of work. The tug *Cocheco* and tug *Clara Bateman* are also out of commission, and the tug *Howell* is the only boat at present in active service on the Piscataqua river.

Mar. 3—*Dover Daily Republican*—Dover's Black Day: A Second Johnstown Unparalled Disaster by Flood and Flame.

$300,000 damage done in ten hours. Business men and corporations receive a terrible set back.

Sunday, March 1, and Monday, March 2, will go down in history as Dover's black days. The devastation wrought by flood and fire inside of twelve hours is unparalleled. The power of an irresistible mass of water was never more fully realized by our citizens than at this time, when the city's debt has been swelled by over a hundred thousand dollars, some of our business men almost financially ruined by losses which no insurance covers, to say nothing of the losses small in comparison that poor and even well off persons who live on the river's bank have suffered.

The city has lost three bridges: the Central avenue, $25,000, the lower Washington street bridge, $6,000, and Watson's $2,000.

Three stores and offices above were torn away from Bracewell block.

From fire the firm of Converse and Hammond will lose $10,000 worth of lumber, lime, etc., and one of their own store houses. All this is fully covered by insurance, the only loss being in the suspension of business.

Crowds thronged the west sidewalk during the afternoon all anxious to see such an unusual thing. At four o'clock all seemed well. The water was high but the bridge appeared safe.

However City Marshall Fogerty was on hand with Stevens and Young ready for an emergency. Along about 4:30 the bridge began to sink. The ice in immense cakes over a foot thick were dashed against the bridge by the angry torrent and at 4:55 two spans, thirty feet or more wide, went down.

The crowd was scarcely off when the woodwork went, the water roared louder than ever, the ice pounded with irresistible force, iron girders snapped like twigs, the woodwork groaned; the immense jam of ice passed through, forcing up those two spans which fell when once it had passed.

At about 7:30 the little story and a half block owned by R.J. Shaw and occupied by a Greek fruit and candy vendor, who has a stock worth about $300, began to wobble and piece by piece dropped into the river until it was gone. This gave a passage for the ice which packed in closer and closer and did fatal work on the Bracewell block piers. At exactly eight o'clock the greatest of all the disasters of the night began. Fred H. Foss's store and the story above it commenced to sink and Roberts Bros. and Flynn's stores also. Then amid the crash of breaking glass and yielding timbers the first story, including these three stores, sank; in an instant followed the second stories. The building fell on the network of wires which fell singing, the poles breaking like pipe stems. Nothing like it was ever seen before. The number of feet going over the dam will give you but little idea of the height of the water. Let us walk up First Street. The water here at its highest was within six inches of the level of the street and it was up to the first floors of the brick part of Bracewell block.

The Cocheco Mfg. Co. will be set back $100,000 or more, as near as can be estimated. Their machine shops have been flooded,

Dover's Black Day, March 1, 1896. The Bracewell Block toppled into the Cochecho River at the Central Avenue bridge. Railroad tracks belong to the Dover, Somersworth and Rochester Street Railway. DPL

their engine rooms likewise, a loss of chemicals and dyes in the Print Works is entailed that cannot be estimated for many days, two of their bridges have gone so that no coal can be carried by rail to the engine rooms, and no steam be given the printery until the new steam pipe is put across the Cochecho from No. 1 mill.

At four o'clock seventy inches of water was pouring over the dam, and at its height from midnight to three o'clock this morning ten feet of water was continually going over the flush boards.

The coal bridge from the shore to the No. 1 mill was washed away, or at least one span during the early part of the night.

The sight from the mill yard bridge just below the dam, was magnificent, as witnessed by the writer while standing there about 5:30 o'clock Sunday evening. The water was up nearly to the bottom of lower boards of the railing, that is on top of the stone wall on the north side above the dam, and must have been about eight feet deep on top of the dam. The volume of water was so great that it ran almost smoothly over the falls in one vast sheet; the ledge beneath it could only manifest itself when huge cakes of ice came over the dam and plunged into the gulf below. Ice, timber and debris of every sort came constantly over the dam. The lower Washington St. bridge was swept away at 10:30 after the bridge above it had washed down the river. It is doubtful if this bridge will be rebuilt; certainly not at present.

Nine carloads of lumber of one kind or another belonging to Converse and Hammond floated away from the upper and glue house wharfs, and the rest that had been removed to a place secure from the rushing waters was burned. The company is fairly well supplied, having $25,000 worth of all kinds in its other storehouses.

The mills have not been running since the crisis. Mills 2 and 3 will start as soon as the water subsides and the belts which were taken off for preservation can be replaced. Washington Street bridge is a complete wreck; the span on the easterly side remains but it is completely broken down and good for nothing to repair; only a few scraps of the other spans remain in sight; the middle piers of stone are also badly broken.

Large cakes of ice were landed along the Cocheco Company railroad track that leads from the coal shed to No. 1 mill; some large cakes were left crushing stone on the city farm.

John W. Place, who lives in the house on the city farm had a lively time of it as the flood nearly surrounded his house and completely flooded the cellar.

C.H. Trickey & Co., dealers in coal and wood, have moved into the treasurer's office in the Court House.

There were fires in both the Printery and No. 1 mill Sunday night caused by lime-heated water. The Company's firemen handled them admirably without the city's aid. The damage was considerable.

Fire Adds Terror

Lumber, Lime and Cement Destroyed.

Converse & Hammond Loses $10,000 Worth of Lumber.

Terrible Conflagration in the Swollen River.

The Brave Firemen Do Telling Work.

In addition to all the wreckage made by water was fire at midnight, Sunday in Converse and Hammond's lumber yard. Water was the cause of the fire too. 1,500 barrels of lime could not be removed to a dry place before the river had swollen and enveloped them. Then the chemical combination of lime and water started a fire which was discovered by Mr. Spurling.

The building in which the fire started had been built about five years ago and was 180 X 35 feet and was used for storing dried lumber, some of the best that the company has for sale. The yard around this building was flooded waist deep and the firemen soon found that they could neither handle themselves nor the hose in so much water. The only thing that could be done was to save the adjacent buildings. In spite of careful work the old Trickey stable, containing about $2,000 of new and old machinery and belonging to the Cocheco Mfg. Co. was destroyed, but the office stable, and other storehouse of Converse & Hammond were saved.

It is estimated the loss of this fire is nearly $15,000 dollars to Converse and Hammond, building, lumber, cement, lime, etc., about $8,000; to the Cocheco Mfg. Co., building and machinery in it $6,000; to John Wesley, building $5,000.

King Fernald lost twenty-five cords of wood piled near the river.

March 6—Converse & Hammond have received word from the Rye Beach Life Saving Station that they have over a car load of lumber that they have saved for them.

March 13—Converse & Hammond have recovered about three-quarters of the lumber that was washed down the river from yards by going along the shore and identifying it.

Everyday come stories of what has been found at this point or that down river, but the queerest of any is one from Newcastle that they found one of the hammered rocks with a hole through it, being a part of one of the piers of the Bracewell Building. The rock weighing about 700 pounds, has been taken to a man's front yard there, and will be kept as a relic.

March 20—One half the bridge from No. 1 mill to the city farm which was used to draw coal over from the Cocheco Company's sheds went away and lodged about the foundation of the site of the lower Washington street bridge.

Meanwhile the Cocheco Mfg. Co. had to depend upon teaming for the coal supply. The teams take it from their shed up round the Soap House through Payne street and Washington Street to the boiler house on Landing. A part of the lower Washington St. bridge is there yet, but the greater portion is a quarter of a mile below the Glue Works in the middle of the channel, where it is in the way of vessels coming up the river.

Those who have been out on this piece of the bridge say it is all whole and will be all right to set in place as soon as the center pier in the river is set up.

Captain Drew, who is to have charge of the tug *H.A. Mathes* on this river, has seen it and said that with one of the Piscataqua Navigation Co. hoisting barges he could take the bridge from its present place and bring it up river without much trouble.

May 8—The Cochecho river channel is filled with sand washed down by the flood and traffic is blocked.

May 22—The schooner *J.S. Colwell* is at Converse & Hammond's dock with a cargo of spruce lumber from Nova Scotia.

Schooner *Franconia* which has been discharging coal at the Trickey wharf went to sea.

July 17—Blasting is now going on in the mill yard in the process of reinforcing the wall on the north side against which the new dam will rest.

July 24—The schooner *Estella* was towed down from this city by the tug *Iva* and lay at the draw pier ready to proceed to Boston.

July 31—The freighting business at the present time is anything but profitable. Coal freights are unusually low; vessels have been chartered at Philadelphia the past week to carry coal from that port to Portland and Bangor at fifty cents a ton with seven cents a ton out for trimming and five cents a ton out for towage, making poor business.

Aug. 7—The friends of Captain Washington W. Hardy of this city will be pleased to know of the arrival of his vessel, the barque *Fred P. Litchfield*, at Melbourne, Australia. Captain Hardy sailed from New York on the eleventh of April and arrived at Melbourne Aug. 2.

Dec. 1—Schooner *Lizzie D. Small* and schooner *Catalina* arrived with coal at Trickey's dock.

The glory days of Dover as an inland port were at an end. No coal arrived by schooner for the Cocheco Manufacturing Company after the flood of March 1896; C.H. Trickey had only five schooners with coal in 1897; Converse & Hammond had only three deliver lumber and United Gas and Electric had just three schooners come up river with coal in 1897. A few more schooners came to the port of Dover, but by the turn of the century, the shipping industry here was essentially finished.

In 1890 Alonzo Quint prophetically wrote: Only fifty years ago we could look out the window of the schoolhouse on the hill and see little packets with their lateen rig come lazily up on the tide. It was less than fifty years ago when we saw the first locomotive halt westward of the uncut arch. Old mills, fifty years ago, had not been superseded and water power alone was used. The old nail factory was in its glory. Shipping into the port of Dover will be a thing of the past by the time the next fifteen years are over.

Specifications of Vessels Calling at the Port of Dover
1830-1896

The following list is compiled from *Merchant Sailing Vessels of the United States, Bureau of Navigation, 1830-1900*. These volumes are in the collection of the Portsmouth Athenaeum, Portsmouth, New Hampshire, and the Old Berwick Historical Society, South Berwick, Maine. Many of the vessels listed made numerous calls to Dover. Vessels mentioned in the text which did not call in Dover are marked with an asterisk (*).

Rig	Name of Vessel	Length	Breadth	Depth	When Built	Home Port
Sch.	A. Benton					
Sch.	A. E. Stevens (Annie)	116.0	28.6	8.7	1869	
Sch.	A.H. Hulbout*	126.0	30.0	10.0	1871	Gloucester, MA
Sch.	Abbie Bursley	125.0	29.0	9.0	1869	Camden, ME
Sch.	Abbie H. Green	128.0	30.8	9.4	1880	
Sch.	Abbie S. Walker	103.7	28.7	8.5	1883	Jonesboro, ME
Sch.	Abel W. Parker	116.1	32.2	7.9	1873	
Sch.	Abner Parker					
St.shp.	Acushnet*	130.5	26.8	8.5	1859	Duxbury, MA
Sch.	Addie	75.2	23.3	7.1	1867	Gouldsboro, ME
Sch.	Adeli (bricks)	51.5	16.0	4.3	1874	Dover, NH
Sch.	Agnes Chamberlain					
Sch.	Alice T. Boardman	96.0	27.0	7.0	1873	Calais, ME
Sch.	Alnomack					
Sch.	Amelia P. Schmidt	128.9	32.2	8.9	1883	
Sch.	Ammie A. Booth	113.8	29.9	9.0	1874	Port Jefferson, DE
St.s.	Ann (Tug)	63.2	13.4	5.9	1863	Dover, NH
Sch.	Anna M. Lamson					

Abbreviations:

Sch. - Schooner; Bk. - Barque; St.shp. - Steamship; St.s - Steamer, screw; St.p. - Steamer, sidewheel; Lgtr. - Lighter; St.Y. - Yacht; Slp - Sloop.

Sch.	Annie V. Lawton					
St.p.	Appledore	87.5	20.5	2.5	1869	Portsmouth, NH
Sch.	Arcola	77.0	21.8	6.8	1867	Bath, ME
Sch.	Arthur A. Hall					
Sch.	Aurora	61.5	21.5	4.2	1868	
Sch.	B. Frank Nealley (D. N. Co.)	123.6	30.2	8.8	1880	Dover, NH
Sch.	B. W. Pierce					
Slp.	Ben Butler				1872	
Sch.	Benj. T. Briggs	92.0	28.0	8.0	1870	Milton, DE
Sch.	Bertha Louise	115.5	28.3	6.7	1890	Boston, MA
Sch.	Bessie C. Beach	128.0	30.0	14.0	1880	New Haven, CT
Sch.	Bison					
Sch.	Boxer	70.0	22.2	6.6	1856	
Sch.	C. R. Flint	130.3	30.2	8.3	1871	New York, NY
Sch.	Casco	61.7	16.7	4.4	1868	Bath, ME
Sch.	Catalina	65.6	20.5	7.3	1857	Wells, ME
Sch.	Ceres	55.3	24.0	6.0	1855	Dover, NH
Sch.	Charles H. Trickey (D. N. Co.)	120.5	32.2	8.1	1878	Dover, NH
Sch.	Charles Henry	66.9	20.3	7.2	1840	Dover, NH
Sch.	Charlestown	76.3	22.8	6.5	1853	
Sch.	Chas. L. Davenport	190.9	38.2	18.8	1890	Thomaston, ME
Sch.	Chilion (bricks)	74.1	22.0	6.9	1869	Dover, NH
Sch.	City of Ellsworth	74.8	23.3	6.7	1875	Ellsworth, ME
Sch.	City of Green Bay	146.0	26.6	11.6	1872	Greed Bay, WI
St.p.	City of Haverhill	141.5	24.0	4.0	1880	Haverhill, MA
Sch.	Clara B. Kennard (bricks)	77.3	25.2	6.3	1886	Dover, NH
St.s.	Clara Bateman*	65.8	16.9	7.0	1863	Portsmouth, NH
Sch.	Clare Rankin	95.1	27.0		1867	
St.shp.	Clipper	90.0	26.0	5.0	1876	
Sch.	Cocheco (bricks)	61.5	20.3	6.8	1839	Dover, NH
St.s.	Cocheco (Tug)	77.0	18.2	8.1	1887	Dover, NH
Sch.	Cora L. Kennard					

Sch.	Cottingham, (John C.)	111.0	28.5	8.8	1872	
Sch.	Crosby	26.0	1.0	4.0	1873	
Sch.	Cyrpus	83.5	24.3	8.9	1846	St. George, ME
Sch.	D. K. Ham	75.5	25.1	5.6	870	Boston, MA
Sch.	D.L. Sturgis	90.0	25.0	7.6	1850	Bath, ME
Sch.	Dauntless	53.6	17.8	3.8	1873	Georgetown, MA
Sch.	Delaware	63.0	20.0	6.0	1850	Thomaston, ME
Sch.	Delia	44.4	14.7	4.0		Gloucester, MA
St.s.	Diana (Tug)	39.9	10.5	4.5	1892	New York, NY
Sch.	Dick Williams	105.8	26.8	8.9	1866	
St.s.	Dione (Tug)	45.5	9.0	2.7	1880	
Sch.	Dover Packet	54.8	18.7	6.7	1825	Dover, NH
Lgtr.	Dover (87 tons)				1891	
Lgtr.	Durham (87 tons)				1891	
Sch.	E. F. Gandy					
Sch.	E. P. Kimball					
Sch.	E. W. Perry (Edward)	122.0	27.4	9.0	1880	
Sch.	Eliza A. Anderson	106.0	26.4	7.0	1869	
Sch.	Ella B. Kimball	111.6	29.3	8.3	1890	Bath, ME
Sch.	Emily A. Staples	79.2	26.0	6.2	1872	
Sch.	Emily S. Baymore	124.0	27.0	9.0	1884	
Sch.	Emma B. Shaw	110.5	29.2	8.5	1867	
Sch.	Empress	88.2	26.4	7.8	1877	Bangor, ME
Sch.	Empress	74.0	24.0	6.8	1856	Penobscot, ME
Sch.	Estella	66.6	19.8	5.7	1872	Portsmouth, NH
Sch.	Eva D. Rose	87.0	23.6	7.3	1880	Philadelphia, PA
Sch.	F. H. Hedges					
St.p.	Fairy	42.5	9.7	4.3	1869	
Sch.	Fannie & Edith	87.5	25.1	7.1	1871	Belfast, ME
St.p.	Favorite	58.0	13.2	6.0		
Sch.	Florida	77.9	28.8	7.5	1829	Brooksville, ME
Sch.	Fleetwing	104.9	23.9	9.3	1865	
Sch.	Fostina	137.0	31.0	11.0	1879	
Sch.	Franconia	92.0	25.5	8.3	1862	

Sch.	Frank McDonnell	123.0	29.6	9.8	1879	Philadelphia, PA
Bk.	Fred P. Litchfield* (Capt. W.W. Hardy of Dover, NH)	177.5	36.1	22.3	1876	
Sch.	Frisbe					
Lgtr.	G. W. Avery (86 tons)				1891	Boston, MA
St.s.	George A. Smart	40.0	10.0	5.0	1889	Dover, NH
Sch.	George Edwards	67.3	20.6	3.9	1871	
Sch.	George W. Raitt (bricks)	79.8	22.0	5.0	1871	Dover, NH
Sch.	Godfrey					
Sch.	Golden Rule	62.0	18.0	6.0	1862	Kennebuck, ME
Sch.	Gov. Ames*	245.6	49.6	21.2	1883	Providence, RI
Sch.	Governor*	86.3	25.0	8.2	1851	Castine, ME
Sch.	Granite State*	251.0	40.0	30.0	1877	
Sch.	Granville	59.2	16.9	7.2	1834	Camden, ME
Sch.	Greyhound	52.0	16.6	5.0	1855	North Haven, CT
Sch.	H. E. Russell					
Sch.	H. H. Chamberlain					
Sch.	H. M. Reed					
Sch.	H. Prescott (bricks)	140.0	34.0	11.6	1882	Bath, ME
Sch.	H. T. Hedges	104.7	28.1	8.1	1868	
St.s.	Hamilton A. Mathes (Tug)	62.0	17.8	7.3	1892	Dover, NH
Sch.	Haratio* (Capt. Hardy of Dover, NH)	115.7	28.6	17.5	1877	Port Jefferson, NY
Sch.	Harry Percy	79.7	22.8	6.5	1869	Bath, ME
Sch.	Hattie A. Lewis (bricks)	62.0	21.8	6.5	1864	Dover, NH
Sch.	Hattie J. Averill	52.0	18.0	5.0	1863	Cohasset, MA
Sch.	Helen	104.2	28.9	9.1	1874	Harrington, ME
St.s.	Howell (Tug)	79.9	20.1	7.9	1873	Bangor, ME
Sch.	Ida Ann	42.0	18.0	4.0		
Sch.	Independence	69.4	20.1	4.9	1853	Machias, ME

Sch.	Index	116.5	31.0	8.3	1870	
Sch.	Iola					
Sch.	Ira D. Sturgis	118.3	30.0	8.5	1873	
Sch.	Ira E. Wright	69.5	19.4	7.9	1882	Rockland, ME
Sch.	Ira H. Sturgis					
St.s.	Iva (Tug)	52.3	14.0	6.2	189	Portsmouth, NH
Sch.	Iva Bell	88.3	25.3	7.8	1870	Bristol, ME
Sch.	Iva May					
Sch.	J. A. Warr					
Sch.	J. Chester Wood (D. N. Co.)	68.6	23.0	6.5	1881	Dover, NH
Sch.	J. D. Ingraham	105.0	25.0	7.0	1865	
Sch.	J. Frank Seavey (D. N. Co.)	144.0	33.9	10.2	1880	Dover, NH
Sch.	J. G. Morse Jr.	92.0	26.4	7.6	1889	
Sch.	J. J. Little	110.0	23.0	8.0	1866	Philadelphia, PA
Sch.	J. M. Harlow	117.0	32.6	9.1	1874	New York, NY
Sch.	J. M. Kennedy	87.5	25.0	7.0	1862	
Sch.	J. Phelps					
Sch.	J. S. Colwell					
Sch.	J. S. Davis					
Sch.	James Henry	67.0	20.6	8.5	1847	Rockland, ME
Sch.	James L. Maloy	102.3	28.5	7.9	1874	Philadelphia, PA
Sch.	James S. Henry	70.0	20.2	7.4	1847	Friendship, ME
St.s.	James Sampson	52.0	14.0	4.8	1878	Dover, NH
St.shp.	Jeannette	80.5	19.6	5.4	1894	Calais, ME
Sch.	Jennie Simmons	114.5	29.6	9.1		
Sch.	Joel F. Sheppard*	155.0	35.2	13.5	1889	Boston, MA
Sch.	John Bracewell (D. N. Co.)	113.6	29.2	9.0	1878	Dover, NH
St.p.	John Brooks*	239.8	34.4	10.8	1859	Boston, MA
Sch.	John Holland* (D. N. Co.)	195.2	40.3	17.8	1980	Dover, NH
Sch.	John J. Hanson* (D. N. Co.)	199.0	34.4	17.5	1885	Dover, NH

Sch.	John Paul*	137.4	32.7	12.3	1891	
Sch.	Jonathan Sawyer (D. N. Co.)	140.0	33.3	10.0	1886	Dover, NH
Sch.	Julia A. Berkele	105.5	25.7	7.9	1886	Farehaven, CT
Sch.	Kate E. Rich	113.3	30.0	9.8	1865	
Sch.	Katie G. Robinson	116.4	29.6	9.3	1873	
Sch.	King Philip	72.0	19.1	7.9	1845	Lubec, ME
Lgtr.	Kittery (86 tons)				1891	
Sch.	Laura E. Roberson					
St.s.	Lester L.	40.5	12.1	4.3	1894	Portsmouth, NH
Sch.	Lillian	56.0	18.0	6.0	1875	Boston, MA
Sch.	Lillie (bricks)	71.3	21.5	5.6	1875	Wells, ME
St.p.	Lincoln* (Tug)	96.3	26.2	7.2	1885	Portsmouth, NH
Sch.	Little J.	71.3	24.5	5.6	1875	Wells, ME
Sch.	Lizzie B. Small	109.3	27.2	8.2	1866	
Sch.	Lizzie J. Call	110.9	30.4	8.2	1886	Portsmouth, NH
Sch.	Louella	32.8	11.0	5.4	1887	Providence, RI
Sch.	Lucy L.	87.0	27.0	9.0	1864	Eastport, ME
Sch.	Lucy Wentworth	78.0	24.1	6.7	1872	Calais, ME
Sch.	Luella	69.0	23.0	7.9	1848	Orrington, ME
St.s.	Luke Hoyt	45.3	11.3	4.6	1863	Boston, ME
Sch.	M. S. Middleton					
Sch.	Mable Hall	95.5	25.6	8.5	1864	
Sch.	Maggie Miller					
Sch.	Maine	105.4	28.0	8.5	1886	
St.shp.	Major	37.3	10.8	3.8	1868	
Sch.	Marcus Edwards	118.0	27.0	9.9	1875	
Sch.	Marion Wentworth	90.0	24.0	7.0	1881	Boston, MA
Sch.	Mary A. Rice	98.0	27.3	6.6	1869	Bucksport, ME
Sch.	Mary A. Stowe					
Sch.	Mary B. Rogers	49.3	23.0	6.3	1875	Arrowsic
Sch.	Mary B. Rogers	79.3	23.9	6.3	1885	Wiscasset, ME
Sch.	Mary Day					
Sch.	Mary E. Crosby	111.3	23.4	8.5	1873	

Sch.	Mary E. H. G. Dow*	203.0	39.9	19.5	1892	
Sch.	Mary E. Whorf	75.0	22.2	7.5		
Sch.	Mary S. Newton					
St.shp.	May Queen	71.4	17	4	1891	Lowell, MA
Sch.	Midnight	27.5	9.5	5.0		Camden, ME
St.y.	Minnie*	57.8	12.2	5.5	1885	
Sch.	Mollie Rhodes	115.3	30.7	9.2	1885	Belfast, ME
St.p.	Moses Taylor*	118.0	21.4	5.5	1859	Philadelphia, PA
St.s.	Mystic (Tug)	50.4	16.5	4.5	1875	Kittery, ME
Sch.	Nathaniel Lank	126.5	33.0	9.3	1883	
Sch.	Ned P. Walker	81.0	24.0	6.0	1881	
Sch.	Nellie E. Gray	79.2	23.4	6.2	1879	Rockland, ME
Sch.	Nellie G. Browne					
St.shp.	Nereus*	228.0	40.0	18.0	1864	New York, NY
Sch.	Nevada	66.0	20.5	7.2	1846	North Haven, CT
Sch.	New Zealand (bricks)	81.8	24.9	8.3	1853	Ellsworth, ME
Sch.	Odell	97.2	26.2	7.5	1873	
Sch.	Oliver	78.5	27.1	7.9	1882	
Sch.	Orion	82.6	23.3	7.5	1835	
Sch.	Pennsylvania	89.0	23.0	8.0	1848	
Sch.	Penobscot	135.6	32.4	11.1		
Sch.	Pierce	62.2	19.9	6.7	1839	Dover, NH
St.s.	Piscataqua (Tug)	78.0	20.3	9.6	1891	Portsmouth, NH
Sch.	Planter	75.4	22.1	6.7	1861	
St.shp.	Portland*	98.0	45.5	8.7	1870	
Sch.	R. B. P. Smith					
Sch.	R. Mason	71.0	22.0	6.0	1873	
Sch.	R. S. Corson	104.0	29.0	8.0	1866	Wilmington, DE
Sch.	R. T. Randlett	124.6	32.1	8.7	1892	Wiscasset, ME
Sch.	Republic	99.5	23.5	8.6	1880	New York, NY
Sch.	Rival	82.2	25.6	7.7	1874	
Sch.	Roberson	92.8	27.6	7.3	1869	
Sch.	Rosa Ada					
Sch.	Rough and Ready	69.0	24.4	5.1	1864	

Type	Name					
Sch.	S. J. Watts					
Sch.	Sadie A. Kimball (bricks)	66.0	21.1	6.1	1884	Dover, NH
Sch.	Sallie E. Ludlam	113.7	30.3	9.3	1873	Philadelphia, PA
Sch.	Sallie M. Evans					
St.shp.	Sam Butterfield* (Samuel)	56.7	10.1	3.8	1891	Portsmouth, NH
Sch.	Samuel Caster, Jr.	119.8	29.3	10.0		
Sch.	Samuel L. Russell	79.0	25.0	7.0	1869	
Sch.	Satellite (bricks)	65.0	20.0	5.2	1874	
Sch.	Silver Spray	77.1	23.3	10.0	1872	Thomaston, ME
Sch.	Sophia A.	57.0	17.0	5.0	1852	
Sch.	Sophia Godfray	109.5	29.3	8.3		
Sch.	St. Elmo	85.5	25.3	7.6	1870	Rockland, ME
Sch.	Strafford	88.7	26.3		1795	Dover, NH
Sch.	Sunbeam	82.9	26.0	6.5	1890	
Sch.	Surprise	150.0	22.0	8.0	1871	
Sch.	Susan E. Nash	82.8	24.2	6.2	1868	
Sch.	Susan Stetson	89.2	25.1	8.2	1867	Bucksport, ME
Sch.	T. A. Lambert*	257.0	47.0	22.0		
Sch.	Thomas B. Garland (D. N. Co.)	126.6	32.0	11.4	1881	Dover, NH
St.shp.	Tom Thumb	2.5	4.0		1836	
Sch.	Triton	56.0	25.0	6.7	1875	Boston, MA
Sch.	Triton (bricks)	76.4	25.0	6.7	1869	Dover, NH
Sch.	Triton (bricks)	74.0	22.0	7.0	1875	
Sch.	Veto	72.0	22.0	7.4	1866	
Sch.	Village Bell	50.0	15.8	5.0	1856	
Sch.	W. L. Elkins (William)	121.0	31.0	8.0	1873	
Sch.	War Eagle*	85.0	26.0	8.0	1868	Dover, NH
Sch.	Warren B. Potter	126.0	32.0	8.0	1879	
Sch.	Warren Edwards					
Slp.	Washington	57.7	15.0	4.4	1837	Dover, NH
Sch.	Willard Sauisbury	105.0	27.0	8.0	1855	Milton, DE

Sch.	William Penn	62.5	20.1	6.7	1838	Dover, NH
Sch.	William Thomas	73.6	24.2	7.6	1849	
Sch.	Wilson and Willard	62.7	21.3	5.7	1848	
Sch.	Wm. F. Collins	128.2	30.3	9.1	1882	Boston, MA
Bk.	Wm. W. Crapo* (Capt. W.W. Hardy of Dover, NH)	215.0	41.8	24.0	1880	New Bedford
Sch.	Z. D. Walker					
Sch.	Z. S. Wallingford	33.6	12.5	3.9	1874	Dover, NH
Sch.	Zimri S. Wallingford (D. N. Co.)	127.7	30.3	9.1	1882	Dover, NH

Notes

Introduction

1. Lydia Stevens, "Dover Landingfrom 1792 to 1842," p.150.

Chapter 1

1. Alonzo H. Quint, "History of Dover," Chap. CXI, in *The History of Rockingham and Strafford County, New Hampshire*, pp.758-887. John Scales, *History of Dover, New Hampshire*. George Wadleigh, *Notable Events in the History of Dover, New Hampshire from the First Settlement in 1623 to 1865*.
2. Quint, p.760.
3. Wadleigh, pp.5-6.
4. Mary P. Thompson, *Landmarks in Ancient Dover*, New Hampshire, p.64.
5. Wadleigh, p.12.
6. Ibid., p.26.7. Ibid., p.29.

8. Scales, p.69.
9. Ibid., p.71.
10. Ibid., p.72.
11. Thompson, pp.195-197.
12. Wadleigh, p.154.
13. Ibid., p.173.
14. Quint, p.813.
15. Wadleigh, p.173.
16. Ibid., p.186.

Chapter 2

1. Quint, p.814.
2. Gordon Grimes, "A History of Dover, New Hampshire 1790-1835," p.22.
3. Stevens, p.152.
4. Richard E. Winslow, *The Piscataqua Gundalow*.
5. D. Foster Taylor, "The Piscataqua River Gundalow," Historic American Merchant Marine Survey, (Survey #171, sponsored by the Smithsonian Institution of the U.S. National Museum,

1937), p.12.

6.   Stevens, p.151.

7.   Dover v. Portsmouth Bridge, pp.26-28.

8.   Ibid., p.32.

9.   Ibid., p.33.

10. Ibid., pp.35-60.

11. Wadleigh, p.199.

12. Ibid., p.202.

13. Grimes, p.83.

14. Michael Reade, "Interlinear Almanacks," Diary excerpts in Robert Whitehouse notebooks, Dover Public Library, Dover, New Hampshire, Vol. 7.

15. Stevens, p.150.

16. Quint, p.817.

17. The variant spelling, Cocheco, used here only in reference to the Cocheco Manufacturing Company, is attributed to a clerical misspelling when the firm's incorporation papers were filed in Concord in 1827. The original spelling, Cochecho, is used everywhere else in this work.

18. See Chapter 3, "The Town of Dover v. the Portsmouth Bridge" for a detailed account of this court action.

19. Wadleigh, p.213.

20. Grimes, Vol. 2, Appendix 4.

21. *New Hampshire Republican*, August 22, 1826.

22. Ibid., July 26, 1825.

23. *Strafford Enquirer*, April 22, 1828.

24. Wadleigh, p.229.

25. Reade, February 1831 diary entry.

26. Wadleigh, p.231.

27. Grimes, Vol. 1, p.172.

28. Quint, pp.815-816.

29. Stevens, p.152.

30. Dover v. Portsmouth Bridge, p.21 and p.34.

31. Stevens, p.152.

32. Dover v. Portsmouth Bridge, p.27.

33. Stevens, p.152.

34. Ibid., p.153.

35. Ibid.

36. Reade, diary entries 1835.

37. Dover v. Portsmouth Bridge, p.59.

38. Ibid., p.25.

39. Wadleigh, p.240.

40. Reade, diary entry 1838.

41. Dover v. Portsmouth Bridge, p.21.

42. Ibid., p.25.

43. Ibid., pp.25-26.

44. Ibid., p.34.

45. Ibid., p.26.

46. Quint, p.815.

47. *Dover Enquirer*, September 21, 1865.

48. Ibid., October 26, 1871.

49. See Chapter 5 "The Dover Navigation Company" for a detailed account of this group's activities.

Chapter 3

1.   Dover v. Portsmouth Bridge, p.2.

2.   Ibid.

3.   Ibid., pp.2-3.

4.   Ibid., pp.3-4.

5.   Ibid., p.4.

6.   Ibid., p.6.

7.   Ibid.

8.   Ibid.

9.   Ibid., p.7.
10.   Ibid., p.8.
11.   Ibid., p.9.
12.   Ibid.
13.   Ibid.
14.   Ibid., p.10.
15.   Ibid., p.11.
16.   Ibid..
17.   Ibid..
18.   Ibid., p.12.
19.   Ibid., p.20.
20.   Ibid., pp.20-21
21.   Ibid., p.21.
22.   Ibid., pp.22-23.
23.   Ibid., p.24.
24.   Ibid., pp.25-26.
25.   Ibid., pp.26-29.
26.   Ibid., pp.29-31
27.   Ibid., pp.31-32.
28.   Ibid., pp.32-33.
29.   Ibid., pp.34-35.
30.   Ibid., pp.35-36.
31.   Ibid., pp.36-37.
32.   Ibid., p.40.
33.   Ibid., pp.40-42.
34.   Ibid., p.42.
35.   Ibid., p.43.
36.   Ibid., pp.45-46.
37.   Ibid., pp.53-54.
38.   Ibid., pp.56-57.
39.   Ibid., pp.57-58.
40.   Ibid., pp.59-60.
41.   Ibid., p.70.
42.   Dover v. Portsmouth Bridge, 17 NH 200 (1845), p.207.
43.   Ibid., pp.200-201.
44.   Ibid., p.211.
45.   Ibid.
46.   Ibid., p.234.

Chapter 4

1.   Wadleigh, p.230.

2.   Dover v. Portsmouth Bridge, p.25.
3.   *Boston Herald*, December 17, 1853.
4.   *Dover Enquirer*, February 4, 1869.
5.   George Thom (1819-1891), Brigadier General, U.S. Army, and Chief Topographic Engineer for coast defense construction and harbor improvements in New England ca. 1865-1883.
6.   *Dover Enquirer*, August 4, 1870.
7.   Ibid., January 19, 1871.
8.   Ibid., March 2, 1871.
9.   Ibid., June 29, 1871.
10.   Duelline was an extremely volatile nitro-cellulose explosive, a forerunner of the more powerful dynamite, that was so sensitive it had to be mixed just before loading. It could not be transported safely and was taken off the market about 1890.
11.   *Dover Enquirer*, July 13, 1871.
12.   Ibid., July 27, 1871.
13.   Ibid., September 14, 1871.
14.   Ibid., September 21, 1871.
15.   Ibid., October 19, 1871.
16.   Ibid., December 21, 1871.
17.   Ibid.
18.   Ibid., April 18, 1872.
19.   Ibid., May 22, 1873.
20.   Ibid., July 17, 1873.
21.   Ibid., September 4, 1873.
22.   Ibid., October 9, 1873.
23.   Ibid., October 1, 1874.
24.   Ibid., August 26, 1875.
25.   Ibid., September 2, 1875.

26. Ibid., September 30, 1875.
27. Ibid., May 18, 1876.
28. Ibid., July 20, 1876.
29. Ibid., August 17, 1876.
30. Ibid., May 3, 1877.
31. Ibid., May 17, 1877.
32. Ibid., July 12, 1877.
33. Ibid., August 16, 1877.
34. Ibid., August 23, 1877.
35. Ibid.
36. Ibid., November 15, 1877.
37. See Chapter 5.
38. *Dover Enquirer,* July 18, 1878.
39. Ibid., August 18, 1881.
40. *Dover Daily Republican,* April 1883.
41. *Dover Enquirer*, July 19, 1883.
42. Ibid., August 16, 1883.
43. Ibid., May 29, 1885.
44. Ibid., October 19, 1888.
45. Ibid., December 27, 1889.
46. Ibid., June 6, 1890.
47. Ibid., July 27, 1894.
48. *Dover Daily Republican,* March 3, 1896.

Chapter 5

1. *Dover Enquirer*, December 26, 1884.
2. Ibid., January 29, 1886.
3. Ibid., January 25, 1890.
4. Ibid., January 29, 1892.
5. Ibid., February 8, 1895.
6. A.E.G. Nye, *Dover, New Hampshire: Its History and Industries*, p.31.
7. *Leading Business Men of Dover, Rochester, Farmington, Great Falls and Berwick,* p.19.

8. B. Frank Nealley, *Report of the Schooner John Bracewell.*
9. *Dover Enquirer,* March 7, 1878.
10. Ibid., June 6, 1878.
11. Ibid.
12. Ibid., July 18, 1878.
13. Ibid., October 23, 1879.
14. Ibid., December 30, 1880.
15. Ibid., September 1, 1881.
16. Ibid., March 10, 1893.
17. Ibid., November 20, 1888.
18. Ibid., March 29, 1889.
19. Ibid., April 24, 1879.
20. Ibid., May 1, 1879.
21. Ibid.
22. Ibid., May 15, 1879.
23. Ibid., June 5, 1879.
24. Ibid., August 26, 1880.
25. Ibid., August 20, 1886.
26. Ibid., September 1, 1893.
27. Ibid., October 23, 1879.
28. Ibid., December 18, 1879.
29. Ibid., March 25, 1880.
30. *Dover Daily Republican*, April, 1883.
31. *Dover Enquirer*, December 16, 1887.
32. Ibid.
33. Ibid., June 30, 1881.
34. Ibid., December 20, 1889.
35. Ibid.
36. Ibid., January 6, 1881.
37. Ibid., August 18, 1881.
38. Ibid., July 27, 1882.
39. Ibid.
40. Ibid., May 17, 1883.
41. Ibid., June 21, 1883.
42. Ibid., May 18, 1894.
43. Ibid., July 23, 1886.
44. *Dover Daily Republican*, April, 1883.
45. *Dover Enquirer*, April 11,

1884.
46. Ibid., December 7, 1888.
47. Ibid., September 20, 1889.
48. Ibid., May 5, 1893.
49. Ibid., November 14, 1884.
50. Ibid., April 10, 1885.
51. Ibid., January 20, 1886.
52. Ibid., March 28, 1890.
53. Ibid., December 25, 1885.
54. Ibid., April 2, 1886.
55. Ibid., August 20, 1886.
56. Ibid.
57. Ibid., August 27, 1886.
58. See Chapter 6 for an account of the exploits of Capt. Benjamin Reynolds.
59. *Dover Enquirer*, March 27, 1896.
60. Ibid., April 27, 1888.
61. Ibid., December 7, 1888.
62. Ibid.
63. Ibid.
64. Ellen Scales, "Dover Sea Capains"
65. *Dover Enquirer*, April 25, 1890.
66. *Portsmouth Times,* November 7, 1890.
67. *Dover Enquirer*, November 7, 1890.
68. Ibid., January 29, 1892.
69. Ibid., July 28, 1893.
70. Ibid.

Chapter 6

1. Scales, *History of Dover,* p.72.
2. *Dover Enquirer*, May 24, 1842.
3. Bell can be seen at the Woodman Institute, Dover.
4. Sailor's speaking trumpet on display at Woodman Institute, Dover.
5. One of these swords is on display at the Woodman Institute, Dover.
6. It should be noted that at the time the Peirce Brothers, Andrew and Thomas, lived in Dover, a second (unrelated) Andrew Peirce also lived in town. This other Andrew Peirce had a long political career and was elected Dover's first mayor. On March 11, 1856, this Peirce also engaged in navigational pursuits, purchasing several vessels with Captain Robert Rogers and building a 500-ton barque, the *Strafford*, on land which is now Henry Law Park.
7. Model at Woodman Institute, Dover.

Chapter 7

1. *Dover Enquirer*, April 20, 1865.
2. Ibid., April 9, 1868.
3. Ibid., May 14, 1868.
4. Ibid., June 24, 1869.

Bibliography

Adams, John P. *Drowned Valley: The Piscataqua River Basin.*
    Hanover, N.H.: University Press of New England, 1976.
—*The Piscataqua River Gundalow.* Durham, N.H.: By the Author,
    1982.
Brighton, Ray. *Port of Portsmouth Ships and the Cotton Trade 1783 -
    1829.* Portsmouth, N.H.: Portsmouth Marine Society, 1986.
*The City of Dover, New Hampshire: A Series of Comprehensive
    Sketches.* Biddeford, Maine: Historical Pub. Co., 1901.
Dover v. Portsmouth Bridge. Testimony before Commission, July
    1842. Dover, N.H.: John T. Gibbs, Printer, 1842.
Dover vs. Portsmouth Bridge. 17NH200, 1845.
Grimes, Gordon. "A History of Dover, New Hampshire 1790–1835."
    Honors thesis, Dept. of History, Bowdoin College, 1971.
*Leading Business Men of Dover, Rochester Farmington, Great Falls
    and Berwick.* Boston: Mercantile Pub. Co., 1890.
Nealley, B. Frank. *Report of the Schooner John Bracewell.* Dover,
    N.H.: Privately Printed, 1910.
Nye, A.E.G. *Dover, New Hampshire: Its History and Industries.*
    Dover, N.H.: Geo. J. Foster and Co., 1898.
Quint, Alonzo H. "History of Dover." In *The History of Rockingham
    and Strafford County, New Hampshire,* pp.758-887. Compiled
    by Hamilton Hurd. Philadelphia: J.W. Lewis, 1882.
Saltonstall, William G. *Ports of Piscataqua.* Cambridge: Harvard
    University Press, 1941.
Scales, Ellen. "Dover Sea Captains." Paper presented at the
    Northam Colonists Historical Society meeting at Mrs. Parker's,
    1915.

Scales, John. *History of Dover, New Hampshire.* Vol. I. Manchester,
     N.H.: By Authority of the City Councils, 1923.
Stevens, Lydia. "Dover Landing from 1792 to 1842." *Granite Monthly*
     39 (May 1907): pp.150-156.
Thompson, Mary P. *Landmarks in Ancient Dover, New Hampshire.*
     Durham, N.H.: Dover Historical Society, 1892.
Wadleigh, George. *Notable Events in the History of Dover, New
     Hampshire From the First Settlement in 1623 to 1865.* Dover,
     N.H.: Tufts College Press, 1913.
Whitehouse, Robert A., comp. "Notebooks on Dover History." 15 vols.
     Dover, N.H.: Dover Public Library, 1982.
Winslow, Richard E. *The Piscataqua Gundalow: Workhorse for a
     Tidal Basin Empire.* Portsmouth, N.H.: Portsmouth Marine
     Society, 1983.

Newspapers

Dover Daily Republican
Dover Enquirer
New Hampshire Republican
Strafford Enquirer

Symbols Used in Photograph and Advertisement Captions and Their Sources

CD	Charles Dame, Dover, N.H.
CLW	Clyde L. Whitehouse Collection, Dover
DLW	Donald L. Whitehouse, Brookville Florida
DPL	Dover Public Library, Dover
EH	Edgar D. Hall, Dover
ES	Elizabeth Sawyer, Durham, N.H.
GB	*Great Bay: A Visual History.* UNH Publication, 1970
JPA	John P. Adams, Newington, N.H.
MMM	Maine Maritime Museum, Bath, Maine
OBHS	Old Berwick Historical Society, South Berwick, Maine.
RAW	Robert A. Whitehouse, Rollinsford, N.H.
TH	Thom Hindle Collection, Dover
WI	Woodman Institute, Dover
DE	*Dover Enquirer*, Dover
NHR	*New Hampshire Republican*, Dover
SE	*Strafford Enquirer*, Dover

Index

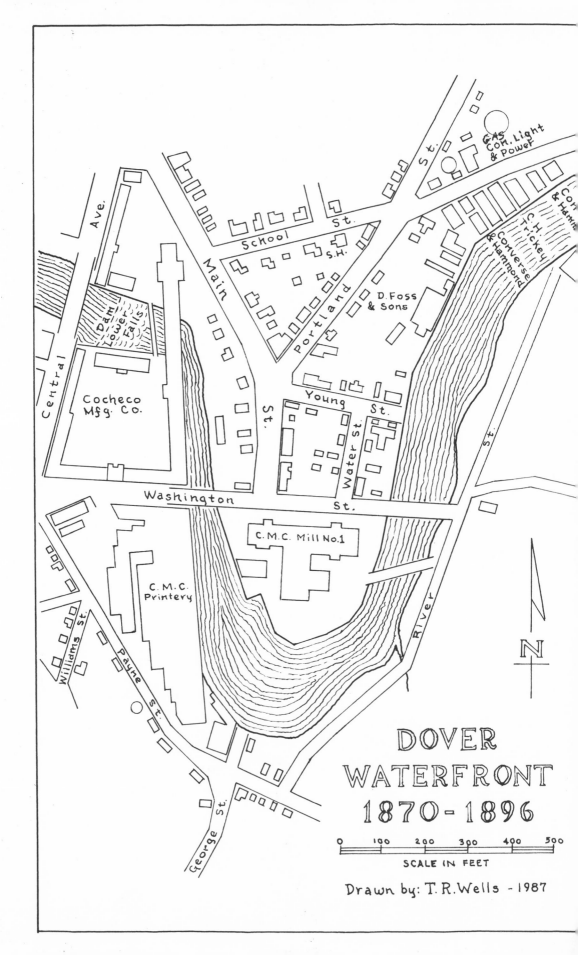

DOVER
WATERFRONT
1870-1896

0   100   200   300   400   500
SCALE IN FEET

Drawn by: T.R.Wells - 1987